Japanese Industrial Competition to 1990

Japanese Industrial Competition to 1990

by
Mary Saso
Stuart Kirby

Abt Books
Cambridge, Massachusetts
EIU Special Series 1

Library of Congress Cataloging in Publication Data

Japanese industrial competition to 1990.

(Economist Intelligence Unit special series)
Contents: Japan's role in the 1980s/by Stuart Kirby—Japanese industry,
how to compete and how to cooperate/by Mary Saso.
1. Japan—Economic conditions—1945-—Addresses, essays, lectures. 2.
Japan—Industries—Addresses, essays, lectures. 3. Economic
forecasting—Japan—Addresses, essays, lectures. 4. Japan—Social conditions—1945- —Addresses, essays, lectures. I. Kirby, Stuart. Japan's role in
the 1980s. 1982. II. Saso, M. (Mary) Japanese industry, how to compete and
how to cooperate. 1982. III. Series.
HC462.9.J33 1982   330.952'048   82-13822
ISBN 0-89011-583-4

Originally published by The Economist Intelligence
Unit as Special Report Nos. 110 and 81.

© Abt Associates Inc., 1982

All rights reserved. No part of this publication may
be reproduced or transmitted in any form or by any
means, electronic or mechanical, including
photocopy, recording, or any information storage or
retrieval system, without specific permission in
writing from the publisher: Abt Books, 55 Wheeler
Street, Cambridge, MA 02138.

Printed in the United States of America

The Authors

Professor Stuart Kirby was born in Japan and has devoted much of his life, as an academic and economic consultant, to Japanese affairs. He has traveled and worked throughout the world but his main concentration has been on Asia. When he has not been working in Japan, Professor Kirby has made frequent visits there.

He has been professor of economics in a number of universities, including Tohoku, Hokkaido, Hong Kong, the Asian Institute of Technology in Bangkok, Aston (Birmingham) and is a Senior Associate of St Antony's College, Oxford.

Professor Kirby is the author of a number of books, of which several are on Japan and China, and over 300 papers and articles. He is fluent in Japanese and many other languages and dialects.

Mrs. Mary Saso has lived in Japan for the last five years and during that period carried out extensive research into Japanese industry. Previously she worked as an economist in Western Europe and Africa. Mrs. Saso's extensive experience in both the developed and less developed world has given her a deep understanding of all the stages of industrial development.

Contents

Part 2: Japan's Role in the 1980s

List of Tables

Part 1: Japanese Industry: How to Compete and How to Cooperate

List of Figures

Part 1: Japanese Industry: How to Compete and How to Cooperate

List of Tables

Part 2: Japan's Role in the 1980s

List of Figures

Part 2: Japan's Role in the 1980s

Part One:
Japanese Industry:
How to Compete and
How to Cooperate

Chapter 1

The Typical Structure of a Japanese Manufacturing Company

Although the intention is to sketch a representative profile of an industrial enterprise in Japan, an important qualification must be stated at the outset. No aspect of Japan's economy or society is as homogeneous as first appearances and many commentators suggest. Indeed even the most general typifications which are considered to underpin the Japanese economy, such as groupism and consensus formation, are subject to major exceptions in practice. Therefore divergent aspects to the profile will be highlighted, so as not to present a potentially deceptive picture.

Analyses of Japan's industrial structure have recognised at least one major non-homogeneous feature and that is the distinction between large and small firms. Since the two groups have faced different labour and capital markets, in which the small and medium sized enterprise has been able to obtain cheaper labour inputs, but more expensive capital, the designation of a "dual economy" has become popular. Such dualism has been indicated by wage differentials, discriminatory interest rates, and productivity gaps. During the period up to 1975, rapid economic growth, accompanied by diffused technological progress and successful rationalisation, has diminished to some extent the significance of the distinctions previously evident. However since the advent of radically new technological processes requiring substantial investment in facilities, the productivity gap has tended to widen again. Therefore the distinctions between large and small firms will be kept in mind throughout this chapter.

The distinctive features of Japanese industry –

In presenting those aspects of a Japanese industrial enterprise which are most prevalent, stress will be given to the ones which have contributed to Japan's industrial success or differ significantly from characteristic aspects of a Western firm. In this way it may be possible to gain some insight into the reasons for Japan's industrial achievements without resorting to explanations based on precepts arising from centuries of Confucianism, or adopting sinister theories of a "Japan Inc".

When considering aspects of Japan's industrialisation different from those in the Western pattern, it would be useful to bear in mind whether or not – or rather to what degree, if a simple dichotomy is invalid – the divergence theory of social evolution is appropriate. It has been generally assumed under this theory that technological advances shape social institutions over time so that industrial societies increasingly resemble one another. In the case of Japan, however, an alternative "culturalist" theory has predominated increasingly since the 1950s, in which it is suggested that unique Japanese personality traits have engendered specific institutional practices, particularly in personnel management. Therefore, under the "culturalist" theory, it becomes almost impossible for an industrial firm in the West to learn from, let alone imitate, these aspects of a Japanese firm which have contributed to its achievements.

3

Rather than subscribing to either of the above contrasting theories, Ronald Dore's revised version of the convergence postulates seems to be most appropriate.[1] In particular, Ronald Dore in his work has convincingly demonstrated that the 'late development effect' applies not merely to capital equipment, in which technologies are embedded, but also to social technology and ideologies. Moreover the resulting patterns of social organisation reflect those trends of a rising desire for social equality and, later, divergence from 'market oriented' labour practices to 'organisation oriented' objectives, which are coming to typify twentieth century developments in modern economies.

Therefore it is not necessary to assume that Japanese organisational forms are completely inappropriate for the West, nor should it be believed that such forms are wholly anachronistic and will soon fade away as Japanese industrial society converges towards its predecessors in the West. Instead there is much to be gained from a careful examination of Japanese industry and its past and prospective developments.

CAPITAL STRUCTURE

In looking at the balance sheets for a wide range of companies in Japan, the most striking feature is the comparatively low net worth ratio. In general stockholders' equity is well below 50 per cent of total assets. As may be seen from Table 1, the net worth ratio, even in manufacturing, has in aggregate actually dropped over the past 15 years from 23.1 to 19.3.

Table 1

Aggregated Financial Results of Japan's Corporations
(percentages; fiscal years)

	All industries			Manufacturing		
	1965	1975	1979	1965	1975	1979
Net worth ratio[a]	19.0	13.9	14.3	23.1	17.0	19.3
Return on equity[b]	17.4	13.5	28.4	15.6	8.3	30.1
Return on capital employed[c]	3.4	1.9	4.1	3.7	1.4	5.8
Return on sales[d]	2.3	1.3	2.5	3.3	1.2	4.0
Pay out ratio[e]	56.8	73.3	24.1	63.1	116.6	21.7
Quick ratio[f]	66.6[g]	71.3	72.0	70.0[g]	74.0	76.1

a Equity/total assets at close of fiscal year. b Ordinary income/equity.
c Ordinary income/total assets. d Ordinary income/sales. e Dividend
payment/net income. f Current assets less inventories/current liabilities
g Current assets do not include negotiable securities.

Source: Tōyō Keizai, Keizai-Tōkei Neakan, 1981.

1. Dore, R British Factory-Japanese Factory. The Origins of National Diversity in Industrial Relations. George Allen and Unwin, London, 1973 pages 11-13.

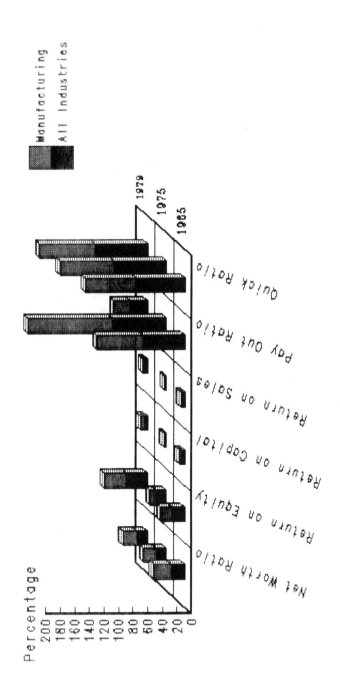

Figure 1a

5

Rather than just relying on aggregates, certain figures drawn from various randomly chosen companies at the most recent closing of their fiscal years may be illustrative. For example, Nachi-Fujikoshi Corp, which manufactures and deals in machine tools, hydraulic and pneumatic equipment, and other capital equipment categories, has been established since 1928. Yet its capital and surplus as of November 30, 1980, stood at Y23,719 mn in relation to total liabilities and capital of ¥87,352 mn (i e 27 per cent). In the case of Matsushita Electric, which needs no introduction, total stockholders' equity as of November 20, 1980, had attained just over ¥1,000 bn compared with total liabilities and stockholders' equity of almost ¥2,500 bn (44 per cent).

In the distribution sector, one of the most successful of the superstore chains, Ito-Yokado Co, Ltd, had in 1980 stockholders' equity amounting to ¥103,047 mn, nearly 34 per cent of its total liabilities and equity of ¥304,131 mn. Even in the case of Seven-Eleven, Japan Co, Ltd, which has only been established for eight years under a licence for convenience store operations from the Southland Corporation of the USA, stockholders' equity in 1980 is still just below 50 per cent with a net worth ratio of ¥10,129 mn to ¥21,606 mn.

Net worth ratios tending to rise –

It appears from a wide sample of balance sheets that total liabilities to net worth have been in the region of 3 to 1. However in major companies leverage is in general now closer to 2 to 1, and is probably approaching a 1 to 1 ratio. With regard to recent changes in the balance sheets of the companies mentioned above, in just one year between 1978/79 and 1979/80 the net worth ratio had risen considerably for almost every company. For example Nachi-Fujikoshi's ratio rose from 21.84 per cent to 27.15 per cent, Matsushita Electric's from 43.12 per cent to 44.06 per cent, and Seven-Eleven, Japan's from 30.66 per cent to 46.88 per cent. Ito-Yokado did register a decrease in its net worth ratio from 35.80 per cent to 33.88 per cent, but this was partly due to foreign currency exchange losses of ¥5,127 mn on the US dollar denominated long term debt; the value of issued common stock itself increased by almost ¥1,000 mn during the year.

– as companies seek foreign shareholders

At this point it should be remarked that most companies' efforts to raise their net worth ratios do not necessarily arise out of a belief that high gearing is detrimental to the company's interests. The peculiarities of Japan's financial markets, as will be explained later, usually render such considerations invalid. Instead those companies listed on the Tokyo Stock Exchange are eager to attract more foreign indirect investment in the wake of more or less full scale liberalisation, since the Foreign Exchange and Foreign Trade Control Law took effect on December 1, 1980[1]. It is generally believed that overseas investors would be hesitant to buy stock where substantial long term debt exists and so the popular ostensible target among Japanese companies is to raise the net worth ratio to 60 per cent. Such companies cite the reasons underlying this target as stemming from a desire to

---

1. Indirect investment in Japanese companies is considered in more depth in chapter IV of this report.

improve the soundness of the company's financial structure. Yet it is arguable
that the particular conditions pertaining to Japan's financial market - particularly
those of low interest rates and close connections between banks and companies -
render these seemingly worthy reasons worthless.

THE FINANCIAL MARKET

Government policy has meant low interest rates on loans -

In order to evaluate the appropriateness of Japan's financial market for industrial
development, it is necessary to consider briefly its development since 1945. So
as to allow plenty of latitude for industrial development in the face of a completely
inadequate securities market at that time, the Bank of Japan lent liberally to the
major commercial banks, on which companies relied heavily for funds. Since a
normal open market mechanism would have allowed interest rates to reach
unmanageable levels on account of the scarcity of funds in conjunction with high
demand for credit, the government employed a low interest rate policy.

This policy was associated with the feature of indicative financing by which the
government and the Bank of Japan steered commercial bank loans towards high
priority industries, particularly the export and basic industries, at artificially
low interest rates   (keisha seisan hōshiki). The justification, which permitted
a consensus to be reached, was that the basic industry sector would otherwise fail
to attract funds in competition with more immediately profitable enterprises.
Although indicative financing may no longer be practised by the government, a
rigid interest rate structure, whereby all interest rates have to be artificially
adjusted after an engineered change in the minimum lending rate, is still in operation. Moreover any loan is contracted at a given interest rate which does not alter
for the life of loan, whatever fluctuations occur in interest rates. However the
recent internationalisation of financing has not only diversified financial assets,
but also raised the elasticity of interest rates.

- and low yields on corporate bonds

It was not only in respect of long term loans but also through bonds that special
relationships, which seem to indicate companies' being dependent on commercial
banks, developed. The government's reliance on deficit financing over the years,
rather than reforming the tax structure to yield more revenue, has resulted in a
substantial government bond market. In order that issues of other bonds should
not distract subscribers to government bonds, bond interest rates at issue have
deliberately been constrained so as to maintain a balance with yields on the government's bond flotations.   Recognising that bond prices would be lower in the
secondary market, a syndicate of major banks and securities companies has been
rationing bonds to chosen companies as well as determining the interest rates.
The corporate bonds have consequently been purchased by banks at interest rates
comparatively favourable to companies and retained until maturity, just as though
they were long term loans.

In addition to the influence exerted by commercial banks over companies, due to their power to dispense favourably both bonds and loans, equity participation is also practised. In this way a group of varied companies has come to be associated with a particular bank, such as the Fuyo Group centred around Fuji Bank. The financial linking of a group is known as keiretsu-yūshi and is considered to have been one of the features of Japan's post 1945 economy which promoted a high rate of economic growth.

The keiretsu designation is often, somewhat confusingly, applied to two other kinds of industrial grouping in Japan. The first kind is that of the inheritors of the zaibatsu which were combines developed up to 1945 which achieved notoriety because the US occupation administration adopted their dissolution as one of the main planks for dismantling Japan's war oriented economy. In the 1950s the earlier zaibatsu, such as Mitsui and Mitsubishi, were re-established, though with less binding ties. These postwar groupings resemble the true keiretsu in that there is a bank as one of the major members, but they are somewhat more structured with regular group meetings held. The final kind of grouping is that formed by a large enterprise and its subsidiaries, which often supply components or services to the parent company. This kind of grouping also usually includes the feature of subcontracting about which more will be said later (see page 27).

In outlining three apparently distinct categories of groupings above, a misleading impression of rigid, well structured formations may have been conveyed. In fact, cases in which a company seems to belong to two or more groupings are not infrequent. Moreover the existence of a grouping does not preclude intense competition between the members should they be in similar fields. While bearing these qualifications in mind, an overseas prospective licensor, licensee, or joint venture partner would find it useful to consult a compendium such as "Industrial Groupings in Japan - 1980-81" (4th edition Dodwell Marketing Consultants).

In examining further the typical capital structure of a Japanese company, the first two types of groupings will both be known as keiretsu for convenience, while the parent companies of the third grouping usually themselves belong to one of the keiretsu. For example Toyota is a member of the Sanwa group. It should be mentioned in passing that not only do preferential financing and cross shareholding link the members of a keiretsu, but also various non-financial arrangements - such as combined research, joint use of a certain general trading company, and vertical integration - exist to different degrees for different companies.

The formal links within a group are not strong

It would be useful at this point to look for a few examples of keiretsu groupings in order to understand the extent of ties in loans granted and shareholdings. (See Table 2.) The first striking aspect is how low are the ratios which indicate a company's share of indebtedness to the lead bank and the bank's shareholdings in that company. Apart from the two oil companies (Mitsubishi Sekiyu and Maruzen Sekiyu), the ratios generally lie below 10 per cent.

Table 2

Selected Keiretsu: Loans and Equity Ties, 1980

Lead bank		Mitsubishi Bank	Fuji Bank	Sumitomo Bank	Sanwa Bank
Major Debtors[a]	1	Mitsubishi Sekiyu 117,840 29.6%	Mitsui Bussan 90,135 4.8%	Sumitomo Kinzoku Kogyo 89,935 10.1%	Maruzen Sekiyu 112,336 16.4%
	2	Mitsubishi Shoji 77,734 5.4%	Nihon Kokan 89,933 8.3%	Mitsui Bussan 73,453 3.9%	Nissho Iwai 72,244 9.9%
	3	Mitsubishi Jukogyo 77,590 10.7%	Maruko 72,411 6.5%	Sumitomo Shoji 70,274 12.5%	Mitubishi Shoji 66,005 4.8%
Major Shareholdings[b]	1	Tokyo Power[d] 12,625 1.2%	Nihon Kokan 126,862 4.3%	Kansai Power[d] 19,703 2.7%	Kansai Power[d] 19,449 2.7%
	2	M Jukogyo 122,368 5.3%	Tokyo Power[d] 11,939 1.1%	Shin Nippon Seitetsu 110,994 1.7%	Shin Nippon Seitetsu 108,516 1.6%
	3	M Shoji 65,523 6.5%	Shin Nippon Seitetsu 118,874 1.8%	Sumitomo Kinzoku Kogyo 95,436 4.1%	Kobe Steel 91,750 4.5%
Major Shareholders[c]	1	Meiji Life Insurance 106,088 5.95%	Yasuda Life Insurance 78,572 4.41%	Sumitomo Life Insurance 94,548 5.31%	Nihon Life Insurance 74,131 4.16%
	2	Tokyo Marine & Fire 83,666 4.70%	Daiichi Life Insurance 50,657 2.84%	Nihon Life Insurance 71,095 3.99%	Meiji Life Insurance 57,628 3.23%

a Debt of companies listed to lead bank in ¥ mn and as percentage of company's total debt.   b Shares held by lead bank in companies listed, '000 and as percentage of company's total shares.   c Shares held in lead bank by companies listed, '000 and as percentage of lead bank's total issued shares.   d Nominal value of shares ¥500, or ten times that of shares in other companies shown.

Source: Tōyō Keizai, Kigyō Keiretsu Sōran, 1981.

The next interesting feature is that some companies appear to belong to several different keiretsu groupings. In particular Mitsui Bussan, though its lead bank is naturally Mitsui, holds first place in the extent of loans granted to it by Fuji Bank and it is also indebted to each of the other lead banks. (Its ranking is fourth in Mitsubishi and Sanwa.) Similarly Mitsubishi Shoji is indebted to Sanwa Bank. Therefore the keiretsu relationships are not at all exclusive, for a group member also borrows from banks other than its lead bank. Indeed usually less than 20 per cent of a member's loans are from its lead bank. However the group member knows that it can depend on the lead bank for assistance at time of crisis.

With regard to cross shareholdings, Table 2 indicates that the holdings of the lead bank in its members rarely exceeds 5 per cent. Similarly, while insurance companies as integrative investors dominate the banks' shareholders, Mitsubishi Jukogyo holds holds only 3.64 per cent of Mitsubishi Bank's shares and Nihon Kokan only 2.74 per cent of Fuji Bank's shares. Nonetheless other data indicate that the extent of cross shareholding, when measured by the average percentage of shares held in a company by all group members, has been increasing since the oil crises during the 1970s. The strengthening of relations has been not so much for the purpose of aggressive business ventures as to protect and solidify present positions.

Keiretsu structure facilitates gearing without tears

The existence of the keiretsu structure is one of the major reasons why Japanese companies have been able to maintain highly leveraged financial structures without undue risk. Indeed apparent risk exposure is also evident when looking at the current ratio of current assets to current liabilities, which Western bankers consider should be in the region of 2 to 1. Yet in the case of a wide variety of major companies in Japan the ratio lay between 0.82 and 1.60 to 1 in 1980. Similarly Table 1 indicates relatively low quick ratios, although there has been some improvement since 1965. If a company does collapse, the lead bank or associated general trading company will take remedial steps so as to minimise the damage to investors - as in the case of Toyo Pulp, in 1976, whose debts were covered by Mitsui Bussan. Such apparent risk can be borne partly because the lead bank in the keiretsu grouping can be regarded as a subordinated creditor over whom other creditors can expect their claims to take precedence; another reason is that the rising stock market, especially in the late 1960s, lifted the market value of stock to well above book value. Indeed companies were reluctant to expand through augmenting equity because the practice has generally been in Japan to issue new stock at book value, instead of near its market price, with the consequence that equity financing is a relatively expensive method. Moreover, since interest payments are deductible from corporate tax liability, higher dividend payments on an expanded equity capital seem unnecessary in periods of high growth rates of corporate profits.

Capital structure encourages pursuit of long term growth

The features of the capital structure of most Japanese companies which differ from those in the West have been rational not just in terms of historical develop-ments and different risk perceptions; such features have also contributed to rapid growth in sales and investment. While there is some controversy on Western managements' objectives, one common argument is that short run profits should be maximised for the benefit of stockholders. In Japan, on the other hand, not only has equity been of less importance to the typical firm's capital structure, but also stock ownership has been more widely diffused among shareholders, as required by the commercial code. Consequently Japanese management has been able to emphasise long run growth even at the expense of immediate profits.

Indeed growth in sales has often been vital for a Japanese company in order to reduce average fixed costs per unit. Interest charges on debt should really be considered as a fixed cost, as indeed is also a considerable part of the labour cost in Japan. In addition investment on new plant and equipment, as well as extra capacity, contributed to relatively high depreciation charges. Consequently Japanese companies have been accustomed to operating with rather small profit margins on sales (see Table 1) which could be sustained mainly on account of rapid sales growth, which brought scale economies.

Before concluding this section, the nature of the ties between members of the keiretsu groupings should be given further examination to see how company performance is affected. However, since the ties vary considerably both between different groupings and within a group itself, where companies are not usually equidistant from the lead bank, to generalise may appear somewhat futile.

The role of the lead bank

Although the extent of cross stockholding seems from Table 2 to be more limited than might have been expected, the structure of a group is usually maintained by other means. In particular the chief executive officers of companies within a group are generally represented in some kind of association which holds meetings fairly regularly. The other major link between group members arises from the role of the lead bank.

While the bank is willing to act as a subordinated creditor, in return it is usually involved in the company's long term strategic planning. In the West the notion of control by a bank is generally viewed as being detrimental to the company's interests in favour of the financier's objectives and, thereby, as fostering conservatism. Yet in Japan a contrary opinion tends to be held in which the lead bank encourages group companies to invest as a way of maintaining the growth of its major customers and keeping their loyalty. Recently, however, there have been indications that the major commercial banks, despite their keiretsu ties, are failing to compete effectively with provincial banks. For example, it was reported in April, 1981, that Bridgestone Tyre had turned to the provincial banks after the major banks had rejected its request for a short term lending rate below the general prime rate of 6.75 per cent. At that time Bridgestone had ¥27,000 bn in bank deposits with only ¥15,000 bn in outstanding loans. Therefore a few provincial banks agreed to extend Bridgestone short term loans at the favourable rate of 6.5 per cent.

Banks' risk exposure shared by the Bank of Japan

While this discussion has been focused on the company's capital structure, the presumed risks for banks attendant on lending to companies which are highly leveraged have not yet been considered. In fact the Bank of Japan, with the Ministry of Finance to some extent, developed a system in the 1950s which amounts to "soft" intervention, to guide commercial banks in expanding or contracting their loan programmes. At the same time, not only do the banks themselves rely heavily on loans from the Bank of Japan, but the latter also effectively guarantees commercial bank loans to large companies. The system of window guidance (madoguchi-kisei) has been one of the features of Japan's post 1945 economy which represents a crucial plank in monetary policy. Such intervention is considered acceptable because business risks are thereby diffused and so do not hinder investment growth. There are several recent examples of intervention by the Bank of Japan and the Ministry of Finance, such as in 1979 when a chain of bankruptcies was prevented following the collapse of the Taiko Sogo Bank.

Japanese commentators have described the whole corporate financing system in Japan as "multi umbrella", because risks are covered at each stage. Thus, rather than investors directly participating in stockholding, indirect financing became the norm by way of the banks, general trading companies, and government finance corporations, particularly the long term credit banks. It remains to be seen whether the merits of this system in spreading risks will continue to outweigh the costs in terms of more intervention in business and higher capital costs than occur under direct investment.

MANAGERIAL SYSTEMS

Since the 1950s much has been written about Japanese managers in the English language. Probably the most useful kind of text is that in which an attempt is made to evaluate whether it is either desirable or feasible for Western managers to adopt certain Japanese managerial practices[1]. At the same time such books often provide only a superficial understanding of the cultural roots of Japanese management. In order to gain a sociological and anthropological grasp of the managerial system and work ethic in Japan, the books by Robert Cole, who has himself worked in Japanese factories, are to be recommended[2]. Cole's experiences in working on the shopfloor are invaluable in that he has been able to perceive the thin line between consensus and coercion. Another writer with work experience in a Japanese company is Rodney Clark, whose perspective is perhaps more from the managerial side than Robert Cole's[3]. The books mentioned here by no means cover the whole range of publications, but one would need to tolerate a certain amount of repetition and be wary of the frequent relating of near myths, if intending to read everything that is available.

---

1 Two recently published examples are: Ouchi W G,Theory Z: How American Business Can Meet the Japanese Challenge,Addison Wesley, 1981. Pascale R T and Athos A G,The Art of Japanese Management,Simon and Schuster, New York, 1981. 2 Cole R E, Japanese Blue Collar, University of California Press, Berkeley, 1973. Cole R E, Work, Mobility and Participation, University of California Press, Berkeley,1979. 3 Clark R, The Japanese Company, Yale University Press,New Haven, 1979.

The myth of the samurai

One of the ways of mythologising Japanese management, and thereby denying that certain managerial practices could be adapted for Western companies, is to emphasise the samurai principles, which were revered during the early stages of Japan's industrial growth in the late 19th and early 20th centuries, known as the Meiji period.[1] Such principles are based on Confucianism, so that a religious fervour came to be attached to the slogan of wakon-yōzai (i e Japanese spirit with Western technology). While Confucian precepts may have been widely practised at one time and may be of some influence today, the truth is that many of the most successful of Japanese managerial practices only came to the forefront after 1945 and moreover were often based on the diligent studies of Japanese management trainees at US business schools.

The trap of contrasting an ideal Japan with Western reality

Another aspect of the mythologising of Japanese management is when commentators, probably unintentionally, compare management ideals in Japan with actual practice elsewhere. Certain ideals, such as the apparent lack of superficial privileges for Japanese managers in their using the same facilities as the blue collar workers, do make an important psychological contribution in not aggravating disharmony in management-labour relations. However this egalitarianism in the workplace is probably more greatly appreciated by blue collar workers overseas, as in the Sony colour television factory at Bridgend, Wales, because of the contrast with management practices in British factories. In Japan, on the other hand, a common dining room is taken for granted, so that its removal would seriously disturb relations between labour and management, which are often finely balanced, especially in this era of slower growth.

In sum it is necessary to be aware that Japanese managerial practices are flexible and pragmatic in response to both changing economic conditions and social objectives. Indeed it is the quality of adaptability which is one of the most striking features, despite the appearance of rigid hierarchical ranks and a fondness for supposed traditions.

MANAGEMENT-LABOUR RELATIONS

Paternalism in response to pre-war tension –

One such apparent tradition is the idea of the enterprise as a family in which the management takes benevolent care of the workers. Yet paternalistic practices in Japanese industry did not begin to develop until the 1920s and then only in response to an upsurge in social tension, which was often directed against the zaibatsu as the despoilers of the rural economy and society. Thus it was the severe problems attendant to rapid urbanisation and industria lisation which finally compelled managers to adopt permanent employment practices and to provide limited welfare facilities for their workers.

Similarly another significant development in management practices during the 1950s followed upon extreme labour unrest and trade union activity in the late 1940s and early 1950s. At that time the "family cult" management exercised in the pre-war period was to some extent replaced with the idea of a "common destiny" for management and labour. This theme was expressed by Dōyūkai, an influential committee concerned with Japan's economic development, in propositions such as the "social responsibilities of business leadership". Ironically, the most evident manifestation of a belief in a common destiny came from the side of the workers, rather than of the management, in their acceptance of enterprise unions.

– to the active pursuit of harmony with labour

However, the fact that enterprise unions have been often in agreement with management objectives reflects upon the latter's deliberate choice of pursuing a path harmonious with labour, namely <u>rōshikyōchō-rosen</u>, rather than one of conflict, <u>rōshitaiketsu-rosen</u>. The well known distinction between these two terms in Japanese is indicative of the realisation on both sides that a choice can, and even should, be made between two alternatives, rather than just drifting into either unhappy compromises or turbid disagreements.

Since the 1970s macroeconomic factors have led to yet another reassessment of managements' role in which profit maximisation objectives have become overt. Consequently management is concerned with rationalising the company's operations by cutting out underemployed labour, which is bound ultimately to affect general labour-management relations. It is already noticeable that the famous <u>amae</u>[1] (dependency and sympathy between different hierarchical rankings), which was thought to be a quintessential part of the Japanese personality, is becoming diluted in company internal relations.

Formal consultation and profit sharing now commonplace

However the breakdown in some of the former relationships of trust between labour and management is being counterbalanced by the development since the 1960s of more formal schemes for labour-management consultations. In addition, employee stock ownership plans (ESOP) have now been implemented by 78 per cent of all listed Japanese companies, according to Nomura Research Institute's 1980 survey. The usual system is for employees to form a shareholders' trust, <u>kabunuski-kai</u>, with deductions from monthly pay checks remitted to the trust and the company contributing up to 5 per cent. Such schemes are often instigated by management in order to enhance employee loyalty to the company. Indeed, although most ESOP trusts in Japan hold voting rights exercised through the trust chairman, there are reportedly no cases of votes against the management.

---

1   The West first became generally aware of <u>amae</u> in Doi T, <u>The Anatomy of Dependence</u>, Kodansha, Tokyo, 1973.

The discussion so far on managerial systems in Japan has tended to be focused on the development of managerial practices to cope with labour relations. How management actually functions internally also should be considered in respect of decision making and career incentives. Yet, although certain distinctions can be made with respect to common Western systems, in general, after the brushwood of superficial distinctions has been cleared away, corporate organisation appears to be very similar to that in the West. Despite their self evident success, in terms of company sales and profitability, Japanese managers continue to be keen to adopt and try out recent Western innovations such as project-type matrix organisations. Thus the main element of success can still be considered to be management's flexibility and willingness to learn.

Nonetheless the few distinctions should be examined not only because of their possible contribution to managerial efficiency, but also because Westerners negotiating licensing or joint venture arrangements need to understand the background to their opposite numbers.

The slow search for consensus -

One feature of management decision making in Japan which has received a lot of attention is the slow and seemingly circuitous route to reaching a consensus. The first stage involves nemawashi in which opinions at all levels of the managerial structure in any concerned divisions should be sounded out. In practice the direct personal consultation will take place between the less senior staff of the concerned divisions. The proposed decision is then drafted (ringi-sho) within the division and passed up through all levels to receive approval. Since an informal consensus has already been reached through nemawashi, the approval, indicated by each manager affixing his seal, often amounts to little more than automatic rubber stamping[1].

- is increasingly held to cramp initiative at the top -

Although the ringi-seido does assist in furthering coordination and communication, especially in providing a route for the submission of ideas from lower staff members, it has been criticised among Japanese for leaving top management in the position of being unable to initiate new ideas. Moreover, since only supporting information and data are included, upper management levels may feel that they are being kept in the dark and cannot propose alternatives. Other criticisms are that the ringi-seido amounts to a piecemeal approach to decision making without proper analysis and that subsequently responsibility cannot be pinpointed. In defence, it is frequently pointed out that the decision making may be slow, but the execution, once the ringi-sho has run its course, is quick because a full

---

1   Yoshino M, Japan's Managerial System. M I T Press, Camb, Massachusetts, 1968 pages 254-265.

consensus has been reached. Another argument in favour is that the system to some extent permits decentralisation of decision making, while maintaining formal authority at the top.

- by Sony among others

Nonetheless it has been recognised among the management of the more dynamic companies, such as Sony Corporation, that present economic conditions require systematic advance planning and leadership from the top management. It is notable that in the case of the innovative and highly successful "Walkman", the Sony chairman, Akio Morita, acted as project manager and, against the initial advice of sales staff, brought it on to the market in about six months from the planning stage.

Therefore it is likely that, although the ringi-seido may be retained in the government bureaucracy, it will be increasingly streamlined or discarded in manufacturing enterprises.

CAREER INCENTIVES AND HIGHER MANAGEMENT

Promotion by seniority -

Concerning promotion prospects with attendant career incentives among managerial staff, it has generally been presumed that the college graduate - almost all managers are such graduates - on entering a Japanese firm can expect to be regularly promoted in line with those entering the firm at the same time whatever their respective abilities. However, as with the ringi-seido, commentators have tended to generalise from the more evident example of the government bureaucracy to private enterprises.

-gives way to a distinction between rank and authority

Even in the bureaucracy, promotion prospects must inevitably become considerably more hazy and dependent on competition, once employees have reached their mid thirties. In industry it is clearly recognised that there are distinctions between rank and function, so that, while someone of mediocre ability can expect to receive higher ranking over time, promotion to positions of higher authority cannot be expected. Indeed about 30 per cent of all large scale enterprises in 1981 promote to middle management positions on the basis of competitive examinations and it is expected that this figure will rise during the 1980s. Meanwhile the merit system will diminish the importance not only of an employee's age, but also of educational background. At the same time the advantage to the operation of the enterprise in permitting ranks to be raised is that it provides a rationale for the mediocre employee to render loyal service to the enterprise with some degree of career planning on his part.

Actually, enterprises have recently begun to implement radical changes among top management posts. The first step is usually the creation of the post of chairman or adviser, into which an aging president is moved. Such chairmen, however, still retain the useful function of maintaining contacts with bankers and other business leaders. This allows younger leaders, who often are highly experienced in business affairs and are well versed in the engineering skills specific to the firm, to be promoted to the posts of president and vice president.

This trend in reshuffling top management was particularly noticeable in April, 1981, when leading Japanese companies implemented major changes in preparation for expansion in the forthcoming fiscal year. For example, Fujitsu Ltd, whose business in computers and telecommunications has grown rapidly, appointed 55 year old Takuma Yamamoto president, while Hitachi Ltd promoted Katsushige Mita, 56, from vice president. Both Yamamoto and Mita graduated from the celebrated engineering departments of the University of Tokyo; so it is considered that their appointments as president reflect priority being given to technological research and development.

Engineers on the board

It remains to consider briefly the typical composition of the board of directors of a medium to large scale Japanese firm. The most salient feature is that not only have almost all the directors spent their whole careers with the company but also a substantial proportion continue to be full time operating executives. In addition the directors would usually be highly experienced in the kind of engineering, or other skills such as law, appropriate to the company.

While this kind of structure of the board may result in rather confined and restricted viewpoints, along with some indications of long standing internal factional rivalries, there are substantial advantages in that the directors are fully conversant with the company's operations and are sympathetic to employees.

Although this section is separated from that which follows by the use of words "managerial" and "labour", in the large scale companies conditions of employment, apart from remuneration scales, for manual and clerical workers are usually comparable with those for managerial staff. Therefore their employment conditions may safely be included in the following section. Indeed the fact that one does not have to make radical distinctions is indicative of the sense of near social equality among all members of a company, which is a significant contributory factor to the company's success.

LABOUR CONDITIONS

QUALIFICATIONS TO LIFETIME EMPLOYMENT

In order to understand some of the reasons for the substantial employee welfare benefits and for the features of the wage structure whereby there are significant differentials between different age groups, one should begin by examining the apparent prevalence of lifetime employment, - shūshin-koyō. At the same time it should be understood that shūshin-koyō is merely a principle, which is subject to modifications in practice, and that, even as a principle, there are likely to be radical changes in the 1980s as the population rapidly ages and economic growth slows down (see Chapter V).

Shūshin-koyō means that when a graduate from school or college enters a company in the April immediately after March graduation, he may anticipate staying with that company until at least the mandatory retirement age of 55 or 60 years. It should be noted that 'she' has not been mentioned because the female labour market is considerably more fluid. In fact it is the possibility of employing women, often as part timers, at times when manpower capacity is being stretched, which is one of the factors permitting companies to offer more or less guaranteed employment for permanent male employees.

Another factor which enables permanent employment for some employees to be practised, despite business fluctuations, is the existence of temporary workers, mid career recruits on probation and subcontractors. In some companies temporary workers, including seasonal workers from farming areas, may only be employed in the most menial tasks, but in other companies the hiring of temporary workers to work alongside permanent employees may be a useful expedient for coping with fluctuations in demand. Moreover mid career recruitment in certain companies, such as Sony Corporation, is not marginal to the employment structure, especially where the recruits bring advanced and poachable skills. Subcontractors also assist in altering the wage bill in so far as extra work may be undertaken under the instructions of the parent company. This, of course, implies that lifetime employment tends to be more characteristic of the large companies than of small and medium sized firms.

Finally business fluctuations can be reflected in the wage bill through the twice yearly bonus scheme. Depending on a company's performance, bonuses, which can represent up to six months of an employee's annual salary, are altered freely by the management, although unions do enter into bargaining on the size of the bonus.

TRAINING EMPLOYEES

In spite of the above ways in which a company can effectively alter its wage bill so that it no longer represents a fixed cost, lifetime employment may still appear to be economically irrational. However since the company must invest considerable amounts in initially training a recruit, due to the non-vocational character of most college courses, there is an incentive to retain that employee. Such on the job and off the job training also inhibits skilled employees from seeking positions elsewhere - not out of a sense of loyalty but because his skills are usually specific to his original company.

Training becomes more elaborate -

Employee training has become increasingly elaborate in line with the more advanced technologies being used. Whereas the norm used to be a month long orientation course in April, many of the larger companies have recently begun year long courses. At Kawasaki Steel the management trainees are required to familarise themselves with all aspects of an integrated steel mill's operation by direct contact with the manual labourers. At most companies, in addition to the customary on the job training, one to one instruction is promoted in which recent recruits are assigned to work under a single, more experienced, worker, who, knowing his own employment is guaranteed, is willing to give instruction.

- and provides a range of skills

On the job training in Japan does not concentrate on the acquisition of a single skill, but endeavours to provide employees with a range of skills, which renders reassignment between different departments more feasible. Thus a slackening off in the demand for the products of one area need not lead to redundancies. Indeed, because of workers' expectations of permanent employment, management recognises that union resistance to redundancies and the consequent decline in work motivation would often be more costly than retraining and reassignment.

Thus automation has not meant redundancy -

In particular, it appears that the increasing usage of numerically-controlled (NC) machine tools has not adversely affected employment, as might have been expected. In June 1981, the Ministry of Labour published a report arising from a survey conducted from 1977 to 1980 on about 4,900 machinery and equipment manufacturing companies[1]. Of the responding companies, which included both large and medium scale employers of 30 workers or more, 47.1 per cent had introduced NC machine tools; of these 48.4 per cent had increased the number of employees on their payrolls between 1977 and 1980. Moreover, although the companies with NC machine tools had reduced the number of employees by 2.5 per cent overall, those which had not yet introduced NC machine tools reduced their employees by 4.4 per cent over the period.

- and unions are readier to accept change

In this context, unions are willing to accept technological changes, including automation, because the lifetime employment principle does in the general, but not exceptional, case preclude redundancies. However such reassignments may often ignore whether or not the marginal productivity of the worker in his new position is positive.

WAGE STRUCTURE

Seniority system eases adjustment to new technologies -

It is the above aspect of the relationship between productivity and the Japanese employment system which is often criticised as being too loose or even non-existent. Yet, although there may not appear to be a direct correspondence between relative wage levels and relative marginal productivities at one point in time, over a considerable time period a correspondence does exist. As may be seen from Figure 1, high relative wages in a man's middle age, when his productivity, apart from the experience factor, could be lower, tend to be matched by rather low wages during his twenties. Thus the wage profile is quite steeply graded - to

---

1   Ministry of Labour, Microelectronics no Koyō no Eikyō ni Kensuru-Chōsa, June, 1981.

FIGURE 1.

AGE AND WAGE PROFILE

Male workers in manufacturing industry

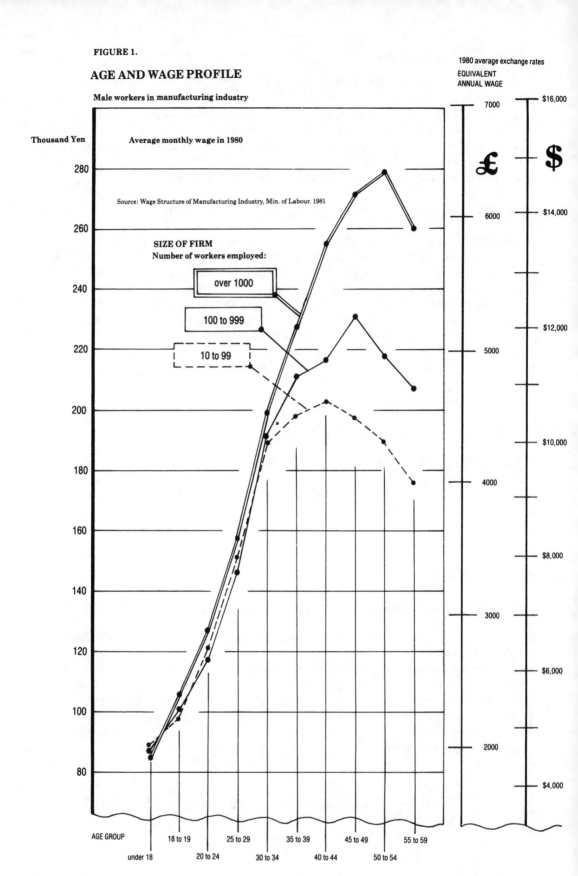

1980 average exchange rates

EQUIVALENT
ANNUAL WAGE

20

FIGURE 2.

AGE AND WAGE INCREASE PROFILE

PER CENT

Male workers in manufacturing industry in Japan

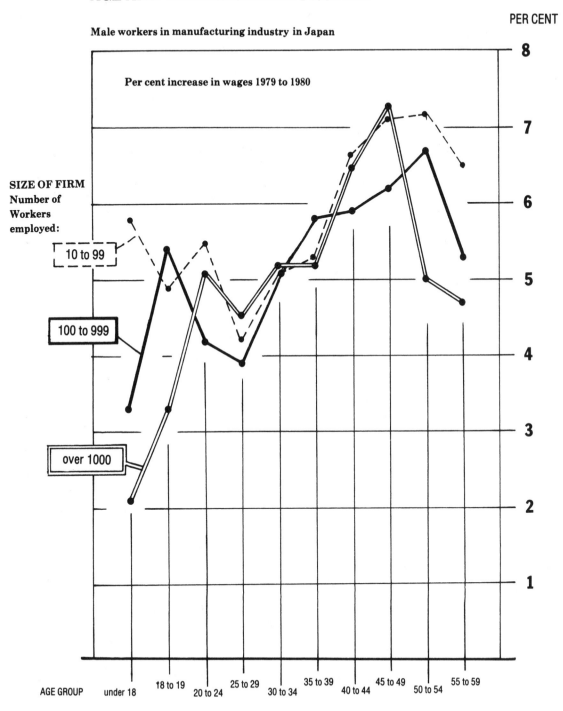

Per cent increase in wages 1979 to 1980

SIZE OF FIRM
Number of
Workers
employed:

10 to 99

100 to 999

over 1000

AGE GROUP under 18 18 to 19 20 to 24 25 to 29 30 to 34 35 to 39 40 to 44 45 to 49 50 to 54 55 to 59

Source: Wage Structure of Manufacturing Industry, Min. of Labour. 1981

an extent greater than in a Western industrialised country. It is thereby postulated that the discounted sum of a worker's lifetime earnings reflects the discounted sum of his whole productivity while with the firm. Apart from the justification of the longer term perspective of productivity, which assumes also that a worker will stay with the company, there is an interesting rationale based on making technological changes acceptable to workers[1]. Under more advanced technologies, older workers possessing the earlier skills might be disadvantaged. Therefore the seniority based payments offer some protection against consequent erosion of wage differentials and so assist in easing the required adjustments. Seniority based wages (nenkō-joretsukei chingin) have usually been considered to be a distinctive and essential part of the Japanese employment system. However Figure 1 demonstrates that nenkō-joretsukei chingin have been substantially modified recently. The data were derived from a Ministry of Labour survey on about 600,000 workers at 27,000 manufacturing companies, carried out in June, 1980. The survey report shows clearly that seniority based wages no longer apply to workers aged over 50 years, even in large scale enterprises. In enterprises employing less than 100 employees, where in any case lower productivity is reflected in lower wages, the peak of a worker's earning ability is now reached before the age of 45 years.

– but peak earning age is falling below 50 –

This is a fairly recent phenomenon in large scale companies, as shown in Figure 2 where the changes in wages between 1979 and 1980 are compared. (In practice the changes would have depended on the spring, 1980, wage bargaining.) In that year the highest rates of increase were experienced by workers in the age bracket of 45 to 49 years in the large scale manufacturing enterprises. Since much lower rates of increase were given to those over 50 years in the same enterprises, it is likely that within a few years the peak earning period for workers in the larger companies will also shift to below 50 years.

– as priority shifts to job-related payments

Indeed wage structures in Japanese companies have never been wholly seniority based. Therefore the trends noted above indicate a shifting of priorities towards job-related payments, which have always existed in part. There have usually been at least five components including the basic salary. The additional components are one based on merit, one based on the job performed, a bonus scheme, and family, transportation, and other welfare payments. In addition, various piece-work schemes are in operation, but, unlike in the West, these do not attempt to match payments to an individual's output. Instead the payment is for the performance of the work group. Moreover it has already been recognised in Japan that piecework can be costly in terms of both administration and dissension; so the payments are allowed only a limited degree of variability and are marginal to the total wage payment.

---

1   Yashiro N, 'Nihongata Koyō-Kankō no Keizai Gōrisei" Shukan Toyo Keizai, January 24, 1981.

The appearance of peak earnings in the forties or early fifties of a man's working life, as indicated in Figure 1, may be an indication that performance based pay systems are becoming more prevalent. However, while permanent employment is still the norm, it is unlikely, for the reasons mentioned above, that the seniority based system will be completely abandoned. Instead it appears that the lessening of the gradient of earnings and decline in the fifties age group's relative earnings reflect not only the performance based elements of wage structures, but also the fact that the growing proportion of older workers is placing considerable strain on seniority systems, which result in an increasing wage bill when new recruits do not outweigh retirees.

The age of retirement has tended to rise

The increase in the proportion of older workers arises both from demographic factors and from the extension of the retirement age, which until the late 1970s had generally been 55 years. By mid 1981, however, it appeared from a survey of 965 large enterprises[1] that 26 per cent retired their staff at 55 years, 16 per cent at 57, and 40 per cent at the age of 60. Yet just two years earlier only 19 per cent had established a mandatory retirement age of 60. The Ministry of Labour and unions are keen to hasten this trend, although their target of all enterprises retiring employees at 60 years by 1985 may be too optimistic. It should be mentioned at this point that the larger enterprises often re-employ workers after "retirement", or find them employment with associated subcontractors. However the working conditions, including wages for the re-employed, are usually less advantageous than those experienced before "retirement".

WORKING HOURS

It may sometimes have been suggested that the comparatively early nominal retirement age in Japan reflected exhaustion after working long hours. Indeed, as shown in Figure 3, although large scale enterprises invariably operate according to a 40 hour week, actual hours worked are considerably more than in the West on average, over the year. The reasons lie in the amount of overtime worked and the tendency, though a declining one, of employees to forego their relatively generous statutory holidays, which in 1979 amounted to an average 29.6 days including national holidays. Another factor accounting for the higher number of hours worked on average would be the lower number of working days lost through labour disputes. Between 1960 and 1978, the number of days lost each year in the USA and the UK rose respectively two times and three times, whereas in Japan the days lost fell by more than two thirds. It may also be that lower rates of absenteeism in Japan have influenced the comparative international statistics on working hours.

At the same time, the significance of the data should not be overrated. Workers in manufacturing enterprises in Japan with more than 500 employees worked during the year 94 hours more on average than employees in Great Britain, which is

---

1   Japan Personnel Administration Research Institute Survey, 1981.

FIGURE 3.

HOURS WORKED IN MANUFACTURING

Number of hours worked during 1978. Average per employee.

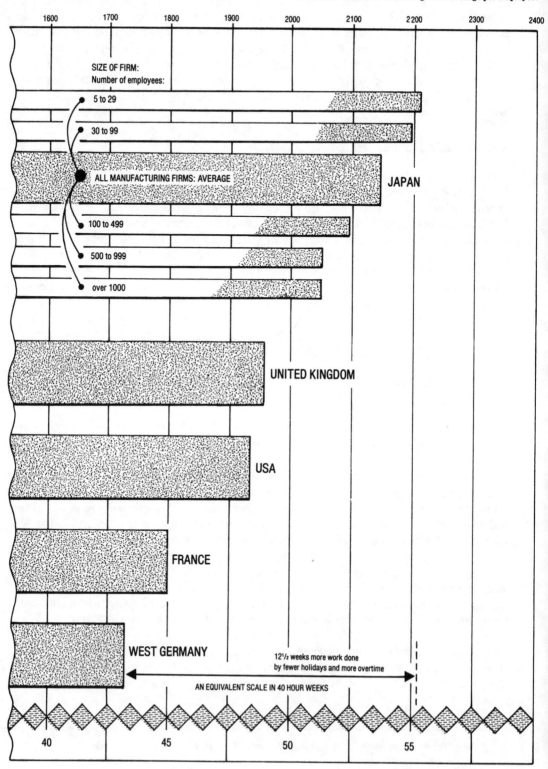

SIZE OF FIRM:
Number of employees:

5 to 29

30 to 99

ALL MANUFACTURING FIRMS: AVERAGE

JAPAN

100 to 499

500 to 999

over 1000

UNITED KINGDOM

USA

FRANCE

WEST GERMANY

12½ weeks more work done
by fewer holidays and more overtime

AN EQUIVALENT SCALE IN 40 HOUR WEEKS

40   45   50   55

Source: Ministry of Labour. White Paper. 1980

equivalent to less than two hours per week. In the smaller enterprises the higher number of hours worked reflects the employees' feeling that lower wages (see Figure 1) can be partly made up for by working longer hours.

Shorter hours might reduce international trade friction

The Ministry of Labour is seeking a reduction in working hours not only for the purpose of securing increased employment opportunities and improving workers' welfare, but also because international trade friction has led to complaints about Japanese being 'workoholics'. As one measure in February, 1981, it was decided that the exemption for small enterprises in the 1947 Labour Standards Law, which now limits scheduled daily working hours to 8 hours, should be abolished in stages up to April 1985.

It may be that the policy target for reducing annual actual working hours to less than 2,000 hours by 1985 is already taking effect. A survey carried out by a policy council of the major unions and released in March, 1981, indicated that on average employees are working 2,016 hours annually. It is interesting that the lowest hours worked - 1,706 - were in technology intensive industries, which suggests that industrial restructuring in Japan will automatically lower the average number of hours worked. (See Chapter V, page 97ff of this report for a discussion on Japan's industrial restructuring.)

ENTERPRISE UNIONS AND INDUSTRIAL RELATIONS

Unions' strength reflected in pay and conditions

The survey on hours worked by the unions' policy council was based on returns from 902 enterprise unions and so may not adequately have covered the smaller enterprises, which are often non-unionised. The contrast in working conditions between large and small enterprises reflects the considerable inherent strength of unions in Japan. Much of that strength emanates from the protection unions receive under the Labour Conciliation Law, Labour Standards Law, and Labour Relations Adjustment Law, which were first promulgated in the early years of the postwar US occupation. Ronald Dore believes that unions thereby benefited from an early social democratic revolution[1]. The result has been that in large scale Japanese enterprises there is no discontinuity in the benefits to workers and to managers. Indeed the number of days of sick pay and the holiday entitlement are a function only of the number of years worked, not of status or rank. Moreover there is evidence that, in comparison with Western Europe, wage differentials between white and blue collar workers tend to be narrow[2].

---

1 Dore R, op cit pages 115-119. 2 Koike K, Nihon no Jūkuren, Yuhikaku-sha, 1981.

FIGURE 4.

CHANGES IN MANUFACTURING: 1970 to 1978

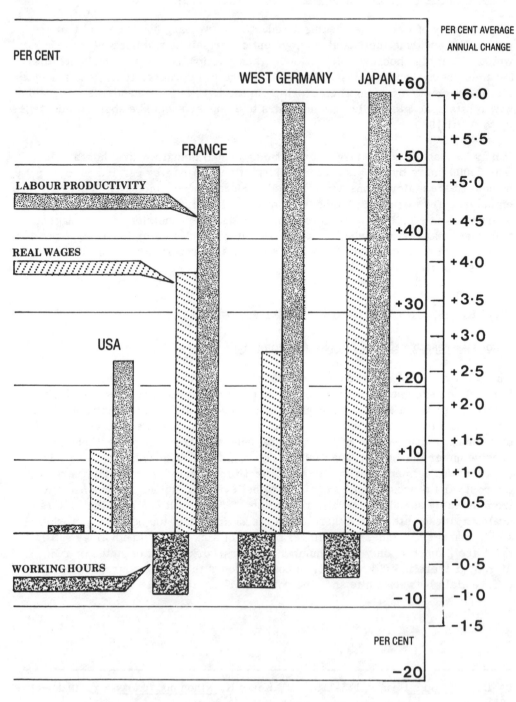

Source: Ministry of Labour. White Paper. 1980

Unions' legal protection has permitted bargaining to be carried out with a clear awareness of relative strengths. Thus a union does not need to resort to shutting down the company with a long drawn out strike. Instead the union can achieve much by embarrassing the management with one day strikes, a slowdown or a work to rule.

Potential labour disputes are further eased by the explicitness of work rules and wage structures. Any firm employing more than ten workers is required to submit its work rules to the Labour Standards Office. The rules must then be posted up in places accessible to employees. Such rules cannot contain clauses which are designed for simple or quick dismissal procedures. Moreover any redundancies which have been finally agreed upon by the union must be accompanied by generous severance benefits.

Thus it may appear that the choice of a rōshikyōchō-rosen (labour harmonising path) by the management may be under legal compulsion with no alternative. The right of union representation on all management committees which might bear some relation to labour conditions would suggest that unions can bring considerable influence on management decisions. However, considerable overtime is worked even in large scale companies, despite many workers' expressed indignation or at least resignation - for overtime mark-ups tend to be quite low at between 25 per cent and 50 per cent of the regular payment. This dissatisfaction would seem to indicate that union power may be more notional than real.

Enterprise unions have good reasons to put job security first -

It is often argued that the power of unions in Japan is weakened because of being enterprise based, rather than across crafts. Such enterprise unions are likely to be as concerned as management that the enterprise is not forced into bankruptcy. However this argument tends implicitly to assume that trade unions in the West are more bent on destroying capitalist enterprises than on protecting jobs. Another related argument is that workers are loyal to their enterprises on account of the Japanese quality of groupism. Yet apparent groupism is probably more an indication of self interest, since the wage structure profiles (see Figure 1) indicate the rewards to be gained from staying with the same company. Moreover, due to extensive on the job training, one's skills tend to be company specific and not easily marketable. Indeed groupism qualities evidently do not apply to the numerous self employed, especially in the retail sector, in Japan.

- but have secured big real wage gains

Thus, for rational reasons, enterprise unions in Japan have been concerned with job security. At the same time, between 1970 and 1978, Japanese unions secured, through coordinated, efficient and meticulous bargaining, higher increases in real wages than in Western industrial countries (Figure 4). Since 1978, the annual spring bargaining (shuntō) has increasingly emphasised extending the retirement age and shortening working hours. As can be seen from Figure 4, between 1970 and 1978, despite Japan's higher gains in labour productivity, working hours were reduced more in France and West Germany.

Important fringe benefits tie workers to companies

The concern of enterprise unions for job security in large scale enterprises is heightened by the substantial non-pecuniary benefits. Large Japanese companies provide dormitories, apartments, and houses at subsidised rents, or with low interest mortgage payments, to their employees. In addition, health insurance is arranged and wages include supplements for the number of family members. Finally, there are usually generous lump sum retirement payments. On the other hand, some commentators feel that such benefits effectively tie the worker to the company, almost against his free will. Satoshi Kamata worked, with a temporary employee status, in a Toyota factory located in Toyota City[1]. In that area employment opportunities with companies other than Toyota Ltd would mean lower wages along with the loss of housing facilities. Kamata's experiences suggest that workers are pushed to their limits under the various rationalisation schemes, which were introduced during the 1970s. Indeed conditions on the factory floor may not be as rosy as often depicted. On asking a group of recent management trainee recruits at another automobile company whether they had enjoyed their obligatory stint in the factory as part of the training, they reacted with highly adverse comments.

Therefore it remains to be seen whether labour-management relations will continue to be as harmonious during the next decade. Slower growth and higher worker expectations, especially in respect of the small and medium sized companies, may result in a loss of confidence and trust in management.

SMALL AND MEDIUM SIZED ENTERPRISES

No longer the "pre-modern" laggards

The large number of small companies operating in the Japanese economy has been a source of concern to the government, which consequently established a specialised Small and Medium Sized Enterprises Agency. Until the 1970s the prevailing opinion was that this 'pre-modern' sector of the economy was unstable - as reflected in higher labour mobility than among large companies - and suffered from low productivity due to an inability to benefit from scale economies. Consequently there was a fear that bankruptcies would become endemic to the small enterprise sector.

However the 1970s have seen a change in the prevailing opinion, which now views the small and medium sized companies as a vital and vigorous part of the Japanese economy. The Small and Medium Sized Enterprises Agency has demonstrated that the proportion of total employment opportunities contributed by smaller companies has increased as larger enterprises have sought to rationalise employment practices in the wake of the oil crises. Moreover some smaller companies'

---

1   Kamata S, Jidōsha Zetsubō Kōjō Gendaishi Shuppankai, Tokyo, 1973.

contribution to value added has risen, as they also have benefited from the semi-conductor revolution. Hence, by their use of integrated circuit technologies – implying higher capital intensification - productivity and wages have risen in these smaller firms so that the differentials with large companies have become narrower in such cases.

In particular, the "system house" industry, which comprises small software and hardware manufacturers and importers, is making a major contribution to the Japanese microcomputer industry. A Nihon Sangyo Shimbun survey found that the usual age of directors in the "system house" industry lies in the mid thirties, because most of the firms have been established in the 1970s. Although such firms were originally based on the mere buying and assembling of parts, including integrated circuits, entrepreneurial drive has led them into customising hardware. Consequently such firms as Sord Computer Systems, Inc, aim to achieve 30 per cent annual growth in sales on the basis of solid ties with corporate clients.

Nonetheless entrepreneurial drive and modern technologies suited to small scale processes may not be sufficient for survival when these firms face the problems of capital availability and lack of resources for research and development. Such requirements may be partially fulfilled through the guidance and support of a 'parent' company. In addition small business associations sometimes have joint R and D programmes.

Subcontractors vulnerable when times are hard

At the same time there is evidence from both the Fair Trade Commission and the Small and Medium Sized Enterprises Agency that when business conditions turn down, 'parent' companies will delay payments or reduce prices for work completed by subcontractors[1]. It has been reported that recently suspected cases of contraventions of the laws designed to prevent such practices have been between 2,700 and 2,900 each year. This is probably one of the factors contributing to the recent high level of bankruptcies in Japan. At the close of the fiscal year in March 1981, private credit survey agencies (Teikoku Databank Ltd and Tokyo Shoko Research Ltd) reported that the total of 18,212 firms going bankrupt during the year was the highest ever recorded.

Despite the fact that poor management is also a contributory factor to bankruptcies among small businesses, one may still conclude that the continued existence of smaller enterprises, including subcontractors, in the Japanese economy illustrates that groupism, as suggested by long term employment with large firms, is only a partial explanation of Japan's corporate environment.

---

1 Asahi Shimbun, February 18, 1981.

THE ROLE OF THE SUBCONTRACTOR

The third kind of grouping of Japanese companies referred to earlier (page 5)
was that of a major company and associated smaller companies, which may or
may not be subsidiaries. Such groupings permit an implicit vertical integration
to operate in that the smaller companies supply intermediate parts and services
to the major company, or engage in on site auxiliary operations (ukeire).

In Japan the mutual ties, and resulting benefits, between a subcontractor and its
'parent' company are popularly designated as representing 'two people with three
legs' (ninin sankyaku), as in a 'three legged' race. The usual system is that the
'parent' firm offers an annual, renewable contract in which the design, specifications
and quality of the components or services required are clearly indicated. In the
1970s rationalisation, especially in the automobile industry, led to a further refine-
ment, known as kamban-hōshiki (literally, 'signboard system'), in which the ukeire
subsidiary has to deliver components directly to the required place on the assembly
line at a specified time in the day. This practice allows the 'parent' company to
pass on the costs and risks associated with inventory storage to the subcontractor.

One way flow of benefits?

In other respects also it appears that the benefits associated with subcontracting
tend to flow in one direction only. One of the means by which a large company is
able to guarantee permanent employment to its labour force is that in times of
slack demand the resort exists of keeping employees occupied on making the
components which had been previously supplied under contract. However, while
this may have been an expedient when production processes were less sophisticated,
it cannot be considered as a significant adjustment mechanism at present.

A more widely practised employment adjustment mechanism is to post temporarily
redundant employees to associated subcontractors. In addition employees of those
companies where the retirement age is 55 years may be found post retirement
employment in subsidiaries, some of which will have been established with this
purpose in mind. Yet, in spite of this apparently close relationship through employment ties, just as in the relationship of keiretsu companies to their lead bank, a
subcontractor may be doing work under contract for several large companies.

The above has focused on the benefits for the 'parent' company in the subcontracting relationship. There may also be a significant drawback in that companies
which are heavily dependent on reliable component supplies prefer not to invest
overseas where a network of subcontracting relationships could not be established
easily. This is probably one of the major factors behind the evident preference of
Japanese automobile manufacturers for trade rather than direct overseas investment. Another aspect of the subcontracting relationship which might at times be
detrimental to the interest of the 'parent' company is that in comparable industries
the gross value added registered by a Japanese manufacturer tends to be less than
in the West.

In general, however, it is the smaller company which is disadvantaged to the
benefit of the large enterprise. Apart from examples such as the "system house"
industry mentioned earlier, in the late 1970s there was a slight widening in the
labour productivity differential between large and small firms. The latter have

not benefited so much from the revolution in production technologies and have been
the receptacle for surplus labour in the Japanese economy.

THE ROLE OF THE GENERAL TRADING COMPANY ABROAD

The trading company's catalytic role –

One common feature of Japanese overseas direct investment, particularly in
South East Asia, has been tie-ups between a Japanese manufacturer, a general
trading company and a local partner. As in the case of the subcontractor relationship, this three way tie-up has received the designation of 'three people with four
legs' (sannin yonkyaku)[1]. The implication is that such a structure permits a
diffusion of risks along with distinct contributions from each of the three partners.

– in bringing together Japanese manufacturer and local partner –

The role of the local partner is to facilitate adaptation of the managerial system to
the prevailing cultural mores, while also perhaps distracting the focus of any
latent hostility against the Japanese. In addition the local partner has often been
an important plank of the production process, since early Japanese overseas
direct investment tended to be in labour intensive standard technologies, such as
textiles. The motivation to engage in production overseas lay in labour shortages
in Japan coupled with import barriers against trade in these lower technology
products. Therefore the local partner would often be the manufacturer in whom
the Japanese company invested through, initially, long term supply contracts for
components and materials coupled with technology transfer agreements. Such
arrangements could include stockholding and directorship positions. Since the
result is tantamount to vertical integration, comparisons have been made with the
subcontractor relationships within Japan[2], although the linkages are usually in
the reverse direction.

– was important in the 1960s, less so in the 1970s

The role of the general trading company (sōgō-shōsha) has been mostly an
integrative one, particularly in providing information to the other two prospective
partners. The general trading company's employees have been more likely to
possess the necessary language skills and knowledge of the local economy than
employees of the manufacturing company. However the influence of the general
trading companies in overseas manufacturing projects declined during the 1970s.
The trading companies' initiative in overseas investment in the late 1960s was

---

1   Kojima K. Kaigai Chokusetsu-Tōshi-Ron. Diamond-sha, Tokyo 1977, page 328.
2   Yoshino. M.Japan's Multinational Enterprises, Harvard University Press,
Cambridge,Massachusetts. 1976, pages 49-50.

too often a hasty response to the raising of import barriers in less developed countries. Thus they engaged in import substitution investment without adequate and comparative project appraisals, so as to maximise profits in the short run. With overseas investment now taking place in advanced technologies, initiatives by the large manufacturing company have become more dominant.

The manufacturing company was often a small one

An interesting feature of the earlier phase of overseas investment in standard technologies was that the third party contributing to the four legs, along with the local partner and general trading company, was often a small or medium sized Japanese enterprise. Due to rising wages in Japan, the labour intensive smaller manufacturing companies found that they could compete more effectively by producing in neighbouring low wage countries. At the same time they lacked the required resources in both capital and overseas management skills, which were supplemented by the general trading company and the local partner. Since the small companies were operating with standard technologies there was no need to protect proprietary knowhow with 100 per cent ownership of the overseas manufacturing company.

Wholly owned subsidiaries now more common

In describing this structure of three partners in a joint manufacturing venture overseas, it should be remembered that, as in many aspects of Japan's industrial structure, there are alternative and increasingly common structures for overseas investment (see Chapter II, page 59ff). Indeed, as may be seen from Table 3, in the precision machinery field more than 60 per cent of overseas investments (by number of local corporations) are in wholly owned subsidiaries, while even for textiles the relative proportion is not quite 13 per cent. Since the technologies for manufacturing precision machinery are advanced and often specific in the firm, the Japanese manufacturer is motivated to maintain 100 per cent equity interest in its overseas subsidiaries.

Table 3

Japanese Equity Interest in Overseas Corporations, 1979/80
(Number of corporations; percentages bracketed)

| | Total | Percentage Japanese interest | | | Average Japanese interest (%) |
		100%	50-99%	Under 50%	
Agriculture, forestry & fishing	128	27	35	66	
	(100.0)	(21.1)	(27.3)	(51.6)	62.5
Mining	67	27	11	29	
	(100.0)	(40.3)	(16.4)	(43.3)	63.4
Manufacturing	1,765	445	574	746	
	(100.0)	(25.2)	(32.5)	(42.3)	60.8
of which:					
food	91	15	29	47	
	(100.0)	(16.5)	(31.9)	(51.6)	55.4

(continued)

Table 3 (continued)

Japanese Equity Interest in Overseas Corporations, 1979/80
(Number of corporations; percentages bracketed)

| | Total | Percentage Japanese interest | | | Average Japanese interest (%) |
		100%	50-99%	Under 50%	
textiles	279	36	101	142	
	(100.0)	(12.9)	(36.2)	(50.9)	54.1
lumber etc	43	7	15	21	
	(100.0)	(16.3)	(34.9)	(48.8)	59.5
chemicals	237	46	73	118	
	(100.0)	(19.4)	(30.8)	(49.8)	55.6
iron & steel	98	7	33	58	
	(100.0)	(7.1)	(33.7)	(59.2)	45.9
non-ferrous metals	50	11	17	22	
	(100.0)	(22.0)	(34.0)	(44.0)	57.6
general machinery	135	49	36	50	
	(100.0)	(36.3)	(26.7)	(37.0)	64.8
electrical machinery	308	121	94	93	
	(100.0)	(39.3)	(30.5)	(30.2)	69.0
transport eqpt	118	25	35	58	
	(100.0)	(21.2)	(29.7)	(49.1)	56.8
precision machinery	59	36	12	11	
	(100.0)	(61.0)	(20.3)	(18.7)	81.9
sundry goods	347	92	129	126	
	(100.0)	(26.5)	(37.2)	(36.3)	65.0
Commerce	1,194	789	238	167	
	(100.0)	(66.1)	(19.9)	(14.0)	85.0
Others	215	108	53	54	
	(100.0)	(50.2)	(24.7)	(25.1)	76.2
Total	3,369	1,396	911	1,062	
	(100.0)	(41.4)	(27.3)	(31.3)	70.4

Source: Miti, Waga-Kuni Kigyo no Kaigai Jigyo Katsudo (Overseas Business Activities of Japanese Enterprises Survey), Tokyo, December 1980. The figures are based on the returned questionnaires of 3,369 overseas corporations with Japanese participation for the 1979/80 fiscal year.

General trading companies assemble project consortia

Nonetheless a role does remain for the general trading company, particularly in helping to absorb the risks associated with plant exports and other turnkey projects. In bidding for large overseas projects, it is common for the general trading company to organise a consortium with Japanese manufacturers. In ordinary trading activities as well, the general trading company assists the small Japanese exporters in the role of a mediator in negotiations. Moreover it may further act as a financial intermediary in arranging credit for the suppliers and importers from the Export-Import Bank of Japan (Yugin). Nor can one ignore the general trading companies' own extensive trading activities. The nine largest companies each deal in over 20,000 different commodities. Consequently it is barely surprising that, for example, C Itoh & Co, Ltd accounted for about 6.7 per cent of Japan's total imports and 6.6 per cent of exports during the fiscal year ending in 1980. Recently general trading companies have been playing an increasingly important role in bringing imports to Japan. Thus between the fiscal years ending in 1979 and 1980 Nissho Iwai Corporation's transactions in imports increased by 28.9 per cent so that import transactions' share of Nissho Iwai's total trade rose from 20 per cent to 29 per cent.

Adaptability characterises Japanese manufacturers

The preceding discussion concerning the structure of a Japanese manufacturing company and the relationships with subcontractors and general trading companies should have demonstrated that one outstanding feature is the degree of adaptability in response to changing economic conditions and social expectations. It may appear on the surface as though employment practices follow rigid, traditional patterns, but in reality the allocation of labour as a resource is reasonably rational and flexible over a longer time perspective. Similarly there is nothing particularly traditional about managerial practices. Instead one may consider that Japanese management is usually characterised by an adaptive ability to introduce innovations and to rationalise production processes, while minimising any resulting disruption of employment.

At the same time one cannot conclude that among the Japanese there is an innate capacity for compromise and consensus. The fact that a consensus is often reached in union-management bargaining on wages or other issues is rather a reflecting of a balancing of countervailing forces in which unions' rights and access to resources are established and respected. It is not only that the status of the bargaining institutions, and the wage and welfare structures, are respected, but also that in a Japanese company individuals - whether as manual or managerial staff - receive mutual respect. Consequently a manual worker takes as much pride in his work as anyone else, which leads to a stronger work ethic than is common in the West.

Chapter 2

Japan's Industrial Performance: 1960~1980

One does not have to look beyond the industrial production indices in order to understand that even since 1960 Japan's industrial structure has been remarkably transformed, and has been accompanied by high growth rates in most sectors (Table 4). The degree of transformation is most strikingly illustrated by a comparison of the index for textile output with that for electrical machinery, which indicates a shift from labour intensive, standard technologies to capital intensive, innovative technologies. It is also noticeable that the basic materials industries, while registering steady growth since 1975, have shown a vulnerability to recessionary conditions that was not experienced to the same degree in the machinery and equipment sector. In particular, the production of fertilisers and organic chemicals has suffered on account of oil price rises, the last half of 1980 seeing the seasonally adjusted production index for fertilisers dipping below 80 and for organic chemicals dropping to 100. On the other hand in the same period the index for telecommunications and electronic apparatus parts rose to over 300, while for the category of 'other applied electronic equipment' (whose 1955 weighting is only 11.2) it reached an outstanding 2,700. In passing it should be noted that the production index for shipbuilding is now varying around 50 (see page 48).

The above figures indicate that Japan's industrial growth has been highly sensitive to changes in relative factor costs. Therefore one must conclude that it is again a capacity for adapting and innovating, in addition to appropriately flexible institutions and structures, which has been a major factor in Japan's high growth rates and resilience in the face of world economic recessions. This capacity needs to be examined in greater detail while drawing on the features described in the preceding chapter.

Many of the factors which have been major contributors to Japan's continued industrial growth since 1960 are interrelated - such as technology and productivity. However, so as to simplify the presentation, the factors are divided into categories, while bearing in mind that there are overlaps - particularly in causation.

THE UNDERLYING CONDITIONS

EDUCATION

It has been generally realised that during the 1950s the standard and diffusion of education in Japan was at a level considerably above that of other countries at a similar stage of development and, indeed, of countries now industrialising.

Table 4

Selected Indices of Industrial Production, 1960–80 (1975=100)

	Weights[a]	1960	1970	1974	1976	1978	1980 1 Qtr[b]	2 Qtr[b]	3 Qtr[b]	4 Qtr[b]
Foodstuffs & tobacco	899.3	39.9	89.9	98.4	101.5	107.8	117.4	106.9	104.0	110.5
Chemicals	953.9	22.3	86.8	109.9	111.5	131.3	150.3	151.5	137.7	139.7
Textiles	897.1	47.9	105.2	106.1	108.4	107.7	109.6	108.9	104.9	104.9
Iron & steel	659.9	22.4	94.2	116.9	109.5	110.1	128.5	128.3	122.5	120.1
Fabricated metal products	504.6	24.4	96.9	123.0	116.8	135.4	142.8	139.7	125.6	123.3
Machinery & equipment	3,724.0	16.5	87.7	116.2	113.7	131.3	166.3	172.0	175.1	182.1
of which:										
industrial machinery	1,284.6	22.1	105.2	126.3	109.9	126.0	158.9	161.9	154.8	163.0
electrical machinery	1,103.8	14.6	87.1	118.0	128.3	155.2	198.5	207.9	218.0	226.4
transport equipment	1,179.3	12.8	73.2	104.6	102.2	106.8	126.9	130.6	132.5	132.3
Total manufacturing	9,928.0	25.3	92.2	112.1	111.2	123.0	143.7	143.9	140.7	142.9

a Derived from 1955 data; those of manufacturing and mining total 10,000.   b Seasonally adjusted.

Sources: Prime Minister's Office, Statistics Bureau, Nihon Tokei Nonkan (Japan Statistical Yearbook); Miti, Research and Statistics Department, Tsusen Tokei (Industrial Statistics Monthly).

Consequently industry could depend upon all employees having received a sound and rigorous education. Moreover the educational system in Japan, with its emphasis on achievement in examinations, has tended to foster highly disciplined and well motivated attitudes. What has been less widely recognised is that the relatively homogeneous nature of education meted out to the Japanese has effectively attenuated the development of rigid class structures differentiating between the manual worker and managerial staff. As long ago as the Meiji period in the late 19th century a universal education system was established so that, whatever a man's later status, he had had broadly the same cultural conditioning as others of a lower or a higher status. The consequent widespread feeling of egalitarianism has permitted, for example, reasonably frank labour-management consultation to be held over equipment investment plans and productivity proposals.

Although it has not been definitively demonstrated that higher levels of education among manual workers cause higher productivity, the success of quality control circles, which require a grasp of statistical knowledge and an analytical approach to problem solving, would suggest that education has become generally embodied in human capital. A clearer direct contribution of a universal meritocratic education system is in bearing more or less the whole burden of occupational allocation. Consequently, although it has been calculated that the private rate of return to a university education is relatively low[1], university entrance is still highly competitive; for by that means one's later occupational status is determined. There is a high correlation between educational qualifications and occupational status.

CONSUMERS' CONTRIBUTION

Instead of just achieving high consumption levels, the Japanese have rather been noted for their consistently high household savings rates. Even in 1981 the ratio of household savings in Japan to disposable income remains the world's highest and is nearly four times larger than that in the USA. Recent data indicate that, despite stagnation in the growth of real incomes during the late 1970s, household savings have continued to rise. For example, in 1980 average annual take home pay rose nominally by 6.1 per cent, but average household savings increased by 10.3 per cent.

Table 5

Average Total Savings per Household in Japan

	1978		1979		1980	
	¥'00,000	% change	¥'00,000	% change	¥'00,000	% change
Post & bank deposits (ordinary & time)	26.0	14.0	28.5	9.6	32.1	12.6
Loan & money trusts	1.8	-	2.4	33.3	2.3	-4.2
						(continued)

1   Sellars S. 'Japan's Labour Market and Higher Education', unpublished paper, University of Sussex, 1979.

Table 5 (continued)

Average Total Savings per Household in Japan

	1978		1979		1980	
	¥'00,000	% change	¥'00,000	% change	¥'00,000	% change
Life insurance	6.6	3.1	6.9	4.5	7.6	10.1
Postal annuity	0.5	1.3	0.5	-	0.7	40.0
Securities	4.1	20.6	4.3	4.9	4.2	-2.3
Property accumulation savings	0.6	20.0	1.1	83.3	1.3	18.2
Total	39.6	11.9	43.7	10.4	48.2	10.3

Source: Bank of Japan's Central Committee for Promotion of Savings.

It is not the purpose of this report to analyse the personal motives behind such high rates of saving, but it may be noted in passing that, according to recent questionnaire surveys, almost 80 per cent of respondents state their motivation to be a provision against illness, accidents, and other emergencies. Thus the employee welfare benefits provided by large companies and the familial atmosphere of smaller companies must be marginal in relieving the anxieties of most people. Therefore one cannot judge Japanese companies to be paternalistic, even though this is a common misconception.

The high savings rates during the 1960s do not necessarily require an explanation based on personal motives. Since high economic growth led to annual increases of 11 to 12 per cent in nominal disposable income, the value of past savings compared unfavourably with present income. Therefore in order to maintain a savings balance in proportion to the rising standard of living, it was necessary to deposit a larger percentage of annual income towards savings. Savings rates also rose in line with people's acquisition of real assets, particularly houses.

The rising standard of living further contributed to the development of mass markets for durable consumer goods. Especially with respect to the sale of electrical consumer goods, the sudden rise in the number of people with the means to purchase refrigerators, televisions, etc, enabled manufacturers to increase output rapidly and thereby to benefit from economies of scale. At the same time the rapid rise to prominence of a few makers in any one field - with the result that nationwide advertising is required to reach consumers effectively - may have brought about a significant entry barrier to competitors, especially prospective importers.

THE GOVERNMENT'S ROLE

The rise in consumers' living standards during the 1960s appeared to be on the initiative of the government with its announced shotoku baizō (income-doubling plan). Although one cannot conclude that it was just the hand of the government which brought about industrial growth, through 'administrative guidance' the government did play a part. Not only the influence of the government itself, but also the cohesion and strength of the cooperative zaikai (literally 'financial' world, that is, major business leaders) meant that appropriate institutional features were established for Japan's economic development. At the same time the zaikai leaders were not always in agreement with the government, which left scope for adjustment and consultation.

A well defined official strategy –

A Council on Industrial Structure (Sangyokozo Shingikai) was established under the auspices of Miti (the Ministry of International Trade and Industry) in 1964. During the 1960s and 1970s, this so called Sankoshin became the main policy making body on all aspects of industrial structure and industrial policy, ranging from finance to pollution to technology to international economics and many other topics, each of which was placed in one of 21 sectional councils. In this way the government strategy for industry, which culminated in a drive for industrial readjustment in the late 1970s, could be well defined.

– and various forms of guidance to implement it

After definition of a strategy, there still remains the need to find a means for implementation. One way employed up until at least 1965 was that of governmental restrictions and influence on technology imports. The purpose was to avoid duplicate imports which might have led to excess capacity. This objective was reinforced by 'administrative guidance' (gyosei-shido) on investment plans which would create new capacity or bring new firms into an industry. 'Administrative guidance' did not usually depend on statutory means, but on an authority emanating from a ministry or government agency, in addition to various policy instruments.

The use of controls over technology imports has already been mentioned, and this was supplemented during the 1950s and early 1960s by foreign exchange allocation for purchases of intermediate inputs. In Chapter I (page 4) reference has been made to the government's partial control over financing facilities, which took a positive form in giving access to low interest loans mostly financed by postal savings from the public Japan Development Bank. All these policy instruments, however. have become of much less importance during the 1970s, as resort is now made to guidance through a trade association or an industry's coordinating group.

Enumerating the means by which the government could engage in 'administrative guidance' may have given a misleading impression of considerable authority and singlemindedness. In fact, apart from the counterbalancing strength of the zaikai leaders, there were contrary forces at work within the government as well. Miti and the Fair Trade Commission were often at loggerheads over the former's policy of encouraging mergers between smaller enterprises so as to achieve scale economies.

Former civil servants take posts in industry

Nonetheless it has sometimes been suggested that the government holds the key to less overt ways of influencing industrial activity. The practice of amakudari (literally. "descending from heaven"), whereby ex-bureaucrats are given leading positions in private firms. is often instanced as an indication of 'special' relationships between the bureaucracy and private industry. During 1980 the National Personnel Authority reported that 228 former officials from 20 ministries and agencies entered private companies, including Hitachi Ltd, and Nippon Steel Corp. Since it is only necessary to seek the approval of the National Personnel Authority if the job in private business bears some close connection with one's former official position, the above figures may be only a small fraction of the total extent of amakudari.

A role in overseas resource development

Recently the government's role in encouraging large scale overseas investment projects, especially for exploitation of natural resources, has been evident. In May, 1981, after some disagreement between Miti and the Ministry of Finance over whether the government's equity holding should be 50 per cent or 40 per cent, it was announced that the government would contribute 45 per cent of the equity in a Japanese investment company for a Japan-Saudi Arabia joint petrochemical project. Thereby the government decided, through the Cabinet, that the project should be a national level undertaking.

TECHNOLOGICAL RESEARCH AND DEVELOPMENT

Research spending grew faster than GNP in the 1960s

Since the 1950s there have been substantial changes in Japan's technological priorities, which have been both contributory to and indicative of the adjustments in industrial structure. Unlike the 1950s, when technological imports had been directed towards large scale capital processes for the production of producer goods, the 1960s were characterised by the introduction of technologies for automated production lines and for the improvement of quality and performance of the product. These priorities reflected both the rapid development of a mass domestic market for consumer durables and an intention to produce for competitive export markets. At the same time production in these spheres led to increased demand for iron and steel products and for synthetic macromolecular materials, which stimulated further innovative technologies, such as automated rolling, in the basic materials industries. Moreover complementary research and development (R & D) activities in transport and communication systems led to considerable technological progress. Indeed in the 1960s the growth of research expenditure exceeded growth in GNP, to reach 2 per cent of GNP in 1971.

R & D activity intensified in the 1970s -

By the 1970s the government had already begun to encourage duplicate technology imports, which previously had been subject to strict controls. By 1971 74 per cent of technology imports, by number of cases, were for duplicates. Such technologies permitted not only a greater diffusion of advanced technologies, especially to smaller enterprises, but also improvement in existing technologies. By this time technological priorities were geared to electronics, energy conservation and pollution control, all of which require more pioneering efforts in R & D and, in the case of the latter two, more public expenditure. With respect to electronics research, it is interesting to compare investment in plant and equipment each year with expenditure on R & D for integrated circuits (IC). In 1971, 1972 and 1975,

FIGURE 5.

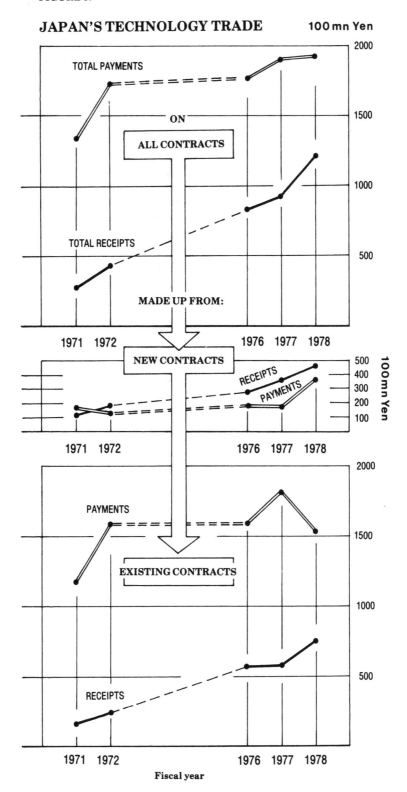

JAPAN'S TECHNOLOGY TRADE   100 mn Yen

Source: MITI, White Paper. 1980

the latter expenditure outweighed plant and equipment investment in the electronics industry by between ¥10 mn and ¥180 mn. Indeed it may be that the stagnant growth in capital spending after the 1973 oil crisis stimulated technological progess; for in the latter half of the 1970s the contribution of technological progress to production growth - particularly conspicuous in the chemical, general and electrical machinery industries - is considered to have been relatively high.

- paying off in technology transfers and exports

The intensification of indigenous R & D activities during the 1970s led to two further significant developments. One was that in terms of newly contracted technology transfer agreements Japan had become a net exporter by 1972, as shown in Figure 5. Although continuing payments for prior contracts still far outweigh receipts, the gap is steadily narrowing. The other interesting development is that, whereas in the 1960s those industries with a relatively large export share (defined as the ratio of Japan's share in OECD exports by industry to Japan's total share), such as iron and steel, and textiles, tended not to be research intensive (ratio of R & D expenditure to sales below 1 per cent), in the 1970s it was the research intensive industries, such as precision machinery and electrical machinery and equipment, which had high export shares.

Having briefly examined the trends during the 1960s and 1970s in technological progress, it would be useful to focus on two particular concerns. One is the degree to which Japanese industry has been dependent on foreign technology, and the other is government involvement in research and development.

Is Japan better at catch-up technology than innovation?

As is clear from Figure 5, Japan has been a considerable importer of foreign technologies; yet international trade in technology is generally considered to be both natural and beneficial in stimulating further technological progress. In particular Japanese industry has maximised the benefits from imported technologies through domestic cost effective R & D, coupled with adroit management and investment. At the same time it must be asked why Japanese industry failed to produce indigenously many innovative research development until the 1970s. It has been suggested that qualitatively Japanese scientists and engineers, because of their rather standard undergraduate training, may be more suited to catch-up, than to pioneering technologies[1]. Nonetheless, just as with managerial staff, engineers receive intensive training after entering a company. Moreover the nature of the Japanese employment system brings research staff into close and durable relations with production engineers, which ought to be a conduit for effective R & D.

Another pertinent factor is the customary relationship between a company and certain professors, who have recommended graduates or performed consultancy

---

1   Peck, M J with Tamura S, 'Technology', in Patrick H and Rosovsky H (eds) Asia's New Giant, The Brookings Institution, Washington, 1976 pages 575-580.

services. For example a pharmaceutical company such as Yoshitomi publishes seemingly impartial research reports on pharmaceutical products written by university faculty members.

It is true that Japanese companies have tended not to engage in the kind of high risk, long term basic research which is often characteristic of large US enterprises. On the other hand the smaller size of most Japanese companies may have permitted a wider diffusion of advanced technologies, as in the case of the "system house" industry for micro-computers (see page 26). In addition it has been pointed out that the subcontracting relationship enables technologies to be diffused to small companies.

The role of the government

With respect to the Japanese government's contribution to research and development, it will be seen from Table 6 that the government's share in supplying funds is considerably lower than in the West. However a Western government's research contribution tends to be devoted to military research, whereas in Japan the government plays an active role in industrial technological research - especially on computers during the early 1970s. Correspondingly private industry's research contribution in Japan is relatively high. This is partly due to governmental promotion through preferential tax measures, including tax reduction on income from technology exports and deductions for increased experimentation and research expenditures. In addition governmental subsidies have been made available, with the emphasis on energy related research, in the late 1970s.

Table 6

Users and Suppliers of R & D Funds: International Comparison[a]
(percentages)

	Japan 1978	USA[b] 1978	UK 1975	West Germany 1977	France[b] 1977
Users					
Industry	64.2	70.3	62.7	68.4	60.3
Government	13.6	13.9	26.6	15.2	22.8
Non-profit research institutes	2.3	3.2	2.4	0.2	1.4
Universities etc	20.0	12.6	8.4	16.2	15.5
Suppliers					
Industry	65.0	46.1	40.8	55.6	41.1
Government	28.0	50.4	51.7	41.3	52.7
Non-profit research institutes	0.4	1.5	2.6	0.2	0.6
Universities etc	6.4	2.1	-	-	-
From overseas	0.1	-	4.9	2.9	5.6

a Categories and definitions differ between countries. b Figures include funds for research in the humanities and social sciences.

Source: OECD data.

FIGURE 6.

Japan's R&D Expenditure NATURAL SCIENCES

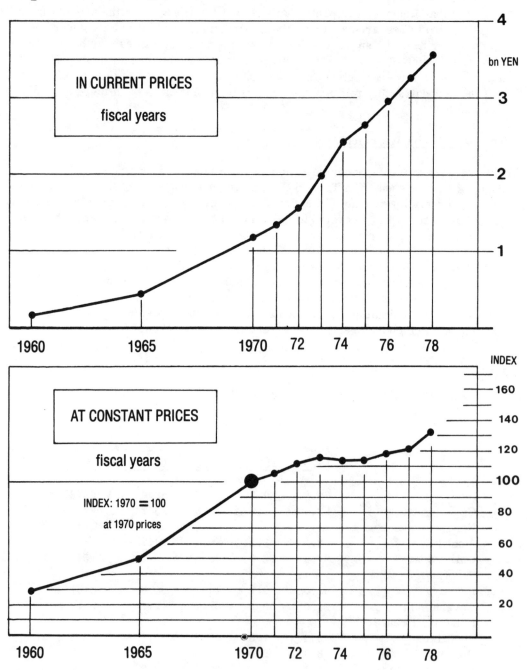

Source: Science and Technology Agency. White Paper. 1980

FIGURE 7.

TRENDS IN OBJECTIVES
FOR TECHNOLOGICAL
RESEARCH IN JAPAN

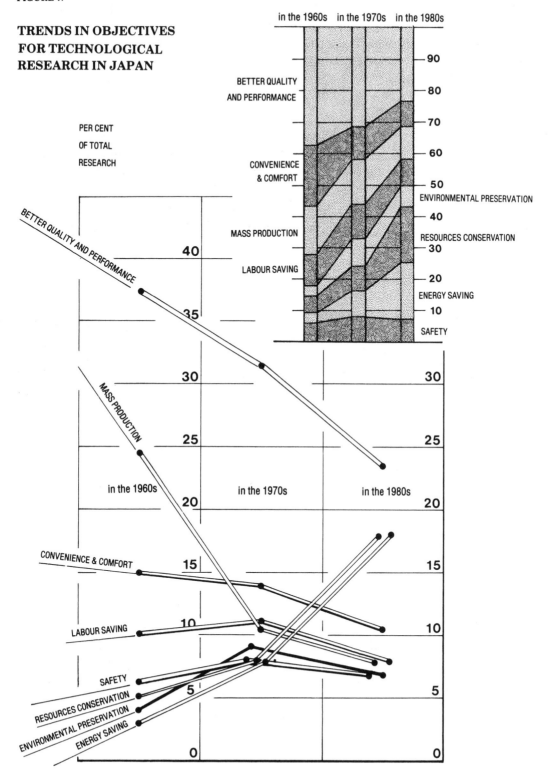

Source: Science and Technology Agency. White Paper. 1980

45

Finally it should be mentioned that the government laid the groundwork in the 1950s and 1960s with the establishment of agencies and councils, which tended to proliferate, and the enactment of facilitating laws such as the Manufacturing Industries' Technological Research Cooperatives Law. An indication of the power of governmental promotion activities was given, in May 1981, when it was announced that Hitachi Ltd, Hitachi Metals Ltd and Sony Corp had developed new electronic products from amorphous metal material at the request of the governmental Research Development Corporation.

To sum up this section on research and development, two figures have been presented. The first, Figure 6, shows the growth in total outlay on research in Japan since 1960; the second, Figure 7, has been compiled from surveys on private enterprises by the Science and Technology Agency to indicate how the objectives for technological research have tended to alter, according to the degree of priority given, over time. These figures demonstrate that in contrast to Western experience, the momentum for research has neither slackened nor been inflexible in its orientation.

LABOUR PRODUCTIVITY

Naturally technological innovations have been one of the major factors contributing to Japan's well known high growth rates for labour productivity. At the same time the Japanese Ministry of Labour considers that industries are still lagging behind the West both in R & D expenditure and manpower training[1]. Therefore one must consider the other factors which have ensured that the growth of labour productivity in Japan's manufacturing industry has been well above that of Western industrial countries, even after the initial catch up period.

Productivity was boosted –

Between 1960 and 1980 Japanese labour productivity increased more than fourfold, while the USA and the UK barely doubled their labour productivity indices. After the 1973/74 oil crisis, Japan's industry was relatively tardy in rationalising manpower in the face of a sharp drop in industrial output (see Table 4). Consequently labour productivity in manufacturing actually declined between 1974 and 1975 by 4 per cent, as can be seen from Table 7. However since 1975/76 the annual percentage increase in labour productivity in manufacturing has averaged out at around 8 per cent (geometric mean).

– by economies of scale in the 1960s –

In fact the periods before and after 1973/74 represent two distinct phases in labour productivity growth, with different contributory factors and results. During the 1960s plant and equipment investment was carried out with the primary objectives of enlarging capacity and increasing capital intensification, in response to heightened

---

1   Ministry of Labour, Rōdō Makusho (Labour White Paper) 1980.

demand. The result was that scale economies were reaped, and so labour productivity rose from a low base in line with higher capital equipment per worker rates. At that time the ratio, averaging above 18 per cent, of Japan's private capital expenditure to GNP was the highest among the industralised countries being supported by a high savings rate. When looking at production growth in individual industries during the 1960s it appears that the contribution from increased capital equipment was particularly significant in the case of steel, non-ferrous metals, petrochemicals, and shipbuilding, but for textiles and electrical machinery the contribution was, for different reasons, rather low.

- and labour saving investment in the 1970s

Since 1976 the factors underlying continuing high growth rates in labour productivity are more complex; but for simplification the two categories of the capacity utilisation and the output coefficient may be considered. Capacity utilisation was raised through both increased overtime by labour from 1978 onwards and better skills in employing capital equipment. The output coefficient has been affected by advanced technologies embodied in new capital equipment accompanied by labour saving investments, such as NC machine tools, and rationalisation of manpower. It is interesting to compare the employment index for manufacturing in the 1960s, when it was rising as labour was supplied from low productivity sectors, to the period of decline from 1974 to early 1979. These advanced production technologies could be typified by the development of the continuous casting process in the steel industry. The choice of such technologies and labour saving investments, despite general stagnation in plant and equipment investment, has been shown, by various surveys on objectives for investment, to have been deliberate - without usually the prime intention of increasing capacity.

Significant disparities in productivity performance

In discussing the high growth rate of labour productivity in Japan one has to be aware of significant disparities, both between large and small firms and between different industries. The latter aspect is partly illustrated by Table 7 in which the processed foods industry shows only marginal productivity growth, while textiles and the iron and steel industry lag behind the others. The breakdown into more detailed industrial groups demonstrates that, whereas the shoe industry did not achieve any growth in productivity between 1975 and 1980, the index for electrical machinery had risen to 235.8 by October, 1980. These disparities in labour productivity for the production of different goods have been reflected in divergent price movements.

With respect to the differences between large and small firms, Table 8 shows the size of the firm significantly affects the value added per employee and, correspondingly, employees' cash earnings.

Table 7

Selected Indices of Labour Productivity
(1975=100)

	Manufacturing	Iron & steel	Machinery & equipment	Chemicals	Textiles	Foodstuffs & tobacco
Weights [a]	95.35	6.34	35.76	9.16	8.62	8.64
Indices [b]						
1970	76.7	73.0	72.5	79.3	78.6	78.4
1974	104.1	106.7	106.0	106.4	95.9	100.3
1976	112.3	111.3	115.9	113.3	110.5	93.3
1978	127.4	121.4	131.7	136.9	124.2	100.5
1980						
Jan	152.9	151.1	171.6	158.1	134.5	117.1
Jun	152.6	145.4	185.0	155.8	130.8	91.8
Oct	158.2	145.8	192.8	160.5	130.4	105.2

a Weights are based on added value in 1975 Census of Manufacturers. b Indices are derived
from the output indices divided by the appropriate labour input indices, based on input in man-days.

Source: Japan Productivity Institute (Nihon Seisansei Honbu).

Table 8

Manufacturing Value Added and Employee Earnings by Size of Firm

Year	Size: no of employees	Total no. of employees in category	Average value added per employee (¥ mn/year)	Average cash earnings per employee (Yen/year)
1965	1-10	1,598,856	0.48	180,286
1978[a]	4-9	1,519,281	3.03	1,414,432
1965	20-	637,788	0.73	345,113
1978	29	884,525	4.12	1,820,532
1965	100-	1,551,148	1.01	400,991
1978	299	1,649,496	5.91	2,353,501
1965	1,000 and	1,644,946	1.63	561,232
1978	over	1,511,729	8.79	3,360,818

a Between 1965 and 1978 the smallest enterprises were redefined.

Source: Miti, Kōgyō Tōkei Gaisū-Hyō (Industrial Statistics Summary).

Indeed the difference in the growth rates of labour productivity between large and small firms tended to widen between 1975 and 1978 as large firms sought to rationalise their manpower levels. For example, between 1960 and 1973 the average annual rate of increase of labour productivity in firms employing more than 500 people was only one percentage point above that in firms employing fewer than 29. Between 1975 and 1978, however, the difference was in the order of three percentage points. Commensurately the large scale firms were able to reduce their wage costs, while the total cost of labour continued to rise in the smallest enterprises.

Social factors have helped

Before concluding this rather general discussion on labour productivity growth, which will be complemented with specific examples later in this chapter, other factors which contributed less directly should be briefly considered. The human factor, in the shape of high educational levels among manual labour and improved management efficiency in the latter half of the 1970s, has been important in enabling quality control circles to operate effectively. (See pages 54ff for further remarks on quality control.) It has further been argued that cooperative labour-management relations in Japan have enabled higher levels of productivity to be reached, most evidently in facilitating the introduction of automated processes. It may also be true that the wider diffusion of technology among enterprises since the late 1960s has heightened inter-company competition and consequently efficiency. An important external factor is that the international competitiveness of Japanese industry permitted high levels of demand to be maintained, which aided productivity and thereby, in a circular fashion, reinforced international competitiveness. So, high labour productivity growth in Japan has been both the cause and the result of industrial success.

One remarkable aspect of Japan's economic growth is that it accelerated in real terms during the 1960s, even though Japan's relative economic backwardness had already been largely rectified. Moreover in the late 1970s high growth rates were maintained, after output per caput and capital investment growth had reached levels comparable with those in West Germany and the USA. Although there was no growth in fiscal 1974, by 1976 real GNP growth had surged again to 5.9 per cent. The second oil crisis had little lasting impact in that in the fiscal years 1979/80 and 1980/81 real growth rates were 6.1 per cent and 5.0 per cent respectively, the latter rate being 0.2 percentage points above the forecast and initially estimated growth rate. In particular during 1980 industrial production exceeded its targeted growth of 4.5 per cent to reach 4.6 per cent. Thus Japan's Economic Planning Agency has been able to conclude that the economy has emerged from the recession caused by oil price rises in the late 1970s. The renewed vitality of manufacturing industries is attested to by the fact that plant and equipment rose in nominal terms by 28.8 per cent during 1980/81.

INTERFIRM COMPETITION

There is evidence of effective competition –

The extent to which industrial growth encourages competition, and in turn is nourished by it, is an interesting analytical question which is not within the scope of this report. Instead an examination is made of whether market competition does exist between Japanese firms, both in domestic and export markets. It is sometimes suspected, in particular, that collusive arrangements are set up in order to aid Japanese overseas penetration and that the entry barriers to the domestic market are impossibly high. However these suspicions are shown to have little real foundation beyond certain cultural misunderstandings.

The Japanese themselves have often referred to a problem of 'excessive competition' (katō kyōso), which leads to the installation of extra capacity in order to gain a larger market share. This is viewed as a problem because the total additional capacity is in excess of domestic market demand. During the 1960s Miti took the argument of 'excessive competition' as a justification for engaging in guidance on investing in extra capacity. Yet at times of high growth one day's excess capacity could be appropriate for the additional demand not long after, so it is hard to judge whether the argument was reasonable. Nonetheless it has been noted that down-ward price rigidity in Japan is less than elsewhere, which is witnessed to by the real price declines in consumer durables and in microelectronic goods. Thus while competition may not have been excessive, neither has it been dormant.

– despite the existence of the keiretsu groupings

On the other hand it has sometimes been argued that the existence of the keiretsu groupings suggests an insidious way of limiting effective competition. However, as shown in Chapter I (page 5) the links between group members are tenuous enough to preclude the possibility of control and tight coordination. In addition, where more than one member of a group is operating in the same industry, there has not been adequate evidence of collusion. At the same time, one cannot deny that group members must influence one another - particularly through the lead bank or trading company - or there would be a limited rationale for their continued existence. The influence is most likely to be in the form of the lead bank putting a damper on overambitious investment plans - because of its position as subordinated creditor - or in coming to the aid of members in difficulties. This would suggest that some kind of business reciprocity is required, but it usually comes in the form of rather higher interest payments to one's lead bank.

Recession cartels are a special case

It is true that the predominance of a few companies in some industries permits oligopolistic collusion to be practised. However in a high growth economy accompanied by substantial plant and equipment investments, collusive practices cannot be effective in the long run, because each firm will tend to drift away or cheat in order to use its additional capacity. For those industries, however, such as shipbuilding and plastics, which experience recessionary conditions, production cartels have been formed, with government approval, for the purpose of restraining output. For example, under the shipbuilding industry's cartel formed in August 1979, output is limited to about half the peak level of 1975 when ships totalling 17 mn gross tons were built. At the time of government approval for a cartel, output had been brought as low as 4.45 mn gross tons that year, but afterwards production began to rise despite the cartel. The industry's justification for limiting output is that it will improve quality (according to Ichikawa of Mitsubishi Heavy Industries Ltd[1]). through developing ships geared to energy conservation.

The shipbuilding industry's cartel has been viewed sympathetically by the government on account of increased competition from South Korean yards, but other cartels do not receive similar treatment. The Fair Trade Commission (FTC) recommends the annulment of illegal cartel arrangements which number about 100 each year. Where companies refuse to accept recommendations, which arise after evidence is found of collusive practices intended to raise prices or to limit bidders in tenders, penalties are imposed.

Industrial concentration may have declined

The Anti-Monopoly Law under which the FTC operates has been criticised for being applicable only to potential mergers, rather than able to dissolve existing mergers. This may be the result of Miti's policy, especially during the 1950s and 1960s, of encouraging the rationalisation of small enterprises through mergers. Nonetheless, despite this policy, a rigorous statistical analysis has demonstrated there to be little difference in industry concentration between Japan and the USA[2]. Indeed it can be argued convincingly that Japan's high economic growth rates have brought about a decline in concentration since the early 1950s, as evidenced by continued entrepreneurial success in smaller firms, as in the "systems house" industry.

---

1   Japan Times, June 6, 1981.   2   Caves R with Uekusa M, Industrial Organisation in Japan, Brookings Institution, Washington, 1976, pages 20-28.

RESPONSE TO OIL CRISES

Japan rides out the second oil price shock –

Japan's dependence on imported oil has been well documented. In particular, as
an industrialised country with a relatively low service orientation the effects of
the 1973/74 oil crisis on output and productivity were immense (see Tables 4 and
7). However, since the second oil crisis at the close of the 1970s Japanese industry
has maintained its vitality. The reasons lie partly in external factors, such as
the staged rise in oil prices in the second case, and the price stabilisation policies
employed by the government and the Bank of Japan; but Japan's industry itself has
been primarily responsible for the successful recovery.

– thanks to the flexible response of wages –

Japan's Economic Planning Agency (EPA) has postulated that the two main factors
permitting industry's continued growth have been the flexible rates of increases
in wages and the active competition among enterprises. (Keizai-Hakusho – White
Paper on the Economy – 1980.) In 1980 the average spring wage increase was
just 6.9 per cent, but the consequent stagnation in real incomes and depression in
consumer demand resulted in an average 7.7 per cent increase being agreed upon
in spring 1981. It seems that workers' memories of the impact of the first oil
crisis led to moderate wage demands. There was also the coercive aspect in
managements' emphasis on rationalisation by cutting personnel costs, both through
employment adjustment and merit payments, in recognition of slower growth.

– and competitive attention to energy saving

The second factor of competition between enterprises has been discussed earlier,
but here the effect on energy consumption is considered. Again the stimulus of
lower growth expectations led to a greater concern with return on capital employed
rather than mere concentration on augmenting one's market share. Thus competition has led to enterprises seeking ways of saving on energy costs, including long
term investment projects. The consequences have been remarkable. In the basic
materials industries energy input per output has decreased and alternative energy
sources have been employed. The resulting declines in demand for petroleum
products are clear from Table 9.

Table 9

Trends in Demand for Petroleum Products in Japan[a]
('000 cu m; fiscal years)

	1978/79	1979/80	1980/81
Gasoline	33,875	34,511	34,680
	(7.5)	(1.9)	(0.5)
Naphtha	34,968	33,496	26,293
	(–)	(–4.2)	(–21.5)
Intermediate distillates – gas oil, kerosene, A fuel oil	67,963	68,369	66,471
	(8.4)	(0.6)	(–2.8)

(continued)

52

Table 9 (continued)

Trends in Demand for Petroleum Products in Japan[a]
('000 cu m; fiscal years)

	1978/79	1979/80	1980/81
C fuel oil	88,534	87,377	73,955
	(-1.1)	(-1.3)	(-15.4)
Total domestic demand for fuel oils[b]	235,078	233,172	209,618
	(2.5)	(-0.8)	(-10.4)

a Figures in brackets represent percentage increase from
previous year.   b Including jet fuel and B fuel oil.

Source: Petroleum Statistics Monthly and Sanwa Bank.

Part of the reason for the decline in demand lies in the fact that the basic materials
industries' output growth has been rather slow since 1978 (see Table 4). However
the particularly notable 15.4 per cent decrease in demand for C fuel oil in 1980 is
primarily due to the steel and cement industries actually not demanding any fuel
oil as they shifted to blast furnaces and cement kilns using no oil. The aggregate
result of such measures by industrial enterprises is that the elasticity of petroleum
consumption to GNP growth has fallen below unity, whereas it was between 1.0 and
1.2 before 1973.

In a less direct way than those mentioned above Japan's industry has emerged from
the recent oil crisis with vigour on account of the introduction of new high quality
products, such as VTRs in the electronics industry and seamless pipes in the steel
industry. Within a short time such products have established internationally strong
market shares, which have provided growing demand, both directly and indirectly,
for related industries.

PATTERNS OF INVESTMENT AND INNOVATION

Willingness to invest in innovative technologies -

The ability of Japan's industries to recover from oil price rises has been dependent
on active capital investment, which has naturally also been a continuing crucial
factor in industrial growth since the 1950s. Such investment has been assisted by
both the relatively low and controlled interest rates, and by the decreasing relative
price of investment goods. The gains from active investment in plant and equipment have been heightened during the 1970s on account of the productivity factors
embodied in capital goods, as in the use of robots and numerically controlled
machine tools. Moreover by the fourth quarter of 1980 the capital goods industry
itself (excluding transport equipment) had reached a production index of 171.4
(1975=100), with electrical machinery at 190.1. These indices may be compared
with the general trends in industrial production for consumer and investment goods
in Table 10.

At the same time one cannot conclude that it is only investment which has propelled
Japan's industrial growth. Although various analyses have demonstrated that the

capital contribution has outweighed others[1], its presence and its contribution have depended on other factors, particularly the adaptations in employment and the application of new techniques or, more generally, knowledge. In this respect the willingness to invest in innovative technologies has been the really determining factor. It is not important whether or not Japanese research was responsible for the original invention. As examined earlier, in the 1960s the size and scope of Japanese industries did not permit effective basic research to be carried out. Instead Japanese companies have shown a commitment to investment in mass-producing technologies, which initially have low returns, coupled with radical improvements.

- illustrated by the cases of integrated circuits -

The most evident example is the case of integrated circuits, initial investment in which in the late 1960s was cross subsidised from the production of consumer durables in Hitachi and other companies. In return ICs were introduced into consumer durables, as typified by calculators, which permitted mass production. However one cannot ignore the government's recognition of the need for subsidies for IC research in the 1960s, which has since been stimulated through the setting up of cooperative research laboratories. The latter factor has now taken on a higher profile with Miti persuading eight companies, including Fujitsu Ltd and Toshiba Corp, to establish in autumn, 1981, a joint research institute for developing optoelectronics ICs.

- and industrial robots

In the field of industrial robot development also, Miti has not been idle, and it has been reported that an appropriation in the 1981/82 budget will be sought for this purpose, in addition to the existing special depreciation allowances and low interest loans. It hardly seems as though an appropriation is required, for private corporations' activities have led to there being about 70,000 robots in operation in Japan. The claim that this is about 15 times the number in operation in the USA arises from difference in definition. If reprogrammability is included in the definition of a robot, eliminating the fixed sequence robots controlled electromechanically rather than by computer, Japan's lead over the USA would come down to perhaps 3:1. But it would still be a lead; yet it was from the USA in 1967 that robots were first imported, their production beginning the next year under foreign technology licences. Particularly since 1973/74, as investment has become less concerned with capacity expansion in favour of rationalising investment, production of industrial robots has accelerated, as shown in Table 11.

---

1   For example, Denison E F and Chung W K, Economic Growth and Its Sources, pages 99-103 in Patrick H and Rosovsky H (eds) Asia's New Giant.

Table 10

Indices of Industrial Production by Market Grouping 1960-80
(1975=100)

	Weights[a]	1960	1970	1974	1976	1978	1980 1 Qtr[b]	2 Qtr[b]	3 Qtr[b]	4 Qtr[b]
Investment goods	3,285.2	21.7	94.3	118.1	106.8	119.8	140.7	142.5	140.7	140.6
of which:										
capital goods	2,272.8	18.1	91.0	119.4	105.5	121.7	146.4	150.2	152.4	154.7
construction materials	1,062.4	32.0	101.3	115.5	109.6	115.7	128.7	126.4	115.8	112.4
Consumer goods	2,528.2	28.8	86.8	103.9	113.8	131.8	155.9	154.9	155.9	162.7
of which:										
durable	850.4	16.0	83.3	107.4	126.8	160.4	213.7	218.6	226.2	239.6
non-durable	1,677.8	38.5	90.2	102.1	107.2	117.3	126.2	122.5	120.5	123.9
Final demand goods	5,813.4	25.4	91.5	111.9	109.8	125.0	147.3	148.1	147.1	150.3
Producers' goods	4,186.6	26.7	94.1	112.8	112.9	119.9	137.8	137.7	130.8	131.9

a Derived from 1955 data and totalling 10,000.0.   b Seasonally adjusted.

Sources: Prime Minister's Office, Statistics Bureau, Nihon Tokei Nenkan; Miti, Research and Statistics Department, Tsusan Tokei.

Table 11

Trends in Industrial Robot Production[a]

(¥ mn; percentage changes from previous year in brackets)

	1975	1976	1977	1978	1979
Manual manipulators	900	1,500	1,800	1,400	1,900
	(29.4)	(73.9)	(15.0)	(-21.6)	(40.6)
Fixed & variable sequence robots	7,900	7,800	10,300	16,600	26,400
	(10.3)	(-1.1)	(31.1)	(61.1)	(59.2)
Playback, numerically controlled, intelligent robots	1,500	2,900	6,200	7,500	12,100
	(-20.0)	(95.9)	(114.1)	(20.1	(62.2)
Parts & related equipment	900	1,800	3,300	2,000	2,070
	(-45.0)	(96.8)	(80.9)	(-41.1)	(3.6)
Total value	11,100	14,100	21,600	27,400	42,400
	(-2.3)	(26.6)	(52.8)	(26.9)	(55.1)
Volume (units)	4,418	7,165	8,613	10,100	14,535
	(6.0)	(62.2)	(20.2)	(17.3)	(43.9)

a Anomalies are due to rounding; percentage changes are calculated from unrounded figures.

Source: Japan Industrial Robot Association.

It is estimated by the same source that the total value of production rose a further 41.4 per cent to ¥60 bn in 1980 and that the volume of output rose by 22.5 per cent to 17,800 units.

About 130 major enterprises are using robots - particularly in automobile and electrical machinery production - for welding, spraying, metal product fabrication, and other operations. The number of suppliers of robots is around 140, which seems excessive in comparison with the number of purchasers. This disparity reflects the two features of intense competition in a new production field, and producers not specialising, just as in the case of IC production. Investment activity in this field to develop more sophisticated sensors for 'intelligent' robots does not appear to have been affected by the slight anxiety, held by both producers and users, concerning the rapid rate of obsolescence compared with the relatively high unit price for a robot.

Sony's example of demand creation

The above discussion has been centred on exclusively technological innovations in which the final consumer plays only a small role in determining their adoption; but Japanese companies have also shown skill in creating a demand for an innovative product. The case of Sony's 'Walkman' - a high fidelity small cassette player with special earphones - is illustrative. Even though 90 per cent of dealers rejected the idea on initial surveys - because of its high price and inability to record - Sony pressed ahead, charmed by the originality of the 'Walkman'. A Sony representative explained that their notion was to educate potential customers by persuading them that one should "not be a slave to hi-fi equipment, but rather be able to go anywhere and do anything without missing high fidelity sound". The concept of a 'Walkman' seems to have correctly corresponded - judging by expected 1981 sales amounting to 2 mn units - to changes in Japanese society.

Sony's notion of "demand creation" is also applied to a range of products, of which most are barely yet in conception. The Sony staff have coined the idea "personal electronics" (koden) to describe products which are neither household appliances nor electronics associated with telecommunications and computers. It has been denied that Sony's introduction in late 1980 of products in the electronic text editing field, such as the Typecorder, heralds entry into the office automation or micro-computer business. Instead it is suggested that such products are appropriate for koden, to be used by individuals in the home as well as professionals in business.

It should perhaps be mentioned at this point that Sony does not appear to be a 'typical' Japanese company in that, for example, up to one third of its employees are mid career recruits. At the same time there is little that is really homogeneous among Japanese companies, and Sony is just the most evident example of the post 1945 establishment of innovative, fast growing enterprises. In any case a larger established and seemingly more traditional company such as Matsushita serves as another example of how innovations depend on more than technology. Matsushita's engineers work closely with both product planners, in surveying the market, and shopfloor workers, in seeking suggestions for producing a new item, such as the ultra thin "Pepper" transistor radio. While the close relationship, in particular between engineers and shopfloor workers, has been hailed as providing team spirit for the launching of a new product, it has also been questioned whether such a spirit hampers truly inventive R & D, which is thought to spring from the individual. Such a question will probably be answered when Japanese companies' innovations during the 1980s can be surveyed.

QUALITY CONTROL

From the USA to Japan and back again -

The irony behind Japanese industry's seemingly successful quality control activities is that the methods, based on statistical analysis, in detecting and reducing product defects were introduced by an American, Deming, in the early 1950s, and now more than 2,000 US enterprises, which include Ford Motor Co and IBM, have adopted the Japanese methodology. The original motivation of Japanese companies in learning about Deming's methods lay in their sense of industrial inferiority compared with the West. This is a salutary example of how Japanese industry's spirit of enquiry and adaptability has led to its overtaking its original mentor.

- in a modified version

Just as with technology imports, however, the original quality control methodology was altered, and arguably improved, when introduced in Japan. In particular, rather than being directly under management guidance, Japanese quality control characteristically has extensive worker participation. Indeed the appropriated Japanese term for quality control movements, jishu-kanri, literally means "self management". The other significant adaptation is that the scope for quality control is more broadly defined to encompass safety, employee morale and skills, and energy conservation.

Hence quality control activities are often cited as one of the causes of improved productivity. At a less direct level, activities associated with quality control can be considered to have improved company performance by providing more effective and sympathetic channels of communication between shopfloor workers, engineers, and middle level management.

In a context of low differentials and mutual respect –

Naturally the establishment of such effective communication depends upon certain preconditions,which include relatively low wage differentials between shopfloor workers and others in the same age group and a mutually respecting accord among all the employees of an enterprise. Hence it is perhaps not surprising that the introduction of quality control circles into Ford's UK plants was, in April 1981, rejected by the unions concerned. At the same time the Japanese enterprise unions require assurances from management that quality control activities will not result in redundancies. These assurances are respected on the surface, although it may be that indirectly redundancies will be caused.

– Japanese workers seem enthusiastic for quality control circles

Nonetheless shopfloor workers appear to be enthusiastic in engaging in quality control circles, each of which usually consists of 8–15 participants. Their enthusiasm is assisted by overtime payments for circle meetings and monetary rewards for notionally successful endeavours. It is also true that the normal tedium of shopfloor work is relieved by undertaking work which requires following trends in data, and problem analysis and solving. Consequently quality control, as practised in Japan, has made the shopfloor a more human place, despite automation. Manual workers' grasp of the nature of the problems and their suggestions are aided by the fact that job rotation has brought both an awareness of the whole production process and a greater range of skills to the individual.

The circles require organisation and training

Concerning the methodology of quality control circles, there is nothing that is spontaneous, nor are the results quickly achieved. Instead the circles are highly organised, with lengthy initiation and learning periods, which involve training in statistical techniques. Even after the initial training period, the quality control circle uses a manual, produced by its company, which sets out all the steps from problem identification to the final report and dissemination of results. Thus, although the monetary rewards have been criticised as overestimating the productivity gains, they are probably necessary as compensation for the workers' cooperation in an apparently formidable undertaking. Moreover the rewards reflect not merely the immediate productivity gains in reducing the number of flaws, but also the improvements in morale, safety, and other factors such as delivery systems.

To give just a few examples of quality control activities could be misleading, as their organisation and scope vary so much from one enterprise to another. Still, brief descriptions of activities in several companies may be at least illustrative.

Toshiba's experience -

In the case of Toshiba and TDK Electronics, it might have been presumed that the
high degree of automation in the production processes would leave only a marginal
role for the improvement of manual skills. Much, however, has been achieved
through line workers' suggestions on reducing the number of production stages and
on increasing the speed of component insertion through practising using both hands.
The latter instance is indicative of the burden of responsibility placed on shopfloor
workers - at Toshiba 99 per cent of plant employees participate in quality control
circles, but, once administrative staff are included, the participation rate falls to
70 per cent. Other ways in which line workers' suggestions have facilitated
efficiency is through standardising and so reducing the number of different
components.

- and Kayaba Industry's

Shopfloor workers at Kayaba Industry Co Ltd, a major manufacturer of hydraulic
equipment, have engaged in data analysis and trials of suggestions in order to
reduce production times. Their eventual success, in cooperation with technical
staff, led to Kayaba being one of the recipients of the Deming Prize in 1980.
Kayaba is also notable in that small groups, trained in quality control, extend
throughout all ranks of employees. The training for management personnel
incorporates notions of aggressive product development and marketing strategy,
as well as emphasising cooperation between all levels and supervision of quality
control activities. It is interesting to note that Kayaba began a more comprehensive and coordinated quality control system as recently as 1976, even though
quality control activities had been under way since 1964.

In order to obtain a more detailed exposition of quality control activities in various
Japanese companies, reference should be made to the Jetro publication Productivity
and Quality Control (1981). Here the discussion on Japan's industrial growth and
transformation will be concluded by considering a specific example of a manufacturer
for whom quality control has been but one factor in productivity growth.

Matsushita untypical in cutting labour force drastically -

At Matsushita's dry cell battery factory in Tsujido, south of Tokyo, labour productivity since 1970 has risen threefold. One consequence has been a reduction
in the labour force from 600 to 360 employees. Similarly Nippon Steel's productivity
gains have been accompanied by a decline of 18 per cent in the number of employees
between 1971 and 1979. Such examples seem to contradict the evidence cited earlier
(page 16) that automation has not adversely affected employment. However, overall, Japan has been able to maintain comparatively high rates of employment because
it is internationally in the forefront in applying highly automated technology, so that
it has gained increasing world market shares for the products involved.

- after rationalisation in mid 1970s

Matsushita's productivity gains in dry cell battery production have largely sprung
from a drastic rationalisation of the factory layout between 1973 and 1975, followed
in the late 1970s by the installation of a computerised line, in which a process control
computer supervises the delivery and mixing of materials. Moreover an automatic

testing system for flaws is in operation. It is not only immediate flaws that are searched for: the life of the battery is also tested under climatic conditions similar to those in its export markets, particularly African.

The quality control circles at Tsujido are required to make monthly reports. The management suggests that it is because the objectives come from below that the circles are willing to make the effort. Computerisation has aided their efforts in that histograms are automatically displayed along the line.

Quality control circles relieve alienation - temporarily

So far sophisticated automation and productivity growth appears not to have adversely affected labour-management relations. However it is not unremarkable that the Tsujido's labour union's two major demands are for an expansion of employment opportunities and a reduction in the number of working hours, which at present stand at 1,980 in the year. Although the humanisation promoted by quality control activities in Japan's factories may have temporarily relieved the alienation often associated with automation, it is likely that the concept of the corporation as a family, which theoretically held during the 1950s and 1960s, has already become meaningless. It is indicative that a large scale survey report, released by the Japan Productivity Institute in May, 1981, showed that one in every ten Japanese company employees is suffering from nervous anxiety and needs psychological help. Thus it is questionable whether labour-management relations will continue to run so smoothly in the future.

THE THRUST OVERSEAS

EXPORTING FOR EFFICIENT GROWTH

Concerning Japanese exports much has been written and commented upon. A recently published book in which Endymion Wilkinson explores the stereotypes hampering a realistic understanding of trade friction with Japan provides a useful summary of the arguments[1]. Therefore in this section more attention will be paid to the development and prospects for Japanese overseas direct investments than to exports. However a brief examination of the role played by exports in Japan's industrial growth could be revealing.

Within Japan there is considerable dissension as to whether or not exports have been the engine of growth. The prevailing view until the late 1970s was usually that exports are a residual requirement for financing imports of vital raw materials. At the same time it had been considered that Japan's economy was insecurely

---

1   Wilkinson E, Misunderstanding, Europe versus Japan, Chuokoron-sha, Tokyo, 1981.

based on the simple processing of imported materials into products for export markets. Since, during the 1960s and 1970s, the current account including invisible trade veered between deficit and surplus – with even the trade balance itself in substantial deficit in the early 1960s and later in the fiscal year 1979/80 – one cannot conclude that export surpluses have been the primary factor in industrial growth. Indeed it was only in the 1960s that exporting became important to Japanese industries, when an undervalued yen contributed to their advantage.

That advantage was not necessarily misused in so far as the pressures of international competition served to improve efficiency and product quality. Moreover when growth in domestic demand has been stagnant, as during 1980/81 due to a decline in real incomes, exports have enabled industrial expansion to continue. It has been estimated that of the 5.0 per cent real growth in GNP during 1980/81, 3.8 percentage points were accounted for by external demand growth. This result resembles to some extent the situation after the 1973/74 oil crisis when the consequent deflationary impact exerted pressure for an export drive. Therefore such clear examples of export led growth cannot be considered to represent an essential or permanent feature of the Japanese economy.

Yet what is an essential feature is the quality of certain goods, particularly electronic goods and automobiles, coupled with high productivity in their output. In addition it should be noted that Japan's export structure has followed a reasonably consistent pattern of changes in industrial structure, so that, whereas in 1960 machinery and equipment accounted for only 26.5 per cent of total export value, by 1980 the percentage was 62.8. The result of exports' keeping in line with relative productivity changes has been a comparatively high degree of export specialisation. On the one hand Miti argues that this apparent international division of labour is efficient and contributes to horizontal trade, especially when the division is within an individual industry such as medical equipment. On the other hand successful expert specialisation has evidently exacerbated trade friction, when associated with a skewed import structure.

It may be useful to highlight a few recent developments in Japan's export patterns. One is the increasing use of subsidiaries – rather than trading companies – often jointly owned with a foreign manufacturer, for overseas sales. Indeed cooperation with potential competitors is not unusual as in the case of France's Matra watch company assembling Seiko quartz watch movements for domestic sales under the Matra brand name. Another development is that there has been a resurgence in exports from small and medium sized light industries, particularly to the Middle East. As was not the case in earlier periods of Japan's export history, these light consumer products, such as tableware and vacuum flasks, are notable for their high quality. The third development, which will occur soon, is a drive to export industrial robots to Europe and North America. In the opinion of the Nihon Keizai Shimbun (June 3, 1981), Japan's initial competitive advantage in this field will soon be eroded; so Japanese manufacturers are making haste to enter export markets.

DIRECT INVESTMENT OVERSEAS

A shifting regional pattern

Naturally there have been various motives for overseas investment by Japanese companies, their order of importance altering over time. Such motives have included a desire to secure raw materials sources, import substitution investment behind trade barriers, the seeking of lower wages for labour intensive production processes, and the transfer of polluting plants. The nature of these objectives led to investment being primarily located in less developed countries and often using standard technologies, as typified by textile plants in South East Asia. It was not until the 1970s, with the stimulus of trade friction, the appreciation of the yen and a greater awareness of "country risks", that the pattern of investment began to shift towards the Western countries. As may be seen from Table 12, North America and Oceania accounted for a larger share by value of Japan's direct investment overseas in the fiscal years 1978/79 and 1979/80 than during the period 1951-79 as a whole; but because the shares for Europe were lower in the latest years than in the period as a whole one cannot consider that investment in the West has already become highly significant, despite the overall trend.

Minority stakes by smallish companies are common

Moreover Japanese overseas investment in North America and Europe is not characteristically in manufacturing, but in commerce and associated services, as is clear from Figure 8. Another distinction which should be made is that in manufacturing a higher proportion of overseas subsidiaries have minority Japanese ownership - more than half of the companies in the food processing, textiles, and iron and steel industries. It is also interesting to note in the cases of textiles, electrical machinery, sundry goods, and precision machinery, that more than 40 per cent of the Japanese parent companies are small and medium sized. Indeed there has been criticism from Saudi Arabia that too many of the Japanese joint ventures are from small and medium sized companies.

Opportunities in the third world

The Middle East presents Japanese companies with a dilemma in investment planning. On the one hand, securing energy resources, both directly and indirectly through close economic links, became even more important during the 1970s. On the other hand, the same period has witnessed concern over increasing "country risks", which have been dramatically highlighted by the troubles for the Mitsui Group over the immense Japan-Iran joint petrochemical project. The Japanese government's contribution from the Overseas Economic Cooperation Fund has been suspended since the outbreak of the Iran-Iraq war.

The use of development assistance funds, not only for developing infrastructures but also for establishing joint ventures in less developed countries, is likely to become of increasing importance, as Japan is aware of pressures to increase its development assistance. An example is the recently inaugurated steel pipe plant construction cooperation company in Mexico in which the Overseas Economic Cooperation Fund (30 per cent) and Sumitomo Metal are the main investors. An interesting development in this area is the discussion between Japanese and Dutch industries, particularly mechanical and electrical engineering companies, on joint cooperation in less developed countries with development assistance funds being provided by both countries.

62

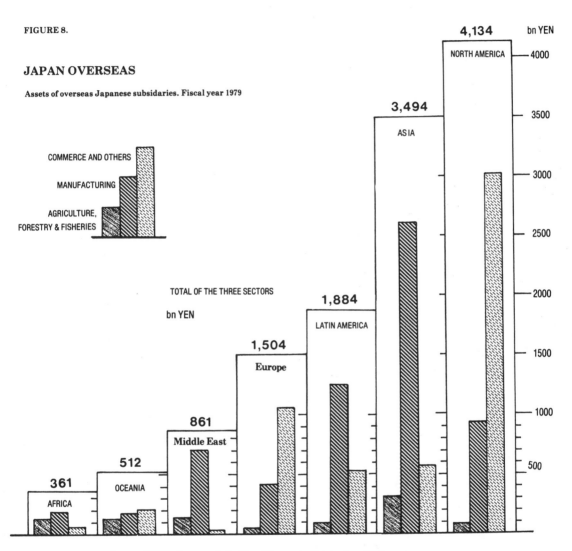

FIGURE 8.

JAPAN OVERSEAS

Assets of overseas Japanese subsidaries. Fiscal year 1979

COMMERCE AND OTHERS

MANUFACTURING

AGRICULTURE,
FORESTRY & FISHERIES

TOTAL OF THE THREE SECTORS

bn YEN

bn YEN

4,134

NORTH AMERICA

4000

3,494

ASIA

3500

3000

2500

2000

1,884

LATIN AMERICA

1500

1,504

Europe

1000

861

Middle East

512

OCEANIA

500

361

AFRICA

Source: MITI, Overseas Activities of Japanese Enterprises. 1980

Total 12,750 bn YEN

Japanese home population 115.9 mn in 1979

ASSETS PER JAPANESE:

£236 or $502 per head

1979 average exchange rates

63

Table 12

Japan's Direct Overseas Investment by Area

	1951/52-1979/80			Fiscal 1978/79			Fiscal 1979/80		
	No. of cases	Value ($ mn)	% of total	No. of cases	Value ($ mn)	% of total	No. of cases	Value ($ mn)	% of total
North America	7,717	8,202	25.8	1,055	1,364	29.7	1,228	1,438	28.8
Latin America	2,458	5,580	17.5	245	616	13.4	208	1,207	24.2
Asia	7,318	8,643	27.2	669	1,340	29.1	759	976	19.5
Middle East	222	2,107	6.6	18	492	10.7	18	130	2.6
Europe (incl USSR)	2,158	3,893	12.2	251	323	7.0	301	495	9.9
Africa	659	1,306	4.1	59	225	4.9	67	168	3.4
Oceania	976	2,078	6.5	98	239	5.2	113	582	11.6
Total	21,508	31,804	100.0	2,395	4,598	100.0	2,694	4,995	100.0

Source: Ministry of Finance, Kaigai Chokusetsu Toshi Todokede Jisseki (Direct Overseas Investment Applied/Authorised in Fiscal 1979), 1980.

Even without the stimulus and support of government funds, Japanese direct investment for manufacturing in less developed countries is going to continue to be of importance. In particular the Asean region still holds the attention of Japanese firms, despite rising wages in the newly industrialised countries. Thus in July, 1981, over 100 firms established the Japan Asean Investment Co, for investment in a joint venture between Japanese and South East Asian businesses, to be known as the Asean Japan Development Corporation (AJDC). The Keizai Doyukai (Japan Committee for Economic Development) has been influential in planning the AJDC, partly with the intention of extending loans to small and medium sized enterprises establishing joint ventures in the Asean region.

Apart from joint ventures, Japanese companies have also been to the forefront in setting up wholly owned enterprises for manufacturing in free trade areas. The justification for total ownership has been to ensure coordination and quality for exporting to third countries – for which advantage can be taken of the preferential tariffs for exports from less developed countries. The main objective in such offshore sourcing investment is to use low cost labour. The Japanese management at the Ricoh Watch factory in the Battan Export Processing Zone of the Philippines emphasised that there was hardly any need for training in skills, as there was a rigid division of labour between different tasks. Since, moreover, the labour force at Ricoh in the Philippines consists mostly of women in their late teens and early twenties, it may readily be understood that Japanese companies investing overseas do not transfer wholesale 'typical' Japanese management and labour practices.

Growing confidence in exporting management methods

Similarly, when investing in the West, Japanese management methods are applied only in so far as they are appropriate and beneficial. Sony management asserts that it would not attempt to form an enterprise union at its Bridgend plant in the UK, where employees belong to trade unions. Tetsuo Tokita, general manager of Sony (UK) Ltd, has emphasised that the incorporation of the 'British spirit' has kept productivity and quality in the Welsh factory comparable with that in Sony factories in Japan[1]. At the Kikkoman Soy Sauce plant in Wisconsin in the USA the management states that the American way of managing business is applied, except on occasions when Japanese business methods are both better for operations and appropriate. This has been the customary policy in the past, but Japanese firms investing overseas are now tending to display more confidence in asserting their own management methods. For example, Nissan's US truckplant, which will begin production in 1983, will reportedly be run according to Japanese management methods.

Investment in the West to avert trade friction

Apart from companies such as Sony, most direct investments by Japanese companies in the West are intended to forestall or avert trade friction. Thus in June 1981, Nippon Electric Co announced a plan to build an integrated VLSI plant in the USA. In the

---

1   Business Bulletin, Marubeni, January, 1981.

automobile industry, tie-ups between manufacturers, such as between Isuzu Motors
Ltd and General Motors, are leading to a radical international reorganisation of
the industry. In addition to the aim of dampening trade friction, there is also the
desire to secure raw material supplies, including energy, from the West. In 1981
Toyo Menka Kaisha Ltd agreed to take over the Texan Chickasha Cotton Oil Co,
in return for a stable supply of ginned cotton. In the energy area Nippon Steel Corp
and Armco Steel Inc have been negotiating a joint venture for coal production in
West Virginia.

Accumulated foreign investment set to rise further

These activities in both less developed countries and the West have resulted in
Japanese direct investment accumulated abroad no longer being comparatively
meagre as in 1970 (Table 13). At the same time, in terms of the proportion of
GNP invested overseas each year, Japan's was the lowest of the countries shown
in 1978 at 0.4 per cent, whereas UK invested 1.5 per cent. Nonetheless the trends
established in the 1970s, along with the advances in Japanese technology and greater
confidence in managerial expertise, are likely to lead to substantial growth in overseas investments during the 1980s. It is considered unlikely, however, that in the
same period Japanese companies would be able seriously to challenge the dominance
of US multinationals.

Table 13

Accumulated Overseas Direct Investments of Leading Industrial Nations

	1970		1978	
	$ bn	% of total	$ bn	% of total
USA	78	52	168	42
UK	20	13	35	9
West Germany	7	5	29	7
Japan	4	3	27	7
Switzerland	8	5	25	6
World total	150	100	400	100

Source: West German Bundesbank.

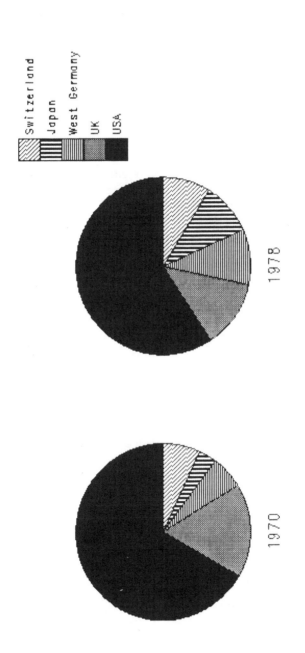

Accumulated Overseas Direct Investments
of Leading Industrial Nations

Switzerland
Japan
West Germany
UK
USA

1978

1970

Figure 8a

Chapter 3

Competing with the Japanese Manufacturing Firm

COMPETING WITHIN JAPAN

During the preceding discussion it will have become evident that the pace of change and degree of adaptability of Japanese industries are characteristically high. Thus to compete effectively the non-Japanese company must be prepared to face rapid changes in competitive conditions and to respond aggressively. It is particularly within the Japanese market that such conditions hold.

In the following a distinction has been drawn between imports into the Japanese market and investment for local manufacture. However the successful exporter to Japan is often the one who has entered into a joint venture or some, reasonably permanent, kind of tie-up with a Japanese company. The investment demonstrates the exporter's long term commitment to the market, which is essential for gaining the confidence of distributors and consumers. Nonetheless the distinction shall be kept, with 'investment' indicating products being manufactured in Japan.

THE JAPANESE MARKET FOR IMPORTS

It is not just Japanese industry which is subject to rapid changes: the Japanese consumer and relevant legislation have also been through some radical transformations since the 1950s. In this way the overseas perception of a "closed market" has become outdated except in so far as it refers to the time which has been lost in gaining an initial foothold in the Japanese market. Thus during the few decades in which mass consumerism "took off" in Japan, restrictive legislation was in force, along with Japanese views of imports as luxuries irrelevant to their daily lives. In value terms Japan's imports of manufactured goods have risen substantially since 1960 (see Table 14). However the ratio of manufactured imports to total imports has failed to increase, apart from isolated surges in 1970 and 1979. Moreover in terms of volume, the index of manufactured imports in real terms declined from 133.5 in 1974 to 100.0 in 1975 and did not rise above the 1974 level until after 1977. Thus it appears that the legislative changes and positive import promotion measures occurring during the 1970s require a substantial lag before becoming effective. Part of the lag stems from the perceptions of overseas exporters, who perhaps lack confidence in entering the Japanese market; so a brief survey of legislation and other measures aiding imports may be appropriate[1].

---

1 For a detailed survey of customs regulation see: Japan Law and Regulations Concerning Customs Duties and Procedures, Japan Tariff Association, 1981.

Table 14

Imports of Manufactured Goods to Japan
($ mn; percentage shares in brackets)

	1960	1970	1975	1977	1979	1980
Chemical products	265	1,000	2,057	3,003	5,178	5,202
	(26.7)	(17.5)	(17.5)	(19.7)	(18.0)	(19.3)
Machinery & equipment	435	2,298	4,286	4,891	8,343	9,843
	(43.8)	(40.1)	(36.5)	(32.2)	(29.0)	(30.7)
Others	293	2,427	5,404	7,318	15,254	16,065
	(29.5)	(42.4)	(46.0)	(48.1)	(53.0)	(50.0)
of which:						
iron & steel	87	276	189	255	899	894
	(8.8)	(4.8)	(1.6)	(1.7)	(3.1)	(2.8)
textile products	–	314	1,310	1,732	3,832	3,180
		(5.5)	(11.2)	(11.4)	(13.3)	(9.9)
non-ferrous metals	118	944	1,284	1,726	3,415	4,480
	(11.9)	(16.5)	(10.9)	(11.3)	(11.9)	(14.0)
Total	993	5,725	11,747	15,212	28,775	32,110
	(100.0)	(100.0)	(100.0)	(100.0)	(100.0)	(100.0)
Volume of manu- factured imports (1975=100)	17.7	72.4	100.0	115.6	167.6	163.4
Manufactures as % of total imports	22.1	30.3	20.3	21.5	26.0	22.8

Source: Japan Tariff Association Gaikoku Bōeki Gaikyō (Summary of Foreign Trade), 1981.

In December 1980, the Foreign Exchange and Foreign Trade Control Law, basically restrictive in principle, was substantially amended so that the basic principle is liberalisation; restrictive or prohibitive measures only applying in case of "emergency". For imports, the validating system has been abolished and the licensing procedure simplified so as to apply only to certain special cases. Restrictions on the means of payment have been abolished. The upshot is that, while specified kinds of goods and goods originating in specified countries still require import authorisation, transactions that do not may proceed directly to customs clearance. It is to soon to assess the impact of these measures but while the law may not have changed radically in substance, the decrease in paperwork required will probably act as an incentive to prospective exporters to Japan.

Japan's tariffs do not compare unfavourably

Concerning import tariffs, the full force of the agreements under the Tokyo round of multilateral trade negotiations, concluded in April 1979, will not finally be felt until after implementation in 1987. Still, certain agreements are being effected somewhat earlier so as to stave off potential trade friction, as in the case of tariffs on ICs which will be lowered to 4.2 per cent in 1982. Table 15 indicates comparative average tariff rates, computed according to the Gatt formula. Such averages are open to some dispute on account of the varied and changing import structures of different countries, but the averages are nonetheless revealing.

Table 15

Comparative Average Tariff Rates Tokyo Round of MTN (1979)[a]

	Basic tariff rate in 1979	Tariff rate after reduction (1981)	Average reduction
Japan	6% approx (11% approx)	3% approx (5.5% approx)	nearly 50%
USA	6% approx (8% approx)	4% approx (nearly 6%)	30% approx
EEC	over 6% (nearly 10%)	5% approx (over 7%)	nearly 25%

a Rates are weighted averages on total imports, excluding petroleum, in 1976. Figures in parentheses indicate the case of only items currently assessable.

Source: Jetro.

Not only in the case of tariffs, but also in respect of items under residual import restrictions, Japan does not compare unfavourably with Western countries, especially as such products are mostly agricultural. At the same time such exemplary indicators of a relatively open market were largely initiated just prior to the Tokyo Round - perhaps in order to sweeten the negotiations.

Positive measures to promote imports

The Tokyo Round also provided the stimulus for import promotion measures which included the establishment of Mipro (the Manufactured Imports Promotion Organisation), and emergency import measures. In May 1981, Mipro opened an office in Washington, whose director was formerly in Miti's North American section. The close connection between Miti and Mipro is thereby underlined, with Miti's role of protecting Japanese industry during the 1960s radically changed - at least superficially. Other governmental bodies, particularly Jetro (Japan External Trade Organisation), which was originally established to promote Japanese exports, and Jica (Japan International Cooperation Agency), have also become involved in the task of import promotion. The bewildering array of organisations with various functions and the changes in regulations would be best understood through referring to Jetro's extensive publications, written in English[1].

Official non-tariff barriers now fewer and lower -

The question of the extent of relative openness of a market becomes more complicated when considering non-tariff barriers. A distinction needs to be made between the barriers that are inspired by various regulations and those rooted in consumer psychology. In the Japanese case reference is also made to the distribution system,

---

1 Publication lists may be obtained from Jetro, 2-5, Toranomon 2-Chome, Minato-ku, Tokyo, or Press Aid Centre, 700 South Flower St, Suite 600, Los Angeles, CA 90017.

although this is not a real non-tariff barrier in so far as domestic manufacturers must also find ways of distributing efficiently. Therefore the nature of distribution channels will be considered separately.

Just as in the case of tariff barriers, Japanese authorities can marshal persuasive arguments to demonstrate that non-tariff barriers emanating from regulations are substantially fewer than previously and can be easily surmounted with a little forethought by the exporter. Technical barriers to trade have been lowered since 1979 through measures such as accepting test data from the country of origin, postponing emission standards on imported automobiles and opening the Japanese industrial standards marking system (JIS) to goods manufactured overseas.

– as US testimony bears out

The rapidity in the changes in regulations affecting both tariffs and non-tariff barriers may be surmised by comparing the conclusions of the two Jones Reports on US–Japan trade submitted to the Sub-Committee on Trade of the US House of Representatives Committee on Ways and Means. The first report, in January 1979, called for the Japanese market to be opened to US goods, but the second report just 20 months later called Japan "a reasonably open market for many products, other than certain agricultural and high technology products".

Nonetheless it must be conceded that the apparent openness of the Japanese market has not led to a consistent growth in manufactured imports. Indeed, as is clear from Tables 14 and 16, their volume actually fell in 1980.

Table 16

Indices of Japan's Manufactured Imports[a]
(1975=100)

Year	Value	Volume	Price
1965	15.9	26.9	59.1
1970	48.9	72.4	67.5
1974	126.2	133.5	94.5
1977	127.2	115.6	110.0
1979	235.5	167.6	140.5
1980	265.3	163.4	162.4
Average annual growth rate (%)			
1965–1970	25.2	21.9	2.7
1970–1974	26.7	16.5	8.8
1965–1974	25.9	19.5	5.4
1977–1979	36.1	20.4	13.0
1979–1980	12.7	-2.5	15.6

a   Manufactured imports in SITC Chapters 5-9.

Source: Japan Tariff Association Gaikoku Bōeki Gaikyō (Summary of Foreign Trade), 1981.

Admittedly a major part of the reason for the decline in the volume of manufactured imports during 1980 lies in the general stagnation in domestic demand arising from a decline in real income. Indeed textiles and other light industrial products imported from the newly industrialising countries were the ones to suffer real declines. The falls of 30.9 per cent in the volume of refrigerators imported from Taiwan and of 12.8 per cent in radios from Taiwan, South Korea and Singapore can be partly blamed upon the remarkably high diffusion rates of durable consumer goods among Japanese households.

Other barriers include exporters' misperceptions

Miti and Jetro are fond of disseminating charts which show dramatic rises in imports as percentages of the number of goods purchased by Japanese households. One such survey shows that between 1968 and 1978 the percentage of footwear purchased accounted for by imports rose from 0.4 per cent to 21.5 per cent, while neckties rose from 1.9 per cent to 18.4 per cent. These figures are impressive but they appear to be in conflict with the data on all manufactured imports, owing to their being highly selective examples. While certain goods have a high degree of acceptability as imports among Japanese consumers, others find great difficulty in penetrating the market. Therefore the exporter needs to pay considerable attention to Japanese lifestyles. Among successful exporters to Japan, it is generally agreed that most of the non-tariff barriers are the result of misperceptions of consumer psychology.

For one thing, it is believed wrongly that the consumer market must be highly homogeneous. The gini coefficient of 0.2655 (1978) for income distribution is the lowest among OECD countries and most Japanese perceive themselves as members of the middle class. However this middle class is highly diverse with inconsistencies in status as indicated by the low correlation (0.31) of education with income (Survey on Social Stratification and Mobility, 1978). Therefore buying patterns are irregular with both highly priced and bargain goods in demand. Moreover within each of these categories there is considerable scope for discriminatory purchases – contrary to the view of standardised consumerism. Thus the Japanese consumer, who tends to have a low degree of brand loyalty, is accustomed to a wide range of choice, and does not automatically equate high prices with good quality. Competition among domestic manufacturers has led to the production of high quality goods, so that the view of imports as being generally of higher quality than domestic goods is long outdated.

An example of discriminating consumer purchases is given in the large choice of brands at Daiei – the largest of the superstore chains in Japan. In the case of soy sauce, which might have been thought to be a standard product, Daiei provides four different brands, enabling the consumer to differentiate between different prices and qualities. The two higher priced brands of soy sauce would be intended for use with raw fish. A Daiei spokesman stressed that, similarly, the marketing of imported goods should be directed explicitly towards some notion of the consumer's likely use of the purchase. Thus thorough market surveys are required – not only because of cultural and lifestyle differences, but also in order to determine how best to adapt and present the goods to prospective customers.

Price elastic demand for imports

The exporter to Japan, therefore, can no longer merely assume that imports naturally belong in the luxury sector of the market - where sales would be all the better with a higher price attached. Indeed between 1966 and 1979, according to Miti's estimates, imports had a high price elasticity of -1.29 to volume. In other words a fall in price leads to a more than proportionate increase in demand. This was strikingly evidenced in 1978 when the large yen appreciation, coupled with tariff reductions, lowered import prices, thereby resulting in substantial increases in the volume of manufactured goods imported between 1977 and 1979 (see Table 16).

The consumer is highly demanding on quality

The equation of imports with luxury goods, formerly presumed to exist, no longer holds, because the Japanese consumer has become highly demanding as to the supposed quality of goods. 32 per cent of the respondents to a public opinion poll held in December 1980 had complaints about products purchased during the past year. It may therefore be suggested that the non-tariff barriers requiring detailed labelling and stringent product safety are in the interests of the exporter to Japan, who would not otherwise be able to compete with local manufacturers already satisfying the regulations. Incidentally, these comments are also pertinent to the Japanese market for industrial goods, where any reject rate above zero is barely tolerable.

More leisure changes consumption patterns

Japanese consumers are not only discriminating and demanding, they are also changing their patterns of consumption as leisure activities become more prominent. Dentsu Incorporated, the major Japanese advertising agency, has prepared forecasts of consumption expenditure up to 1985. Although the growth in consumer expenditure has been low since 1974, higher real growth of 3.6 per cent annually is forecast on account of the education boom, Westernisation and heightened interest in leisure activities. Each of these factors is relevant to the potential exporter because, for example, education implies the will to learn about foreign cultures. Thus, despite imports being somewhat excluded during the period of mass consumerisation based on household goods, different kinds of imports could play a significant role in the present stage where Japanese consumers are seeking a qualitative improvement in lifestyles. Among the highest real annual average growth rates for goods forecast by Dentsu for the period 1979 to 1985 are bread (7.54 per cent), dining out (6.34 per cent), beverages (4.28 per cent), furniture and tools (4.04 per cent), Western clothes (6.04 per cent), automobile related expenses (5.85 per cent), self enlightenment and entertainment (5.43 per cent).

Supermarkets and department stores are important -

The distribution and retail sector repays thorough investigation on the part of the potential exporter. In the retail sector, while small, self employed retailers are still numerous, supermarkets and superstores are continuing to gain larger market shares. During the 1970s such chainstores almost tripled their sales floor space and more than quadrupled their sales. Department stores, which tend to sell slower moving, higher quality items, continued to grow, although less dramatically with sales rising over 2.5 times. Nonetheless department stores, which often import directly, will continue to be an important avenue for imported goods entering the market because of the demonstration effect of department store goods. Such goods also permit a higher level of product differentiation.

– while franchised outlets should be borne in mind

The exporter to Japan might have assumed that the numerous small retailers were irrelevant, and perhaps an impediment, to successful sales. However the recent emergence of franchised convenience stores represents another route for imported mass consumer products. Seven-Eleven, Japan Co Ltd, encourages self employed retailers to enter franchises, which provide initial loans and subsequent survices in return for percentage commissions from the stores' gross profit margins. Inventory orders from the franchised stores are relayed from each store's computer terminal to the head office's central computer. The invoices are thereby centrally processed, while a local wholesaler is instructed to deliver goods to Seven-Eleven stores in its area. In this way the traditional distribution network is used, but in a considerably more efficient fashion.

Both supermarkets and manufacturers are taking control of distribution –

Superstores and supermarkets have gone further in streamlining the distribution system, by setting up their own distribution centres. Many of the goods sold in chain stores are thereby ordered direct from the manufacturer. Even without the mediation of chain stores, manufacturers have been increasingly taking control over distribution channels. This so called systemisation of distribution, while commendable in reducing distribution margins, has provoked concern in that entry barriers to competition have been raised through limitations on sales territories and specific sales policies in ensuring the cooperation of distributors.

– but the stronger wholesalers are adapting

The result of all the above practices is that the traditional distribution network – in which there were three sizes of tonya (wholesalers) through which a good passed to reach a highly fragmented market of neighbourhood stores – has already been substantially bypassed with only the large tonya likely to survive much longer. The surviving tonya are those which have sought sophistication through measures such as strengthening marketing, planning and processing functions. Therefore foreign goods entering the market in this way are unlikely to suffer impediments. Indeed the policy of Wella Cosmetics, whose products have penetrated deeply into the Japanese market, is to use exactly the same distributing system as do their Japanese competitors, which means selling through wholesalers. On the other hand, Airwick Industries Inc – an American household and personal care products maker – has set up its own distribution system. Previously a Japanese distributor had been used, so the change in strategy has required establishing a marketing office with 45 employees by 1982.

Merchandising imports requires investment

Indeed for any successful merchandising of foreign goods in Japan, substantial investment is required, even though the goods are manufactured elsewhere and a Japanese trading company, whether large or specialised, is used for gaining entry.

Jetro's advice is centred around the idea of not treating Japan as a spot market from which one withdraws when competition becomes tougher. At the simplest level, investment can imply the building up of contacts with local distributors and determined advertising efforts. A more binding investment would involve entering into a joint venture or tie up with a local manufacturer for contract manufacture. The latter category will be considered in the following chapter on cooperation, which is, of course, but one way of competing effectively.

Contacts with local distributors and advertising can both be included in promotion, with the former designated as in-channel promotion. Since the Japanese favour business conducted on rather personal terms, in-channel promotion appropriate to Japanese business mores is essential. It may appear that the Japanese wholesaler gains higher margins than elsewhere, but the services provided in credit, bearing risk and maintaining close contacts with many small retailers tend also to be commensurately higher. At the same time, incentives to the wholesaler in the form of rebates, and even gifts, are thought to be indispensable.

Advertising is essential

Competition from domestically produced goods and the discerning nature of the Japanese consumer, who approaches buying decisions with remarkable diligence, make large scale advertising essential. Such advertising need not necessarily be expensive. Using newspaper fold-ins can be just as effective as television commercials in reaching an urban market, because more than 98 per cent of the major daily newspapers are for home delivery subscriptions. Indeed written media advertising is of great importance in Japan where numerous specialist magazines serve a voracious reading public. The general interest, popular weekly magazines may also be the medium for free exposure, as when the Kentucky Fried Chicken company created "news" around its entry into Japan.

Consumers distrust after-sale service on imports

The exporter's commitment to the market must continue long after the product has been sold. One reason why imports fail to gain full favour is the fear that post sale service will be inadequate or lacking altogether. Therefore a servicing system based on a comprehensive guarantee is essential. In Japanese merchandising, the customer has come to expect somewhat more in the way of service than is guaranteed or legally required. Such services may appear superficial in the form of free towels given by shopkeepers, but it extends to providing extensive after-service.

A long term commitment must be made –

The above has given just some indication of the long term commitment required in entering the Japanese market. From the initial market surveys, through modification to design and packaging to meet Japanese tastes, to detailing the market and maintaining good contacts with distributors, the groundwork required is extensive. Consequently it is generally believed that losses will inevitably be suffered for the first few years and thereafter competition will necessitate maximising sales volume, because of low unit profit margins.

<u>- but the ultimate rewards are great</u>

Nonetheless the managers of foreign firms which have succeeded in the Japanese market stress that, in spite of the initial losses, the long term potential for worthwhile profits is good, on account of the huge and diversified consumer market. Even in two preserves, the automobile industry and posts and telecommunications equipment, where it is considered that Japanese markets are hopelessly exclusive, inroads have been made.

In the case of the automobile industry, companies are seeking to purchase overseas parts and components, despite holding their own subcontracting network. In 1980/81 Nissan Motor Co's imports, including parts, materials and machinery, rose in value by 56.3 per cent. Although 26 per cent of the total was accounted for by materials imported from South Africa, one cannot discount the fact that automotive parts represented 54 per cent of Nissan's imports. Another example, namely Suzuki's 1981 contract with the UK's Johnson Matthey Chemicals to purchase car exhaust catalysts, might be considered ironic in view of Japan's strict emission controls deterring would be car imports. In fact Johnson Matthey Chemicals, which "aims to extend sales of car exhaust catalysts currently required by pollution control legislation in the USA and Japan" (company spokesman), has demonstrated how a deliberate objective in meeting the special needs of the Japanese market will reap its rewards.

The settlement in 1981 of the issue of NTT procurements has been well documented. It may be that this will be a worthy precedent for the campaign of both overseas governments and the Fair Trade Commission (FTC) to end existing exceptions under the anti-monopoly law in respect of government monopolies. In the mean time it may be interesting to note that the Japanese market for office use postage metering equipment is dominated by a few foreign makers including Pitney Bowes Inc and Hasler Ltd. Pitney Bowes's commitment to the Japanese market has expanded since the 1950s, with the cooperation of the UK trading company, Dodwell and Co Ltd.

The examples of successful foreign companies, in general, tend to demonstrate that direct investment, involving at least the final manufacturing stages in Japan, is a prerequisite for long term expansion. Therefore a separate section is devoted to this strategy, even though much of the earlier discussion on consumer psychology, distribution, and promotion is also relevant to the foreign firm which chooses to manufacture locally.

MANUFACTURING WITHIN JAPAN

As shown in Chapter II Japan's investment overseas is not yet commensurate with its size as an economic power (in 1979/80, the flow of outward investment was $4,995 mn); but in the same year the flow of foreign investment into Japan was even lower at just 10.9 per cent of this total ($542 mn), while in 1980 it was a mere $299 mn. This is all the more surprising since Miti's 1980 survey of foreign business affiliates shows that the profitability indicators for major foreign affiliated firms have been consistently higher than for major Japanese companies (Table 17). Yet of the companies responding to the survey, whereas in 1973/74 close to 250 were newly formed, in 1978/79 only 179 had been established during that year. This trend is all the more disturbing in that only 30.2 per cent of the newly established foreign affiliates were in manufacturing, whereas in 1973/74 the corresponding percentage was 46.4. Consequently the share of foreign affiliated firms in total industry sales and assets has remained insignificant. Indeed between the fiscal years 1977/78 and 1978/79 foreign affiliated companies in manufacturing industries other than oil products registered a decline in their share of total sales from 2.8 per cent to 2.6 per cent. The comparative figures for all industries and all manufacturing are even less inspiring, as is clear from Table 18.

The proportion of affiliates wholly owned abroad has risen

It is possible that the changes in the Foreign Exchange and Foreign Trade Control Law referred to earlier (page 66) will encourage more foreign direct investment in Japan. Nonetheless the law as it was practised before the amendment cannot have been too much of a deterrent, since the Miti survey found that newly established foreign affiliates in which the foreign partners owned more than 50 per cent of the equity rose from 46.4 per cent in 1973/74 to 67.0 per cent in 1978/79. Moreover those newly formed foreign firms wholly owned by the parent increased remarkably from 32.5 per cent in 1973 to 47.4 per cent in 1978.

They need to minimise expatriate staff –

The increase in the proportion of wholly owned subsidiaries runs contrary to the usual advice that a joint venture with a Japanese partner is invaluable for providing initial contacts and for overcoming some of the language barriers. It may be that foreign firms investing in Japan rather tend to favour maintaining full control, while avoiding possible contract and communication difficulties with a local partner. Nonetheless whether or not the foreign affiliated firm is wholly owned, it is of course necessary to employ Japanese personnel at the management level. Firms which have tried to avoid this option have suffered both from exorbitantly high fixed costs in the form of expatriate management salaries and from inadequate understanding of and contact with the local market. Indeed many of the successful foreign firms in Japan deliberately minimise the number of expatriate staff, while encouraging those who are required to remain beyond the normal contract period for expatriates elsewhere. This is necessary not only because of the time needed to grasp Japanese business and cultural practices, but also because of the long term commitment required in order to penetrate the market and expand.

– but will have to pay well to recruit Japanese staff

At the same time there are still difficulties in recruiting appropriate Japanese personnel. Experienced engineers and management staff prefer to remain with the company which has nurtured them, while the most able college leavers prefer to enter one of the highly rated Japanese companies. A decision to take employment with a foreign firm hinges on whether the firm is perceived to be permanently and reliably established in Japan. The foreign employer will therefore have to provide a salary which includes an inducement payment, in addition to covering the monetary value of the various welfare benefits expected in a large Japanese company.

Table 17

Profitability Indicators for Major Foreign Affiliated Firms in Japan
(percentages; fiscal years beginning in April of year shown)

	Ratio of net profit to total capital employed[a]						Ratio of net profit to net sales					
	1973	1974	1975	1976	1977	1978	1973	1974	1975	1976	1977	1978
Major foreign firms												
All industries	5.1	1.5	0.6	2.2	2.6	2.8	4.6	1.1	0.4	1.5	1.7	2.0
Manufacturing	5.3	1.7	0.5	2.1	2.5	2.8	5.6	1.5	0.4	1.7	1.9	2.2
Manufacturing except for oil processing	5.6	2.7	1.1	2.4	2.4	3.3	7.6	3.0	1.2	2.4	2.2	3.0
Major Japanese firms												
All industries	1.8	1.3	0.9	1.1	1.4	1.5	1.6	1.1	0.7	0.9	1.1	1.2
Manufacturing	2.4	1.7	0.9	1.4	1.5	1.7	2.7	1.7	0.9	1.5	1.5	1.7

a Net profit is defined as profit after tax. Capital employed is defined as liabilities and net worth.

Source: Miti. Gaishikei Kigyō no Dōkō (Foreign Business Affiliates in Japan), 1980.

Table 18

Foreign Affiliated Firms' Shares in Sales and Total Assets in Japan

(¥'00 bn; fiscal years beginning in April of year shown)

	Sales						Total assets					
	1973	1974	1975	1976	1977	1978	1973	1974	1975	1976	1977	1978
Foreign affiliated firms [a]												
All industries	71.2	82.2	86.9	109.3	119.9	113.6	53.7	62.1	63.9	75.4	81.4	79.2
Manufacturing	45.1	54.1	57.1	79.9	87.2	82.0	42.9	48.2	50.5	52.9	66.5	63.4
Manufacturing except oil processing	31.5	31.8	29.3	41.7	49.3	49.7	33.6	32.0	29.8	39.2	43.9	42.8
All corporations in Japan												
All industries	3,553	4,404	4,566	5,298	5,565	6,091	2,580	2,939	3,199	3,529	3,656	4,016
Manufacturing	1,201	1,457	1,483	1,734	1,857	1,963	1,042	1,173	1,304	1,400	1,443	1,514
Manufacturing except oil processing	–	–	1,388	1,623	1,747	1,865	–	–	1,234	1,324	1,368	1,444

a The figures for the foreign affiliated firms are for the surveyed companies.

Source: Miti, Gaishikei Kigyō no Dōkō (Foreign Business Affiliates in Japan), 1980.

The working language should be Japanese

Some foreign firms increase their difficulties in finding capable Japanese personnel
by seeking those with foreign language abilities. However, the Japanese who have
mastered fluent English are not necessarily the best technicians, nor may be the
most adept in handling Japanese business contacts and subordinates. The approach,
adopted by Wella Cosmetics, in which the working language is Japanese seems most
appropriate. Again that requires expatriate management to remain long enough in
Japan to learn the language. Expatriate management must also be willing to
participate in drinking after work for the sake of otsukiai (maintaining good relationships). Also, just as Japanese ventures in the West accept non-enterprise unions,
so should Western managers in Japan promote participatory management and
harmonious labour relations through the customary closed shop enterprise unions.

Licensing arrangements may be an alternative to manufacture –

Obviously there are many potential pitfalls in the way of establishing a manufacturing
enterprise in Japan. Since, moreover, Japanese labour costs are equivalent to
those in the West, foreign firms interested in entering the Japanese market may
prefer to manufacture in a nearby South East Asian country. However Japanese
customers, especially in the market for machinery and intermediate materials,
attach great importance to prompt delivery as well as uniform quality and standards.
For these reasons a combination of import and manufacture in which the final
processing stages are carried out by contract manufacturers in Japan would be a
preferable option. Alternatively the foreign firm may simply choose to sell a
licence, including royalties, to a Japanese manufacturer. Licensed pharmaceutical
products associated with multinational companies are a common way for a relatively
small company, such as Yoshitomi Ltd. manufacturing Bayer products under licence,
to maintain a leading position in the industry. In the apparel and food processing
businesses, also, there is considerable scope for licensing because of the Westernisation of tastes. Thus, the Fukusuke Corporation, which originally produced tabi
(the special socks worn with kimono), signed a licensing and technical agreement
with the Van Heusen shirt company in 1965, when the market for tabi had become
relatively insignificant.

– but manufacturing subsidiaries can ensure adequate servicing

Nonetheless for high technology intermediate products in which proprietary knowhow may be at stake, establishing a manufacturing subsidiary in Japan in order that
the products may be adequately serviced seems to be an advisable option. AVX
Corp. a leading manufacturer of multilayer ceramic capacitors, decided to
establish a plant in Japan during 1981 so as to compete effectively with Japanese
manufacturers of MLCs. Similarly Material Research Corp will open a Japanese
plant in 1982 so as to be able to maintain a closer dialogue with its customers in
the IC industry. MRC has chosen to incorporate a Japanese partner with a 20 per
cent equity holding, presumably to assist in more effective customisation for the
Japanese IC industry. Still, MRC is not limiting its sights to Japanese customers
only, but rather considers that Far Eastern markets and American companies
already in Japan – namely Texas Instruments and IBM – will be better serviced
through a plant in Japan.

Risks and rewards

The managements of companies such as MRC are evidently willing to take on risks in establishing them in the Japanese market. Indeed it is interesting to note that although Japanese companies tend to operate with rather low net worth and current ratios, which would be considered risky in the West, foreign affiliated firms in Japan have ratios comparable with those in Japanese firms (Table 19). At the same time, despite exhortations to foreign firms to expect losses in the first five to ten years of operation and to aim to maximise sales volume rather than unit profits, foreign affiliated firms, according to Miti's survey, have on average earned higher net profit to sales ratios than Japanese firms. For example in 1978/79, for manufacturing firms, the comparative ratios were 2.2 per cent and 1.7 per cent, while in manufacturing excluding oil processing the disparity was even wider with foreign firms' average net profit to sales ratio at 3.0 per cent and Japanese firms' at 1.5 per cent.

Overriding need to adapt to local demand

In concluding this discussion on competition within the Japanese market, the proviso should be made that the preceding has tended to avoid pessimism in attempting to show how the market can be penetrated. In fact, as is particularly evident in the case of agricultural products where various troublesome stipulations for standardisation exist, legal requirements often appear to be excessively fussy. The story of the Jetro employee who, after serving overseas and wishing to import his BMW car into Japan, was confronted with lengthy hassles over altering specifications is not apocryphal. Also, the imperative of presenting Japanese consumers with goods which are well and attractively packaged appears to be an unreasonable requirement in this ecologically minded age.

However while certain requirements could be dispensed with, others are, in the minds of the Japanese, essential. For example, the extreme levels of humidity in the summer would necessitate Marks and Spencers' biscuits being more highly packaged than they are when appearing on Daiei's counters. In the case of automobiles, specifications are often stipulated in order to heighten safety. Since the Japanese have actually succeeded in lowering the death rate from traffic accidents since 1970, despite the greatly increased number of cars, their judgement of what constitutes 'safe' cannot be easily dismissed.

Finally, those entering the Japanese market can only conclude that in sum the best approach is to imitate the Japanese who have succeeded in overseas markets by adapting their products to meet local demands.

Table 19

Safety Indicators for Major Foreign Affiliated Firms in Japan
(percentages; fiscal years beginning in April of year shown)

	Current ratio[a]						Net worth ratio[b]					
	1973	1974	1975	1976	1977	1978	1973	1974	1975	1976	1977	1978
Major foreign firms												
All industries	103.4	106.0	103.0	109.6	112.0	112.2	21.7	19.7	16.8	17.7	20.0	21.9
Manufacturing	103.7	108.8	104.0	111.3	113.5	114.0	22.9	21.0	16.9	17.9	20.4	22.4
Manufacturing except for oil processing	101.4	121.9	116.2	123.8	123.2	122.3	21.8	27.9	26.1	24.7	25.7	27.5
Major Japanese firms												
All industries	107.9	107.9	112.6	113.0	111.2	108.6	15.8	15.3	14.7	16.3	17.1	17.3
Manufacturing	110.7	109.9	115.5	116.6	115.7	112.4	19.3	18.5	17.3	19.4	20.1	20.4

a Current assets/current liabilities x 100. b $\dfrac{\text{Net worth + reserved profits}}{\text{liabilities and net worth}}$ x 100

Source: Miti, Gaishikei Kigyo no Doko (Foreign Business Affiliates in Japan), 1980.

Export concentration follows from productivity advantage

The debate over whether Japanese exports are excessively concentrated in certain industries - with perhaps the deliberate intention of destroying the overseas industry in question - has been vociferous. Officials from European and North American countries have sometimes conducted their arguments in an emotional and misleading way which has distracted attention from the real issues. The substantive issue could be summed up as being that comparative growth rates in productivity in certain industries have altered the terms of trade successively in favour of Japanese exports. Nor need the causes of high productivity growth rates be mythologised. While other factors have assisted in its implementation, more highly automated processes have been the basis of Japan's productivity growth - particularly in the electronics industry in recent years.

The case of electronics

Thus it may be predicted that the present trade friction over automobiles will soon be heightened by conflicts over IC trade. Yet that may not necessarily be so, because Western producers have failed to provide adequate capacity in the electronics industry quickly enough. Thus Nippon Electric Co's decision to establish in 1981 a wholly owned subsidiary in Glasgow to sell electronic parts in Britain and Ireland is based on the expectation that British demand for semiconductors will increase two and a half times over its 1980 level by 1985. In the US market, Japanese semi-conductor manufacturers such as Nippon Electric Company are choosing to invest more in local production including a planned VLSI plant, in order to avert expected friction. Moreover the Finance Ministry in Japan has asserted that Japanese IC makers have been engaging in voluntary export restraint during 1981 - especially by suspending exports of spot ICs other than those under long term contracts.

Is Japan's dominance in cars only temporary?

The issues over automobile trade are more complex than is usually realised because of a misperception of Japanese strength in the long term in this industry. Part of the reason why the Japanese automobile firms have been unwilling participants in export restraints is because they believe that the Western automobile companies could still be strong competitors. Thus the Japanese automobile industry considers its present dominant position to be a temporary one, which will be superseded once the American industry has completed its switch to more fuel economic, small cars and the European industry has sorted out its rationalisation problems. Miti's vice minister for international affairs, Mr Naohiro Amaya, has suggested that "the American auto industry seems to perceive the Japanese competition as stronger than it actually is"[1]. The current worldwide reorganisation of the automobile

---

1   Japan Times, November 9, 1980.

industry mentioned earlier (page 62) may go a considerable way in resolving auto
trade friction. It is after all notable that the presidents of the Japanese firms
affiliated with General Motors, Ford and Chrysler did not view the April 1981
agreement with the USA on export restrictions with alarm as did the presidents
of Nissan and Toyota. Thus Isuzu, Toyo Kogyo, and Mitsubishi Motors Corp
were able to present a case to the Miti minister, arguing that their US partners
desired an undiminished supply of their automobiles from Japan which would provide
profits required for investment in restructuring the US production facilities of their
partners. As it happens the Miti formula, decided upon later, did permit the annual
average of exports in 1979 and 1980 from these affiliated companies to increase;
but the justification lay in a special adjustment, for those exports had fallen
relatively since 1979.

What sort of international competition?

The bilateral agreements on Japanese automobile export restraints reached during
1981 have aroused considerable apprehension in Japan that protectionism will spread,
thereby causing world trade to shrink. It may be that threats of protectionism from
the West are in the short term interests of the non-Japanese industries concerned
in so far as Keidanren (the influential 'Federation of Economic Organisations')
has called on Japanese exporters to try to prevent trade friction caused by foreign
markets being swamped with specific Japanese products (May 1981). However
in adopting the kind of terminology used by foreign critics of Japan's trade practices,
Keidanren's resolution sounds neither convincing nor operable.

Mr Saburo Okita, the government's trade representative, has instead called attention to the apparent failure of many countries to catch up with the rapid transition
to what he calls a "dynamic international division of labour". Evidently, in trade
between equally industrialised nations areas of specialisation should develop in
order to justify the exchange of goods. It may be that such specialisation is feasible
within a given industry, as in the cases of medical equipment, cited in Chapter II
(page 58), and of a UK firm supplying exhaust emission catalysts (page 72).
Whether specialisation among different industries can develop, however, will
probably depend on collective governmental agreements being reached.

International agreements over steel

An approach has been adopted in the steel industry rather different from that in
automobiles, whereby trade agreements, including the US trigger price system,
have been reached without unduly acrimonious debate. It has sometimes been
suggested that the Japanese steel industry feels indebted to the West not only for
technology but also for postwar US capital and equipment supplies; so that it is
more willing to hold back while the US steel industry regains its competitive edge.
Although there may be a little truth in this argument, it is more plausible to
assume that the world steel industry has come to recognise the mutual dependence
between its firms and has therefore reached an accord somewhat akin to an oligopolistic arrangement.

Japan and the Nics

In trade with less developed countries, certain Japanese economists have taken
pride in the apparent stability reached through Japan's moving into specialisation

in knowledge intensive industries, while leaving the way open for the newly industrialising countries to specialise in labour intensive industries. It would be shortsighted, however, to expect the Nics to continue to be satisfied with their role once high growth levels have dropped off. Indeed, although the four Asian Nics raised their share of Japan's manufactured imports to 16.5 per cent in 1979, in 1980 their manufactured exports to Japan fell, even in value terms by 8.5 per cent, so that their share correspondingly dropped to 13.5 per cent. This is probably only natural in so far as one could not expect the economies of Japan and the Nics to be complementary with one another over the long term. Similarly Brazil's growing strength in the Asian export market is likely to upset the delicate balance of complementary interests between Japan and South East Asia. Singapore has already felt the effects of a reduction in Japanese interest, despite its continued campaign to attract Japanese capital and industrial technology. Table 12 demonstrates the extent of the decline in Japan's direct investment in Asia, with a fall of over 27 per cent in authorised investment in just one year between March 1979 and 1980.

Mixed feelings about Japanese investment in industrial countries

As noted earlier (page 59) part of the reason for the decline in new investment in Asia is due to a shift to Western countries. Attitudes towards Japanese investment in the EEC and North America continue to be highly ambivalent. On the one hand there is a persistent call for Japanese investment to provide employment, particularly in the depressed areas of the UK. Various missions - from Scotland and the West Midlands among others - have been sent to Japan to argue their cases based on the availability of highly skilled labour and stable energy supplies. On the other hand a conflict of interests within the EEC has led to severe apprehension about Nissan's proposed plant in the UK, which would facilitate further penetration of Japanese cars into the European market.

Concerning the argument over creating employment opportunities, a legitimate question is whether existing adequate capacity will merely be duplicated. For this reason the British Plastics Federation protested against the Department of Industry's proposals for providing development grants for the establishment of a Japanese plastics processing plant for television components in South Wales. However trade union leaders in the UK have generally welcomed the notion of Japanese investment, despite protests from leaders of industry that established firms may be threatened, thereby possibly leading to redundancies in British firms.

Australia has also decided in favour of encouraging Japanese investment. A new government requirement in Australia, somewhat redolent of a less developed country's import substitution policy, is for increased domestic production of automobiles. Therefore Toyota has responded by establishing a second body plant. Although Toyota has generally been loth to engage in direct investment overseas, in this case it is believed that the expanded investment will improve the competitive position of Toyota's cars in the Australian market. Ironically subsidiaries of America's General Motors and Ford hold strongly competitive positions in Australia, compared with Japanese companies.

The unwillingness of Japan's major automobile firms to invest overseas until recently was primarily due to an apprehension about obtaining reliable part supplies, once they were separated from their close networks of subcontractors in Japan.

Now, with Canadian government encouragement, Toyota is likely to set up an auto parts plant in British Columbia, although a Toyota car manufacturing operation is not yet in sight. As in most of the cases of proposed Japanese investment in the West, political considerations - this time on the Canadian side - have played a part. An opposition leader suggested that the proposed plant was nothing more than a political gimmick to secure a by-election in British Columbia during May 1981.

Thus the whole question of competing with Japanese investment overseas is highly coloured by political manoeuvrings. In general, in spite of the protestations of certain industry leaders, both governments and workers are amenable to more extensive Japanese direct investments. In the case of governments, however, there have been threats - probably not to be taken seriously - to block investments in retaliation for the apparently closed nature of the Japanese system with its close buyer-seller relationships and impediments to capital flows. In the case of labour, it has been suggested that if the quality of skills is less overseas than in Japan, the flow of Japanese investment, especially into the USA, may slow down. A Nikko Research Centre Survey, whose report was released in June 1981, indicated that over 65 per cent of Japanese firms in the USA were dissatisfied with the quality of labour. However since the survey questionnaire was sent to only 88 firms, of whom a mere 55.7 per cent replied, its results are not convincing. The experience of Sony, Kikkoman and others suggests that productivity rates can be matched overseas. Indeed some Japanese managers have commended the diligent work, under clear and agreed contracts, of American labour. Small scale Japanese investments in Atlanta, Georgia, have succeeded, apparently because of the Southerners' accepting the team idea of work.

If the injection of Japanese management and capital into Western economies can bring about such satisfactory results, the implication is that Western firms could do just as well - or better, being on home ground - by improving industrial relations, by encouraging management to acquire shopfloor experience, and by appointing more technologically knowledgeable managers than at present. In the meantime it looks as though politicians in the West will continue to seek overseas direct investment from Japanese firms, which have proved the viability of the above practices.

Competition or cooperation?

One way which the USA has considered for directly imitating Japanese institutions is the proposed establishment of US sōgō shōsha (general trading companies). However sōgō shōsha have been crucial in the Japanese context only because Japanese manufacturing companies have lacked, until recently, the necessary scope and skills for competing effectively overseas. Thus Japanese commentators have been sceptical as to whether American sōgō shōsha would be appropriate for more effective US competition when the other elements which have contributed to Japanese success are lacking. A more feasible alternative might be that proposed by Yoshizo Ikeda, chairman of Mitsui, that Japan's sōgō shōsha should hold equity interests in American exporting companies by means of which management knowhow could be exchanged. Indeed it would seem that generally some form of cooperation will be more effective than all-out competition between Japanese and foreign firms.

Chapter 4

Cooperating with Japanese Enterprises

COOPERATING WITHIN JAPAN

As in the case of competition, discussion of cooperation will be divided into two sections for within and outside Japan. Yet this distinction is rapidly becoming meaningless as major industries, ranging from the pharmaceutical industry to the automobile industry (Chapter III page   80), engage in worldwide reorganisation, involving various forms of tie ups. For the sake of mere order, such reorganisation efforts will be discussed in the 'outside Japan' section.

Four major categories of cooperation within Japan will be considered here, although there are other possibilities. At the simplest level, equity may be purchased in a Japanese company, while at the other end of the scale a joint venture for manufacture could be established. In between are the well tested route of various licensing arrangements and the growing number of shōhin teikei for selling goods directly through major retailers.

The advantages behind some kind of tie up are clear in that they provide contacts and knowledge of the local market. The importance of personal contact in conducting business in Japan cannot be overestimated. Usually one gains an introduction only through mentioning another mutually known person. Moreover it is not enough to rely on communicating by letter or by telephone in establishing a relationship. In a business negotiation the watershed between success and failure occurs during an apparently innocuous occasion - the exchange of aisatsu (greetings). The negotiating parties together with the top level management all meet together, exchange name cards, and discuss nothing. Thereafter compromises may still have to be reached, but the aisatsu meeting has already determined whether or not the final outcome is successful.

How to negotiate in Japan has become a popular topic in books and journals. The implication is usually that the areas of conflict will not be clear and a consensus will emerge without overt debate. However writers on this topic tend to ignore the fact that the Japanese side are naturally quite well aware that they are negotiating with foreigners. Hence they would greet attempts to imitate their own negotiating practices with distrust. Japanese management staff are knowledgeable about, and often familiar with, Western business practices, so they prefer to engage in explicit arguments, rather than superficial hara (literally: stomach) language. At the same time, apart from the pleasure of learning about another culture, it would of course be in the interests of the Western executive entering into a contract in Japan to become acquainted with Japanese business practices.

Just as in the negotiating case, so in deciding upon a formal contract, there is little sense in attempting to follow the traditional Japanese practice - no longer so prevalent - of relying on trust rather than a written contract. Nonetheless, even with a formal contract, special problems do arise, particularly when smaller firms, less involved in international dealings, are involved. An initial problem is in determining which version - the Japanese or foreign language - is binding. Before the contract is signed, there should also be clarification about the limits to the disclosure of corporate information. Inevitably changes in exchange rates and other cost changes are often a source of conflict, after the contract has been signed. Such disputes can be referred to the Japan Commercial Arbitration Association, whose case histories may provide opportunities for salutary study.

While the difficulties emanating from both communication hurdles and some loss of control in entering a tie up should not be belittled, experience has on the whole demonstrated that the knowledge and commitment required for penetrating the Japanese market make some form of tie up worthwhile.

EQUITY PARTICIPATION

Beginning at the simplest form, which often hardly qualifies as a tie up, does provide some inkling of the processes involved. Once again it is the rapidity of recent changes which must be stressed, especially on account of the radical amendments in the Foreign Exchange Control Law, effective from December 1980. While the relevant articles are mentioned here, this cannot be a substitute for a publication such as the Japan Business Law Journal's February, 1981, issue on Interpretation of the Amended Foreign Exchange Control Law. The annual publication of the Japan Securities Research Institute, Securities Market in Japan (Tokyo Shoken Kaikan, Zaikei Shoho-sha Publishing Co), may also be recommended.

Certain restrictions on foreign ownership persist

Concerning equity participation in Japanese firms, the revised law now permits foreign investors to hold an unlimited amount of stock in a Japanese firm, although any individual may still hold no more than 10 per cent. Restrictions are imposed on foreign ownership in the case of eleven designated firms, in which it is considered majority foreign ownership could possibly have a negative impact on the Japanese economy or impair national security and order. Thus the limits on foreign ownership of oil companies range up to 50 per cent, while for Hitachi Ltd and Tokyo Precision Instrument Co, the limits are 30 per cent and 32 per cent respectively.

One restrictive case - a limit of 25 per cent on foreign equity participation in Katakura Industries Co - has already been the subject of a legal battle with the Japanese government early in 1981. The justification for the restriction lies in Katakura's role in the sericultural industry, which is argued to be strategically important to Japanese agriculture. However a Hong Kong investor, whose investment group holds a combined 23 per cent interest in Katakura, points out that the company's sericultural involvement is only marginal to its operations.

It is likely that the looseness of the law's provisions for designating restrictions on certain companies will lead to further disputes. Katakura is the only one of the eleven initially designated which is restricted on account of the nation's agriculture. Six are oil companies, while two are related to nuclear power, one to narcotics, and the last is a maker of aircraft instruments. The range of these companies suggests that other companies could, apparently arbitrarily, be included among the group at any time.

Upsurge of foreign buying in 1980

Even before the revised law became effective, 1980 had seen an upsurge in foreign investors' acquisition of Japanese stocks. In that year acquisitions amounted to $12,172 mn, with disposals at only $7,183 mn, whereas in the previous couple of years disposals had exceeded acquisition. 1980 was characterised particularly by the participation of investors from oil producing countries in Japan's stock market.

Foreign investors have tended conservatively to concentrate their purchases in stocks of large companies, where the share prices are relatively stable. Table 20 shows the ten most popular in the first half of 1981 in terms of number of shares purchased net, but since Sony's shares, for instance, tend to be priced at roughly ten times the amount of Toshiba's, and there are other very highly priced blue chips such as Victor and Kyoto Ceramic, the table is not necessarily a guide to those shares in which the greatest net amount was invested.

Table 20

Stocks Most Popular among Foreign Investors
(Jan-Jun 1981)

Company	Net foreign acquisitions (mn shares)
Nippon Kokan KK.	113.50
Toshiba Corp	81.15
Mitsubishi Electric Corp	74.60
Teijin Ltd	65.45
Matsushita Electrical Co Ltd	55.95
Nippon Steel Corp	54.90
Asahi Chemical Industries Co Ltd	52.30
Kawasaki Heavy Industries Ltd	49.90
Sumitomo Metal Industries Ltd	49.75
Showa Denko KK	45.55

Source: Nikko Securities Co Ltd.

Therefore there is yet untried scope for the foreign investor to seek out medium sized companies - especially in the electronics industry - whose shares' potential for appreciation is high. Such companies are actively seeking foreign equity participation, as evidenced by their expenditure on producing glossy English versions of their annual reports. In order to improve communication further with prospective investors, a few companies, such as Ito-Yokado and Seven-Eleven, Japan, have produced 'slide shows' with an attached English commentary explaining their operations and profit performance.

These activities are just one indication of the internationalisation of Tokyo's capital market. This process would be halted if the government were to invoke discretionary powers against liberalisation of the capital account, under the revised Foreign Exchange Control Law. Again the scope for discretion could be interpreted quite widely as the relevant Article 21 allows cases such as difficulty in maintaining balance of payments equilibrium.

An analysis by Daiwa Securities Co Ltd, has identified four major hindrances to complete internationalisation of the Tokyo capital market, three of which concern the bond market. Thus Daiwa calls for the following measures:

1. fostering short term government bonds as the nucleus of the short term bond market;

2. approving more unsecured bonds issued for fund raising by reputable corporations;

3. increasing the flexibility and liberalising the terms of bond issue;

4. unifying international standards for auditing (as elsewhere, double auditing is required for foreign stocks listed on Tokyo Stock Exchange).

DIRECT RETAILING (SHOHIN TEIKEI)

The radical restructuring of Japan's distribution and retailing system over the past two decades, with the advent of chain superstores, has opened up import routes for mass consumer goods. In particular the largest superstore chain. Daiei, has been to the forefront in seeking to import good quality goods whose prices are reasonable. The usual arrangement is that the retailer agrees to import a minimum amount each year, in return for monopoly selling rights in the Japanese market. Since the Japanese side is bound to import for a given period, whether or not the goods sell satisfactorily, the shōhin teikei is comparatively advantageous to the prospective exporter to the Japanese market.

The advantages for the Japanese side in the arrangement may seem more nebulous. Therefore the future growth of shōhin teikei arrangements is rather indeterminate. A visit to a superstore and to a department store would provide evidence of the reasons why Daiei is at present pursuing such arrangements. The department store's share of the market has been gradually declining, but its apparent verve, which conveys a sense of both innovation and luxury, means that it holds a pre-eminent place in consumers' sensibilities. Seibu, which incidentally markets Sears Roebuck mail order goods, is a good example of a department store whose image is vigorous and exciting. On the other hand, a superstore's growth until the present has depended on its being able to offer cheaper, and hence more standard, goods with high turnover and low gross margins. With the rapid improvement in people's living standards coupled with a desire to improve the quality of life, the prospects for superstores may diminish while department stores could once more surge ahead.

Hence Daiei is diversifying its appeal by including in its stock goods from the UK's Marks and Spencer, the USA's J C Penney and others. An interesting development in prospect is the planned exchange of goods between Daiei and Kroger. In the case of France's Au Printemps, Daiei has gone one step further in opening a store in Kobe, solely as an outlet for Au Printemps' goods. Oddly enough, the associated company - Au Printemps Japan SA - is a wholly owned subsidiary of Daiei, where a joint venture might have been expected with use of the name.

No room for complacency on design or packaging

One drawback to such arrangements is that often the overseas company, which relies almost wholly on the Japanese side for marketing the goods, does not give enough attention to whether the goods are appropriately packaged for the Japanese consumer. Moreover a reasonable level of quality has different implications for different cultures. Thus in Japan it is only the very cheapest skirts and dresses which are not lined, although the general finishing may be judged by some as inadequate. Therefore, one cannot complacently enter a shōhin teikei without ensuring that the product is appropriately designed, unless one wishes the arrangement not to be perpetuated beyond the initial contract period.

Not only retailers but also manufacturers in Japan have entered into arrangements tantamount to shōhin teikei. Sony decided in the early 1970s to complement its product range with imported home appliances. It began by placing advertisements in Western journals calling for products to be marketed with Sony's assistance in Japan. In particular, Sony sought high quality home appliances which were not already available. In this way Sony saw its role not just as a distributor, but also as an "educator" of Japanese consumers in creating demand. Products from Oster, Hoover, and others are now marketed in Japan exclusively by Sony, which purchases an agreed amount at the fob price. This system is being deepened now that Sony is producing some of the goods, such as Oster's crêpe pan, under licence in Japan.

The Japanese retailer or manufacturer identifies with the product

The prime advantage of entering the Japanese market through a shōhin teikei is that, rather than relying on a general trading company, which imports numerous goods, one's products become directly associated with a well known Japanese manufacturer or retailer. Hence it is important to the Japanese company that the imported goods should be successfully marketed, so as not to detract from its own image. Thus even though a small, specialised trading company may be just as well acquainted with the appropriate market segment, there is a lower sense of identification with success. This advantage probably outweighs the disadvantage of losing control over the marketing, as long as the exporter still acquaints himself with the Japanese market and despatches appropriate goods as a consequence.

Certainly the scope for this kind of arrangement is widening, as exporters have come to appreciate the immense investment required in trying to enter the Japanese market on their own. Amdahl Corp of California's business link up with Fujitsu Ltd has provided the route for its new large capacity computer of the 580 series to enter the Japanese market, whereby it could effectively compete with IBM's 3081 Processor Complex. In a completely different field, the Swedish pharmaceutical manufacturer, Kabi, has reached a basic agreement with Sumitomo Chemical for exports of its growth hormone to Japan. As in other cases, Sumitomo is considering whether to discuss importing the associated technology later on.

FRANCHISES AND OTHER LICENSING ARRANGEMENTS

While the future success of all shōhin teikei arrangements may still be somewhat
uncertain, the viability of most licensing arrangements has long ago been proven.
For that reason Japanese companies often intend to engage in further discussions
for the licensing of the technology involved, even after a direct import arrangement
has been concluded. The variety of licensing arrangements is enormous; so, while
the following will discuss a cross section of different agreements, the full range of
possibilities cannot be properly presented here.

Franchising fast food outlets

Many of the arrangements intended for the final consumer have been sought because
of the Westernisation of Japanese tastes. It is therefore thought that a Western
company would provide not only the expertise to satisfy such tastes, but also the
association of being the 'real thing'. The restaurant business, including fast foods,
serves as a good example, because the rapid improvement in living standards is
expected to lead to a real 6.34 per cent increase in expenditure on dining
out in the first half of the 1980s (Dentsu forecast).

Just as in the case of shōhin teikei, Daiei has been notable in seeking franchises
ranging from hamburger chains to a relatively expensive restaurant chain (Victoria
Station). For example, as the Japanese franchisee for Wendy's hamburger chain,
Daiei has agreed to establish a certain number of Wendy's outlets each year in order
to retain its exclusive rights in Japan. A smaller superstore chain, Nichii Co,
has also entered the field by concluding an agreement with Arby's Inc, for receiving
knowhow on the production and sale of roast beef sandwiches. Nichii's commitment
to the franchise is perhaps demonstrated by its having established a new company –
Arby's Japan. Similarly the Ito Yokado superstore chain has firmly established,
since 1973, Denny's Japan Co Ltd, under licence from Denny's Inc of California.
Incidentally franchises have not been the most prominent arrangement in the foreign
fast food business in Japan – both McDonalds and Kentucky Fried Chicken are 50-50
joint ventures with their parent companies.

Licensing in the motor industry

Licensing has been proved to involve less arduous negotiations and controversy
than either joint ventures or direct overseas investment in the automobile industry.
Nonetheless the negotiations between Nissan and Volkswagen for producing the
Passat under licence in Japan have probably been more drawn out than initially
anticipated. While Volkswagen acknowledges that there will not be any direct
employment benefit in West Germany, it is anticipated that the supply of parts will
bring about substantial employment and other benefits to West German industry.
Volkswagen intends that the Passats produced in Japan, probably beginning in 1983,
should be not only sold in the domestic market, but also exported through Volkswagen
channels to South East Asia. Therefore it is presumed that while sales in Japan will
profit Nissan directly, exports to nearby markets will contribute substantially to
Volkswagen profits. It is just as well that such potential fruits have been suggested
for Volkswagen, because the initial announcement of the Nissan-Volkswagen deal
led to sales of VW cars in Japan through Yanase, the major car importer/distributor,
falling by 20 per cent in the early months of 1981. The drop in sales is probably not
just on account of an expectation of cheaper VWs available through domestic production;

in addition the Japanese consumer would feel more secure about the immediate availability of spare parts and reliable servicing facilities. It is likely that when some of the ill feeling generated by trade friction has been overcome, Nissan's purchase of a licence to produce Passats in Japan will be extended by cross licensing arrangements.

The pharmaceutical industry, which invests considerably in R & D for just one drug, is notable for the number of cross licences extended between Japanese and other firms. While the balance is still in favour of Western drug companies exporting their technology to Japan, the continued growth of such exports will depend to some extent on the purchase of Japanese licences in return.

Original equipment manufacturing

One can only include original equipment manufacturing (OEM) agreements within the general licensing category. Such agreements permit the foreign firm's name to be used while the locally manufactured product's quality is equal to that of the original. For example, Olivetti has six major OEM agreements with office equipment manufacturers in Japan. It is rather intriguing to note that one of Olivetti's OEM typewriter makers, Nakajima, also supplies Olympia, Triumph and Sears Roebuck. In the case of Olivetti's OEM agreement with Sharp for plain paper copiers, Sharp's output is destined for Olivetti's European market. Indeed, at present Olivetti does not intend to market plain paper copiers in Japan.

This kind of arrangement has gone one step further in the audio industry, where Sony and NV Philips have jointly developed a compact disc digital audio system. The subsequent decision by both Matsushita and Pioneer-Electronic Corp to sign patent licence agreements for the system with NV Philips has indicated that the 'compact disc' will probably become the uniform system in Japan. Evidently such cooperation is essential so that the development of incompatible systems is as far as possible precluded. Therefore there is a scientific, as well as profit, rationale for international cooperation on high technology products.

Licence acquisitions no longer need prior approval

The importance of licensing to such cooperation has always been well recognised by Miti, which has encouraged the seeking of licences for foreign technology. However, before the December 1980 amendments in the Foreign Exchange and Foreign Trade Control Law, licensing agreements with a duration of more than one year were subject to approval under the Foreign Investment Law. This requirement reflected Miti's desire to control duplicate imports of foreign technology so as to foster a single, powerful company within a particular industry. Now that all licensing agreements are subject only to prior notification the scope for control by the government has been limited, even though powers for prohibiting or recommending changes in the licensing agreement have been reserved. It remains to be seen whether such powers will be exercised, but in the present climate of opinion it is probable that little will be done.

At this point it should be mentioned that government intervention does naturally take place in other forms, and needs particular attention where the foreign licensor of pharmaceuticals is concerned. During 1980, in two stages, more stringent legislation designed to ensure drug safety came into effect. It may be that the new legislation is ultimately beneficial to the licensor of pathbreaking pharmaceutical preparations, in so far as the period over which 'copying' cannot take place and side effects must be closely monitored has been extended from three to six years.

Just as in trade, the issue of legislation over safety standards arouses controversy. Still the regulations, it must be remembered, are in principle applied equally to both domestic and foreign products.

JOINT VENTURES

Multinationals satisfied with a smaller stake -

Somewhat ironically, it appears from the data on foreign affiliated firms in Japan that the leading multinationals are more willing than small firms to enter into joint ventures. Table 21 shows that in 1980 for 62 per cent of the US leading multinationals, defined as those listed among the Fortune 200, operating in Japan, the parent company of the affiliate had minority, or just 50 per cent ownership. The only exceptions are pharmaceutical firms and those in the steel and non-ferrous metals industry. It would seem that the close ties between the USA and Japan, in addition to the fact that US leading firms are more truly multinational, account for the rather different picture presented by non-US multinational companies operating in Japan. Nonetheless 50 per cent or less foreign ownership of affiliates is still evident in the chemical, rubber, and transportation equipment industries.

- than smaller direct investors -

Yet, as noted in Chapter III (page 73) the number of foreign affiliates with majority ownership has tended to increase each year, so that now in over 50 per cent of all affiliates in Japan, the foreign parent has more than 50 per cent ownership[1]. This trend has been accompanied by another in which it appears that the number of smaller foreign enterprises directly investing in Japan has swollen each year. In particular, between 1978 and 1979 no less than 44.7 per cent of newly formed foreign affiliates were capitalised at less than ¥10 mn. At first sight it seems somewhat strange that smaller foreign firms, who it might be thought would particularly gain from fifty-fifty joint venture establishments, should be choosing not to imitate the leading multinationals. At the same time the aggregated figures do indicate an increase in the number of foreign firms operating in commerce and the service industry. Again between 1978 and 1979, 61.9 per cent of newly formed foreign affiliates were in non-manufacturing fields, although the corresponding percentage for all affiliates responding to Miti's survey was 46.8.

---

1   All the following figures are taken from Miti's annual survey of foreign affiliates in Japan (Gaishikei Kigyō no Dōkō).

Table 21

Leading Multinationals Operating in Japan [a]

(Number of companies; March 31. 1980)

Industry	US companies — No. operating in Japan [b]	Over 25% under 50%	50%	Over 50% under 100%	100%	Total [c]	Non-US companies — No. operating in Japan	Over 50% under 50%	50%	under 100%	100%	Total
Food	16	3	11	3	8	25	2	–	–	1	2	3
Textiles	1	–	1	–	–	1	–	–	–	–	–	–
Paper & pulp	6 (1)	1	5	1	1	8	–	–	–	–	–	–
Chemicals	16	5	23	4	12	44	8	3	20	3	8	34
Pharmaceuticals	9	–	10	4	16	30	1	–	2	–	2	4
Oil	14	10	11	–	10	31	2	1	2	–	2	5
Rubber	5 (1)	3	3	–	3	9	1	1	1	–	–	2
Ceramics & quarrying	3 (1)	1	3	–	1	5	1	–	1	–	–	1
Steel & non-ferrous metals	4	1	–	2	3	6	6	–	3	1	7	11
Fabricated metals	4	1	3	–	1	5	1	–	–	–	–	–
General machinery	17	9	11	5	6	31	1	–	–	–	1	1
Electrical machinery	11	10	8	1	8	27	3	1	1	1	2	5
Transport equipment	14 (2)	14	14	2	7	37	2	1	1	–	–	2
Precision machinery	4	1	3	–	2	6	–	–	–	–	–	–
Others	2	1	2	–	4	7	1	–	–	–	1	1
Total	125 (5)	60	108	22	82	272	28	7	31	6	25	26

(The column group "Over 25% under 50%, 50%, Over 50% under 100%, 100%, Total" for US companies and the corresponding Non-US columns fall under the heading "No. of affiliates more than 25% owned by parent".)

a The term "leading multinationals" refers to the 200 US manufacturing and mining companies listed in order of their annual sales by Fortune Magazine and the 100 non-US manufacturing and mining companies listed by Fortune in 1980 (other than the 21 Japanese companies). b Figures in brackets indicate the number of multinationals in Japan owning less than 25 per cent of their affiliates shares. c Totals may not be identical with totals of companies operating in Japan, as several foreign firms have established more than one affiliated company.

Source: Based on the licences granted by the Ministry of Finance.

- although going it alone is the harder way

Perhaps one can presume that in general the trends are commensurate with one another, so that smaller foreign firms investing in Japan tend to be in commerce and services and to take on majority ownership. However, if that is not so, then one must ask why smaller manufacturers from overseas are choosing to go it alone rather than participate in joint ventures.

The complexity of the Japanese market and the comparatively pernickety consumers, in addition to red tape and language hurdles, would suggest that establishing a joint venture is one of the best ways to invest directly in manufacturing in Japan. It may be that smaller firms lack the means to survey the options, but there are various Japanese consulting firms who provide advice and contacts.

Naturally the negotiations for establishing a joint venture can be thorny, especially over management rights. Even in the automobile industry, in which major world firms are entering into various alliances, the path to establishing a joint venture is not smooth. Indeed in 1981 Ford decided to withdraw its investment in the Japan Automatic Transmission Co, which had been a three way joint venture with Nissan and Toyo Kogyo.

The experience of the food processing industry -

In other fields, such as chemicals and the food processing industry, the history of joint ventures between foreign and Japanese firms has been both longer and more satisfactory. In food processing, Ajinomoto, which is pre-eminent in providing monosodium glutamate based spices for Japanese cooking, has cooperated in establishing joint ventures for the processing of Western foods. A recent successful example is the fifty-fifty owned Ajinomoto-Danone Company, whose dairy products entered the market in autumn 1980. Whereas imported cheeses tend only to be sold in supermarkets catering to foreigners or in the speciality food sections of department stores, the Danone varieties of cream cheese can be found almost everywhere, because of the Ajinomoto link. Moreover Ajinomoto-Danone was able to invest considerably in an initial extensive advertising campaign, coupled with instore demonstrations and free sampling.

- the chemical industry -

The chemical industry thrived, until the oil crises of the 1970s, on joint ventures between major Western and Japanese firms. Asahi-Dow Ltd, a joint venture between Asahi Chemical Industry Co Ltd and Dow Chemical Co, was founded as long ago as 1952, with the initial purpose of producing polyvinylidene chloride products. Since then its capitalisation has expanded by 25 times accompanied by diversification. Whereas in the early years there was considerable technological assistance from Dow, by 1964 Stylac, a product of Asahi-Dow's own research and development, was being marketed. With respect to the chemical industry, it is interesting to note from Table 21 that a total of 22 leading multinational chemical companies have no less than 78 affiliates operating in Japan. Of these joint venture affiliates in the chemical industry, only 34.6 per cent have majority ownership by the foreign parent.

The 1980s have signalled a certain amount of reorientation in the chemical industry, in the face of such factors as overcapacity in PVC production. Mitsui Petrochemical Industries Ltd has realigned itself towards producing products for the electronics industry. Thus, along with Mitsui Toatsu Chemicals Inc, an agreement has been reached to set up a joint venture in Japan to manufacture PPO (polyphenyleneoxide) for use in the trim of computers and electrical machinery, beginning from the autumn of 1983. Similarly Mitsui Petrochemical has joined with three other Japanese firms to establish a joint venture with Allied Corp of the USA for initially importing and marketing amorphous alloys used in the production of magnetic heads. It is anticipated that imports will be followed by domestic production, if the crystalline alloys sell as well as expected in Japan.

The above example illustrates that the scope for international joint ventures in Japan can comprise merely importing and distribution with the option of extending activities later on. For this reason, business consultants often recommend joint ventures even when entering the Japanese market merely for trade. Especially in such fields as industrial goods, the intensive and specialised marketing required, coupled with the need for reliable contacts with the purchasing industries, make a joint venture with a Japanese partner more or less indispensable.

– and pharmaceuticals

Similarly in the pharmaceutical industry, where detailed information accompanying sales and contacts with medical institutions are required, joint ventures have in general proved to be a viable way of entering the Japanese market beyond that of merely licensing production technology. As in other industries, major Japanese pharmaceutical companies have been willing to establish separate joint ventures to specialise in a drug line different from their own. For example, Nippon Merck Banyu Co is a joint venture of more than 20 years' standing, between Merck & Co of the USA and Banyu Pharmaceutical UK, the former holding 50.5 per cent of the equity. While Nippon Merck Banyu Co is ranked only 31st in Japan, with Banyu in tenth position in the pharmaceutical industry, Merck still anticipates a rapid growth in sales through being able to introduce its own drugs to Japan through the joint venture.

COOPERATING OUTSIDE JAPAN

Tie-ups preempt trade friction in pharmaceuticals

The pharmaceutical industry's joint ventures provide an illustration of how cooperation within Japan is being extended outside. Once Merck has obtained approval for a particular drug, which has become a costly and lengthy process, a joint venture enables the potential market to be extended further. In the case of the tie up between Takeda and Abbot, Takeda has been undertaking its clinical work in the USA, with the aim of speeding up approval procedures. Now that Japan's pharmaceutical research and development expenditure is ranked fifth behind the USA, West Germany, Switzerland, and France, Japanese pharmaceutical companies wish to expand overseas sales by means of international joint ventures and other tie ups. In this way the pharmaceutical companies may be able to preempt the kind of trade friction which has plagued the automobile industry and threatens some areas of electronics.

Trade friction hinders collaboration in cars

In the case of the automobile industry, trade friction may have played a part in hindering negotiations for cooperation outside Japan. For example, Toyota had originally expressed the pious hope that a joint venture formula could be agreed with Ford, whereby the latter's idle plants in the USA would be used to produce Toyota cars and so perhaps ease trade friction. After protracted negotiations, enlivened by threats of Arabian boycotts of Toyota vehicles and fear of US anti-trust action, the joint venture proposal itself was abandoned as being too risky. In addition it was believed that Toyota's original apparent enthusiasm had waned after the USA-Japan settlement on "voluntary" export restraints in April, 1981. Thus it appears that voluntary trade restraints may unintentionally be inhibiting direct Japanese investment abroad. On the other hand, Honda has decided to bring its Ohio plant into full capacity production six months earlier than the scheduled November 1984 and to increase planned output by 30,000 cars a year, on account of Japan's curbs on automobile exports to the USA.

The precarious state of Chrysler's finances have compelled it to be a more amenable negotiator than either Ford or Toyota. In just one month of 1981, Chrysler entered into new joint ventures with Peugeot, American Motors Corp and Volkswagen of America Inc, as well as with Mitsubishi Motors. There has apparently been some strain in Chrysler-Mitsubishi relations, despite their apparent closeness indicated by Chrysler's being Mitsubishi's exclusive US distributor and owning 15 per cent interest in Mitsubishi. At times there have been rumours of an impending merger between the two, but Chrysler would have to be in even more dire straits, before agreeing to submerge its identity.

Therefore joint ventures seem for the present to be the most viable form of intense cooperation in the automobile industry. However the ultimate success of such arrangements cannot yet be fully assessed. In the case of the 1980 Nissan-Alfa Romeo agreement to establish a fifty-fifty joint venture in Naples for the production of compact cars, output will not actually occur until 1983. The agreement provides for Nissan to supply the body and suspension, while Alfa Romeo is responsible for the engine and transmission. Consequently the compact will tend to be identified as a Nissan model, rather akin to the 'Cherry'.

Since the identification of car types is still rather nationalistically perceived – let alone the strong company connotations – joint venture negotiations may often flounder on the question of the car type itself. Probably for this reason British Leyland has insisted that the Triumph Acclaim – the fruit of a tie up with Honda – will have a British content, particularly in components, amounting to at least 70 per cent of the works price of the car. Moreover, although royalties will be paid – the Acclaim is a Europeanised version of the Honda Ballade – no profits will be remitted to Honda. Nonetheless a key part of the agreement seems to be that all the engines will be imported from Honda initially.

On the other hand, Toyota is expecting to reach an agreement with the UK's Lotus for supplying engines. However an agreement with more potential for cooperation is that between Rolls Royce and Japanese Aero Engines Ltd for sharing the development cost of RJ500 engines. This endeavour, in which Japanese engineers and designers have cooperated with their Rolls Royce counterparts, is worthy of closer study. The agreement provides for the first engine to be test-run in Bristol from early 1982, while the second will be run at Ishikawajima-Harima Heavy Industries Co's Mizuho plant.

Cooperation stands a better chance in intermediate products

It seems as though the scope for cooperation has been wider in the case of goods not directly associated with the final mass consumer market. Thus in the steel industry, where capital costs and technology are of prime importance, various technological cooperation agreements have been concluded between Japanese and other companies. The ties between the British Steel Corporation and Nippon Steel Corp were strengthened in mid 1981 with a package agreement designed to assist BSC with its rehabilitation efforts. In addition BSC is encouraging Nippon Steel to purchase equity in Redpath Dorman Long Ltd (its engineering division); and talks are under way for joint receipt of orders for international projects. Similarly, the US Steel Corporation has been receiving technical assistance from Sumitomo Metal Industries for reconstructing the former's cold rolling mills. Other companies in the US and Australian steel industries have also engaged in technical cooperation agreements with Japanese steel companies, usually with the aim of modernising plant and equipment in the industry overseas. Kawasaki Steel Corp alone has concluded technical assistance contracts with Australian Iron and Steel Pty Ltd, Svenskt Stal AB of Sweden, Bethlehem Steel Corp of the USA and several others.

Carving up the world video market

Japan's present pre-eminence in the steel industry has enabled the above agreements to be negotiated satisfactorily. In the area of video systems, the presence of incompatible systems has led to pressure to conclude international agreements so as to establish a secure market. The latest success appears to be the agreement between Japan's Victor Company and three European companies - the UK's Thorn EMI, France's Thomson Brand and West Germany's Telefunken - to set up a joint venture in which productive activities take place in each country. Thus, beginning in autumn 1982, VTRs will be manufactured in West Germany, and video cameras in France, while video discs will be produced in the UK. Already in 1980, Thorn EMI, along with Victor, Matsushita and General Electric, had formed three jointly owned companies in preparation for launching the video disc developed by Victor on the American market.

Evidently such cooperative efforts are now being forged ahead of the development of potential trade friction, nor are goods with a strong nationalistic identity involved. In the case of computers, cooperation has tended to come too late. However there is still some room for international specialisation through, for example, Japanese companies' marketing their small business computers through IBM. For example, Matsushita withdrew from the large computer market in 1964, but began producing small business computers in 1979.

Cooperation in third countries

Before concluding this survey of various industrial cooperative efforts with Japanese companies, explicit mention should be made of projects in third countries. In addition to proposals linked to development assistance (page 59) there are examples of purely commercial joint venture manufacturing projects in third countries. In 1982 Sweden's Volvo and Japan's Hino will produce trucks in Morocco under an unprecedented tie up between the two companies, although Hino has joint ventures with local capital in Thailand, the Philippines and Saudi Arabia. In the area of plant exports, there appears to be considerable scope for cooperation. The Japan Machinery Exporters' Association intends to send a mission to West Germany and Spain in autumn 1981 and this, together with talks with a delegation to Tokyo from the UK's Engineering Employers' Federation, is designed to promote cooperation in plant exports to third countries.

One that came unstuck

This chapter may have been misleading in surveying the successful examples of cooperation with Japanese industry. A striking, contrary, example, in which much was at stake, is the collapse of the coal liquefaction project planned by Japan, the USA and West Germany. The major reason seems to have been the rising costs, added to the US government's economic recovery plan for shifting alternative energy programmes over to the private sector. It will be interesting, therefore, to see whether the Sumitomo Group's coal liquefaction project fares any better.

A measure of the Japanese government's interest in promoting cooperation to ease pressures over trade is that for the coal liquefaction project the total appropriation for the fiscal years 1980/81 and 1981/82 was so large that only 8.7 per cent had been used by mid 1981, when the project fell through. The government has also proposed holding, in autumn 1981, a Japan-Europe symposium on mutual industrial cooperation. Keidanren has similarly adopted this line as part of its public relations exercise on behalf of Japanese companies. Again in autumn 1981, Keidanren officials will attend a meeting with members of the US "Business Roundtable". While the discussions will include energy and trade problems, stress will be given to mutual investment plans.

The role of the internationally oriented consulting company

Smaller companies may feel that governmental and leading company meetings are rather irrelevant to the actual groundwork of finding contacts and conducting negotiations. In the past decade, however, Japan has seen an upsurge in the number of internationally oriented consulting companies. An example is the Sumitomo Business Consulting Co Ltd, whose major shareholders are 18 members of the Sumitomo Group. Thus its interests are spread throughout the Japanese economy. While such companies are engaged also in assisting small and medium sized Japanese companies to venture overseas, their range of consequent contacts is an aid to the foreign firm entering Japan, whether through trade, licensing or investment. In the case of the Sumitomo consulting company, they also cooperate with official bodies such as the state of Florida, the Nigerian government and the UK's Telford New Town Development Authority in introducing trading partners and Japanese overseas investors. Japanese consulting companies may be relatively new entrants to the international business cooperation scene – the Sumitomo example has been established only since 1971 – but they offer a realistic alternative source for the information previously monopolised by the general trading companies.

Chapter 5

Future Developments in Japanese Industry

TOWARDS FURTHER KNOWLEDGE INTENSIFICATION

Although Miti's role in guiding industrial development has diminished considerably since the 1950s, it still attempts to maintain a prominent profile through the release of policy pronouncements. In keeping with the reiterated, avowed aim - but not necessarily practice - of achieving a national consensus on industrial policy, Miti's Industrial Structure Council is composed of industrialists, labour leaders and academics. In 1980 the council submitted a major report entitled "Industrial Policy for the 1980s" (Hachijū-nendai no Tsūshō Sangyō Seisaku), which serves to indicate both the desired and largely anticipated direction of industrial development in Japan in the near future. While some attention is given to developing a more service oriented and creative economy, the main emphasis continues to be on the knowledge intensification of industry, as an extension of trends in the 1970s.

The Industrial Structure Council defines the objectives requiring further industrial transformation as being energy conservation, ensuring economic security, promoting an international division of labour and meeting the people's needs. This rather broad range of objectives can, it is considered, be satisfied through encouraging industries producing high value-added goods based on "creative" labour and soft technologies. The council has attempted to be more specific than the above would suggest by examining the implications for the major industrial categories. Thus, the processing and assembly industries are called upon to utilise electronic data processing technologies and to develop flexible production modes appropriate for product variations. Already many of the large scale processing and assembling industries have gone far in achieving these goals through computerising production lines.

Scope for new basic materials

In the case of basic materials industries, low sales growth has to some extent inhibited developments. The Industrial Structure Council suggests that, along with promoting further energy conservation, these industries should improve product quality and seek the development and use of new or speciality materials. Certainly, Japan's largest PVC producer, Shin-Etsu Chemicals Co Ltd, has endeavoured to diversify into electronics materials operations with quite considerable success. In just two years between 1978 and 1980 Shin-Etsu's sales of electronics materials almost doubled to reach 16.5 per cent of total sales. In particular high purity silicon and yttrium oxides produced by Shin-Etsu account for predominant shares in the Japanese market.

Nevertheless, the rapid and highly competitive development of new electronics materials means that companies in this field must constantly be engaged in producing improved compounds, such as Shin-Etsu's gadolinium gallium garnet substrates. Thus its research and development expenses at more than 3 per cent of sales may not be adequate for Shin-Etsu to maintain its position, while plant exports and PVC production during 1980 were severely depressed. Although the total production growth of high purity silicon has followed that of semiconductors (Table 22), the increase in Japan's electric power charges in the spring of 1980 has reduced the profitability of domestic production. This has dampened the urge to invest further in expensive high purity silicon production facilities, which may be quickly made redundant through the development of lower cost production technologies.

Table 22

Japan's Output of High Purity Silicon
(tons; percentage increases bracketed)

	1976	1977	1978	1979	1980
A. Multiple crystals: domestic production	277	283	254	331	470
	(29.2)	(2.1)	(-10.1)	(30.0)	(42.0)
B. Multiple crystals: imports	49	50	90	210	280
	(58.1)	(2.0)	(80.0)	(133.3)	(33.3)
C. Total multiple crystals	326	333	344	541	750
	(32.5)	(2.1)	(3.3)	(57.3)	(38.6)
Import dependency (B/C) %	15.0	15.0	26.2	38.8	37.3
Single crystal output[a]	132	123	170	245	337
	(94.1)	(-6.8)	(38.2)	(44.1)	(37.6)
Production of semi-conductors (mn)	625	758	1,120	1,194	2,543
	(106.7	(21.3)	(47.8)	(51.3)	(50.1)

a Single crystals, cut into wafers, are processed from multiple crystals.

Sources: Sanwa Bank Ltd, Economic Letter, July 1981 - compiled from Machinery Statistics, Rare Metals News.

CREATIVE TECHNOLOGY

The impression that Japan lags in true innovation -

Thus the path to more sophisticated knowledge intensification is fraught with the obsolescence hazard presented by rapid technological developments. At the same time the surge in imports of multiple crystals for high purity silicon in 1979 (Table 22) suggests that Japanese companies have been too ready to view a temporary slowdown in sales as a reason to avoid further investment in R & D. In The Economist's July 1981 survey of Japanese industry attention was drawn to a reluctance to seize the initiative in research and to introduce risky new technologies. This kind of criticism has received particularly emphatic support in the July 1981 White Paper from the Science and Technology Agency (Kagaku Gijutsu Hakusho, 1981). An international comparison demonstrates that in terms of science research expenses and of number of scientists, Japan ranks third after the USA and the USSR. Also, in terms of the world total export value of technology intensive products, Japan's share is 12.4 per cent, with West Germany and the USA in the lead. However, in contrast to these apparently commendable achievements, Japan seems to be inadequate in the area of truly innovative, creative technology.

- officially confirmed

The Science and Technology Agency's analysis reaches this conclusion, already well known impressionistically, by distinguishing between various outcomes of scientific research. The division into "epochal breakthrough", "major development" and "improvement on existing technology" must necessarily be somewhat arbitrary at the boundaries, but they are useful categories. The White Paper is then able to demonstrate that "epochal breakthroughs" account for only 7.7 per cent of all technological innovations, while the corresponding figure is 27.4 per cent in the USA and 55.6 per cent in the UK.

As for proposed solutions, the White Paper calls for the development of creative technologies in priority areas including energy, electronics, information, new materials,"life enhancement". The fear is that, although Japan at present is clearly one step ahead in the utilisation of production related technologies, both Western countries and the newly industrialising countries could soon challenge that lead. As one striking example of such a challenge, the Japanese steel industry has expressed its belief that the South Korean steel industry poses a major threat to Japanese mills, both overseas and in the Japanese market.

The role of the government

Since in Japan government spending accounts for 28 per cent of total research expenses, compared to shares of between 40 per cent and 58 per cent in Western countries, the Science and Technology Agency has also stressed a need for expansion of R & D expenditures in the government sector. The comparative shares are more equal, however, if one deducts expenses on research for military purposes. Moreover, before the release of the Science and Technology Agency's White Paper, the Japanese government had already been engaged in various large scale projects designed to promote further research and development. The 1981/82 budget included a new appropriation of ¥3,350 mn for "science and technology promotion adjustment fees". Also in spring 1981, a "fluid research system" was established whereby groups of 20 to 30 researchers chosen from a variety of fields are to be engaged in developing a specific project within a deadline of, for example, five years. Thereafter the research group members will return to their respective organisations, which should cover private enterprises, universities, and national research institutions.

A less pragmatic government policy is the high-flown notion of building in 1990 new towns combining technological industries and related academic institutions along with ordinary residential houses. "Technopolis 90", the designated title of the project, has received ¥20 mn in the 1981/82 budget for preliminary research costs. Even without projects such as "Technopolis 90", it is inevitable that there would be more inter-industry cooperation in research in the 1980s and beyond, as new technologies often require close relations. Thus, for example, in the area of optical fibre communication, cooperative participation in both research and production activities will be necessary for certain industries, such as electronics, textiles. wire, and glass. More generally the wide field of "mechatronics" will see an increasing intensity of cooperation between the machine tool, precision equipment and industrial machinery industries.

1990 appears to be a significant year in governmental promotion of research for it is then that the development of the "fifth generation of computers" is scheduled to be completed. This project involving both the government and private enterprise has now taken on, perhaps inadvertently, a nationalistic character since Miti has pronounced that foreign participation, except in such forums as symposiums, will not be possible. Much interest had been shown by the British and other govern- ments. along with overseas computer manufacturers. in participating; but, in the summer of 1981. the Japanese government justified their exclusion by reference to factors such as the expense of simultaneous translation, and the project's being financed by Japanese taxes.

Private sector steps up its efforts

While the Japanese government's higher profile in promoting truly creative research and development may soon be considerably more significant, private enterprise will continue to play the major role, as the pressure to limit general government expenditure has become so great. Even though enterprises had been unwilling. or unable because of scale factors, to engage in risky research projects, by the late 1970s an EPA survey found that more than 60 per cent of manufacturing companies intended to concentrate on the "development of new products and technologies" as a primary part of management strategy. The most obvious immediate effects have been increased utilisation of IC related machinery and expanded output of "new" electronic appliances, such as VTRs, and of fine chemicals including drugs and photo-sensitised materials.

In the longer term, the R & D objectives of private enterprises are expected to shift towards conservation of resources, particularly energy. Figure 7 (page 42) demonstrated the expected trends in objectives in the 1980s contrasted with the preceding two decades. The Industrial Structure Council expects these priorities, with the impetus of the need for energy conservation, to lead to expenditure on R & D as a share of GNP rising from 1.7 per cent in 1980 to 3 per cent by the end of the decade.

ENERGY CONSERVATION

The imperative need for measures for energy conservation in Japanese industry has been often reiterated. because Japan's dependence on oil from the Middle East in proportion to its total energy supply is the highest among the developed countries. The resulting comparatively high power costs in Japan have severely affected industries such as aluminium smelting. Consequently the six companies in Japan's aluminium industry have further curtailed their smelting output even beyond the stabilisation agreement on capacity in 1979 (Table 23), under the guidance of the Industrial Structure Council.

Table 23

Curtailments in Aluminium Smelting Capacity
('000 tons/year)

Company	Stabilisation planned capacity (1979)	Voluntarily limited output (1981)
Nippon Light Metal	198	159
Showa Light Metal	162	87
Sumitomo Aluminium	296	190
Mitsubishi Light Metal	237	66
Mitsui Aluminium	125	107
Sumikei Aluminium	99	99
Total	1,117	708

Source: Asahi Shimbun, August 5, 1981.

The apparent success of Japanese industry in conserving energy during the 1970s has often been admired, but the prospects are not so promising. Part of the energy savings arose because of the slump in the high energy consuming industries in the late 1970s. More significantly, the actual energy conservation measures taken have been largely where the required changes were fairly easy to make at a low cost and with an immediate effect – for example, by preventing steam leakage, controlling combustion, and using brick insulation to prevent heat loss. Consequently the possibilities for easy conservation measures have been more or less exhausted. If, as suggested by the evidence in Figure 7, considerably more is invested in R & D on energy conservation, industries with high energy consumption may possibly continue to play a strategic role. Otherwise, there would be interesting implications for trade friction, if Japan were to decide to invoke Gatt safeguards, as discussed later (page 106).

Meanwhile the Industrial Structure Council lays its hopes not only on nuclear fusion as a main energy source in the 21st century, but also solar power in households. The purpose would be to divert an even higher proportion of other energy sources than the present 56 per cent to industrial consumption.

EMPLOYMENT STRUCTURE

Services took up the slack in the 1970s –

It has been predicted that during the 1980s Japan's economy will continue to grow – with the forecast growth rates varying somewhat (page 110) – but at a rate lower than in the 1960s, and probably even lower than in those years in the 1970s which were not too adversely affected by the oil crises. Apart from the coming era of slower growth weakening employment absorption capacity in general, higher levels of automation will aggravate this trend. At one time it might have been hoped that the tertiary sector could absorb not only those continuing to leave agricultural pursuits, but also those made redundant by automation in manufacturing. Indeed there has been a recent rapid increase in employment in the service industries, particularly in those companies engaging in computer software and time sharing services, to the extent that in 1980 54.6 per cent of persons employed were in the

tertiary sector. Hence between 1970 and 1980 the increase in employment opportunities in service industries more than compensated for the movement of those
from the primary sector (Table 24).

Table 24

National Income and Employment by Industry
(percentage shares)

	Share of domestic factor income		Share of persons employed	
	1970	1980	1970	1980
Primary industries[a]	6.1	4.4	17.4	10.5
Secondary industries[b]	41.8	37.5	35.2	34.9
Tertiary industries[c]	52.1	58.1	47.4	54.6
Total	100.0	100.0	100.0	100.0

a Agriculture, forestry and fishing. b Mining, construction,
manufacturing. c Services, wholesale and retail trade,
others.

Source: Economic Planning Agency (Keizai Kigaku-chō).

– but will be unable to in the 1980s

One cannot, however, any longer expect employment in the service industries to
grow at the same rate as previously, because in these areas also automation is
becoming a significant factor. For example, in the retail sector the number of
outlets using computerised 'point of sale' systems is expected to jump sharply
in 1982 to a level where it will be worthwhile for manufacturers to cooperate fully
in the system. Similarly, in office work Japanese language word processors have
now been developed, despite the formidable task of coping with both syllabaries
and nearly 2,000 kanji. The willingness to purchase a Japanese language word
processor at over ¥2 mn demonstrates a commitment to improving office productivity that in turn implies rationalisation with attendant redundancies.

Smaller companies may absorb less labour than before

It may be true on the other hand that higher growth of labour productivity permits
a more flexible employment structure whereby growing sectors can absorb surplus
production factors. It would seem, however, that this relationship could only hold
up to a certain productivity growth level, after which the very height of the labour
productivity growth would cause redundancies despite growing sales. In the case
of Japan's economy, this result has been somewhat concealed until now because
small and medium sized enterprises have absorbed excess labour. Table 8
(page 46) reveals, however, that the disparity between large and small firms in
average value added per employee has tended to widen since 1965. For example in
1974 the value added per employee in enterprises with 20 to 29 employees was 51.0
per cent of that in enterprises with over 1,000 employees, while in 1978 the relevant ratio was 46.1 per cent. Over the same period the total number employed by
the largest enterprises fell from over 1.8 mn to 1.5 mn, after a peak of over 2 mn
employees in 1970. Meanwhile the number employed by enterprises with 20 to 29
employees rose by 25.5 per cent.

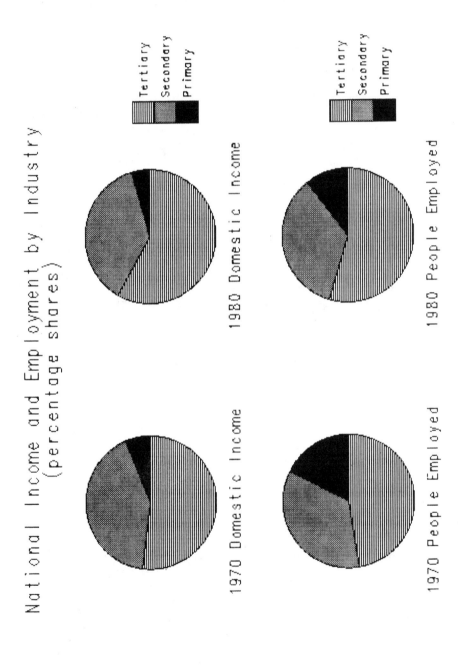

National Income and Employment by Industry (percentage shares)

1970 Domestic Income

1980 Domestic Income

1970 People Employed

1980 People Employed

Tertiary
Secondary
Primary

Tertiary
Secondary
Primary

Figure 9

107

The age structure is changing

The questionable ability of smaller companies to go on absorbing labour is a factor in total employment which will be increasingly aggravated by the ageing of the population accompanied by a more insistent desire to work beyond 55 years of age. As examined earlier (Chapter I, page 20), industry is meeting these demands by revising the system of seniority payments. Already in the early 1980s more than 10 per cent of firms are cutting wages when employees continue to work beyond the former mandatory retirement age, while 80 per cent of firms peg salaries at that age, according to Ministry of Labour data. The extent of these and other changes in the wage structure has led the central Minimum Wage Council to recommend in the summer of 1981 that the present minimum wage system be abolished.

These are likely to be mere stop-gap measures until more radical changes in the employment system are implemented. The nature of such changes is still difficult to predict. Some Japanese commentators consider that companies will abandon even the framework, light as it is, of permanent employment for their core labour force and instead seek more specialised and fluid manpower. The increasing use of female labour, as a temporary, cheap expedient, would aid this kind of transition.

Less radical changes could be instituted by narrowing the differentials between large and small enterprises, particularly in terms of pension benefits. It is striking that, despite general mandatory retirement ages of 55 years until recently, the labour participation ratio of those aged 65 years and older is 26.8 per cent in Japan, compared to ratios of less than 10 per cent in several Western countries. Evidently those who are choosing to retire early under systems giving a lump sum payment before retirement age are continuing to work in smaller enterprises, because their means for livelihood are inadequate. Another measure required would be mid career training programmes to enable older workers to maintain appropriate skills for more sophisticated technologies.

Problems of alienation

Improved pension benefits and mid career training schemes will not be able to solve the likely imminent problem of worker alienation and lower morale as processes become more highly automated. Quality control circles at present serve the function of bringing more personal involvement into the workplace, but the novelty of circle activities could soon wear off. Until now management in the Japanese style (Nihon-teki kei-ei) has reputedly brought about harmonious labour relations; but the Japanese themselves are beginning to question whether their management style actually works in all sectors, or is severely restricted to the elite, permanent labour force (Economisuto, 28.7.81). More significantly there is now some doubt as to whether the style is appropriate for the long term.

Unions were remarkably cooperative during the late 1970s, to an extent greater than in 1973/74. The Ministry of Labour's 1981 White Paper concluded that wage restraint had been responsible for minimising the economic disruption caused by the 1978/79 oil price rises. However, now that it is clear that in 1980 workers' real earnings fell by 0.9 per cent, it must be queried whether unions can continue to accept the fact that workers have borne the brunt of the adjustment to higher energy prices.

Unions push for shorter hours

In the face of widening automation, unions have been aware of the threat of unemployment higher than the 2.29 per cent officially registered in June, 1981 (seasonally adjusted). Thus demands have tended to be concentrated on shortening working hours. For this demand, trade friction is an unexpected ally in so far as employers are sensitive to the charge that a greater labour input leads to an unfair advantage in price competitiveness. That overseas complaint, however, is rapidly losing validity as most large manufacturing firms have instituted a 40 hour week. Indeed the use of robots and computerised production lines makes the issue of labour input appears rather irrelevant.

It may be that industrial robots performing certain tasks will indirectly lead to more harmonious industrial relations to the extent that damages suits filed by workers whose health has been adversely affected by the nature of the job are avoided. The recent strength of the anti-pollution movement in Japan has stimulated various suits such as the one begun in July, 1981, by subcontract workers at Mitsubishi Heavy Industries. The complainants claim that they are suffering from Raynaud's disease as a result of using vibrating tools inadequately equipped with safety devices.

Harmonious labour relations will be harder to achieve

It would seem, from this review of the various factors impinging on management-labour relations, that the prospects for continued harmony are becoming dimmer. Between 1960 and 1973, per caput income trebled, which must have been one of the major contributing factors to harmonious relations. Moreover, during the same period the real prices of consumer durables fell, on account of mass production, so that the rise in living standards was dramatic. Against this background enterprise unions could flourish to the apparent benefit of both sides.

At present the instances of labour determinedly challenging management are still isolated. The intense labour dispute over rationalisation at Sasebo Heavy Industries is usually considered to be an exceptional case, but is nonetheless significant. More daunting are the examples of workers challenging the closed shop enterprise union such as that at Nissan - few though the challengers are. Should both management and labour be unable to accommodate the structural changes brought on by knowledge intensification of industries, such examples may become more frequent. It would be ironic if Japanese style management were to break down just when numerous foreign missions, assisted by the Japan Productivity Centre, are coming to Japan to study management-labour relations.

ADJUSTMENTS IN LIFESTYLES

New products, new markets, new jobs

Yet, despite all the evidence pointing in the direction of potential strains in labour-management relations, it would not be invalid to arrive at an opposite conclusion on the strength of the past adaptability of Japanese industry. This view would be based on the strength in export and domestic markets of Japan's consumer electronic appliances and industrial machinery. Consequently it would be anticipated that the industries dealing in these goods could absorb more labour as sales grow rapidly, even though there would be stagnation in the basic materials industries. In the domestic market, even though the diffusion rates of standard consumer appliances, such as washing machines and refrigerators, are over 99 per cent for Japanese households, there is still a wide market for new types of durables and services - often associated with increased leisure time. For example, in March 1981, the diffusion rate for VTRs was 5.1 per cent, for movie cameras/projector sets 9.0 per cent, and for pianos 16.7 per cent, according to data from the prime minister's office. A Sanwa Bank analysis of goods whose markets are expanding suggests that product strategies will be based on the following three factors: new technologies (such as LSIs in electronic organs); greater market segmentation (where demand can be stimulated by appealing to fashionability); and higher quality lifestyles (as expressed in a demand for system kitchens, auto caravans etc).

A booming future for video sales worldwide -

In the export market, the prospects for the knowledge intensive industries are even more promising. While Japan produces over 90 per cent of the VTRs in the world, the rival manufacturers - the Betamax group led by Sony and the VHS group under Matsushita and Victor - can all anticipate annual output increases of about 20 per cent in the first half of the 1980s. Such expectations are not unrealistic because of the overwhelming competitive strength of Japanese VTR manufacturers in world markets. Matsushita attributed its record sales and profits during the first half of 1981 to sales of VTRs in overseas markets. Consequently, further investment is being undertaken to raise Matsushita's monthly VTR producing capacity to 250,000 sets by the close of 1981. The success of both groups of VTR makers would have presented a bewildering sight to Miti policy makers in the 1950s and 1960s, when they were assiduously attempting to foster single large powerful companies in specific areas, so as to compete with the US giants.

- and computerisation in Japan

Another major facet of imminent structural change lies in computerisation through-out manufacturing industry and the services sector. In the five years subsequent to 1981, Miti's Council for the Promotion of Information Processing forecasts computers in use in terms of installation costs should be increased by an annual average of 15.2 per cent. This would represent a drastic rise in computer utilisation on top of the annual increase of 12.6 per cent between 1976/77 and 1980/81. In particular, the number of microcomputers in use is expected to increase annually by 25.3 per cent.

The extent and impact of the overall structural change emanating from these developments is open to various predictions in terms of the implications for technological developments, energy conservation and employment. Thus the preceding is but one assemblage of views as seen in Japan. The likely consequences in terms of company investment programmes and economic growth will follow, prior to a discussion of the implications for overseas economies.

CORPORATE PERFORMANCE

Despite the fact that many of the large corporations suffered profit declines during 1980/81, commentators view the overall picture as having been commendable, since that year saw the peak deflationary impact of the second oil crisis. Thus, although Nissan experienced a 24.4 per cent fall in operating profits over the previous fiscal year, its sales growth of 10.5 per cent enabled this profit decline to be viewed with equanimity. Surveys of profit performance in general give rather conflicting impressions, depending on whether or not particular firms were included in the survey. The Wako Economic Research Institute's survey of performance from October, 1980, to March, 1981, suggests that overall sales grew by 4.2 per cent for the 386 firms listed in the first section of the Tokyo Stock Exchange, while current profits fell by 10.7 per cent. Another wider survey, comprising 743 companies with the exclusion of banks, insurance companies and brokerage houses, indicates that during the same half year sales grew by 5.3 per cent, but profits dipped only 0.9 per cent from the preceding six months. The disparities in the surveys can lead one to the presumption that on the whole the larger firms, listed in the first section, did not perform so well as the average company.

It is certainly clear that, as would have been expected, the basic materials industries' performance did not match up to that of the assembling industries. In the paper and pulp industry current profits fell steeply by 82 per cent, while in chemicals, textiles and steel, the declines registered 57 per cent, 42 per cent and 29 per cent respectively. Since part of the reason for the plunging profits lay in import competition, the government is now faced with the choice whether or not to permit the industries so affected - especially aluminium, chemicals and textiles - to go into decline, according to its avowed principles of free trade and adapting the industrial structure according to dynamic international comparative advantage. The suspicion is growing in Japan that the government will turn protectionist on the plea that such industries are strategic, just as in the case of agriculture.

Even among manufacturers not in the basic materials industries, performance was patchy. Nissan's results, quoted earlier, are representative of the automobile manufacturers, whose poor profit performance tends to be attributed to voluntary and other restraints on export growth. The more likely reason, however, is the general stagnation in domestic consumer demand. Again as would have been expected, the best performance in 1980/81 was turned in by manufacturers of industrial robots, computers, ICs and consumer electronics.

FUTURE CORPORATE STRATEGY

In the light of the 1980/81 results, predictions are now being made about future corporate performance, based on plant and equipment investment plans. Since manufacturing industries increased their capital investment by an amazing 28.8 per cent in 1980/81, their plans for an average 10.1 per cent increase in 1981/82, according to survey figures from the Bank of Japan, may be viewed as partly complementary to the already substantial investments. Despite their relatively poor performance in the last fiscal year, both the steel industry and non-ferrous

111

metal industry have plans to raise capital investments, by respectively 29.1 per cent and 36.7 per cent, in 1981/82, according to the Long Term Credit Bank of Japan's survey figures.

Such investment plans reflect a growing trepidation in the basic materials industries that the upward trend in the average age of their capital stock during the 1970s has led to their production facilities becoming outdated. Between 1965 and 1972 the average age of capital stock in the materials industry declined from about nine years to seven but since then the average age has increased almost to nine years again. Meanwhile in the USA, although there have similarly been declines in earnings of private enterprises, the average age of capital stock in all US manufacturing industries has registered an almost continuous decline from about eleven years in 1965 to just over nine years (Miti estimates).

Consequently replacement investment is becoming an important motive in plant and equipment investment plans. Since the value in real terms of the capital stock eligible for replacement in the first half of the 1980s will on average be double that of the capital stock eligible for replacement in 1975-79 (Table 25), it has been estimated that replacement investment will increase annually by 11.0 per cent at least.

Table 25

Trends in Replacement Investment (¥ bn at 1970 prices)		1966-69	1970-74	1975-79	1980-85
A.	Capital stock ten or more years old	17,212	29,239	51,017	107,850
	Annual rate of growth (%)		7.1	11.8	14.6
B.	Replacement investment	11,076	21,548	36,390	77,710
	Annual rate of growth (%)	20.8	10.3	11.1	11.0
B/A.	Rate of replacement investment	64.4	73.7	71.3	72.1
	Ratio of A to total capital stock at period end (%)	8.5	6.0	8.2	11.6

Source: Sanwa Bank, Economic Letter, December 1980.

For example, as mentioned earlier, the Japanese steel industry is planning major equipment investments during the year beginning in April 1981. The capital spending plans announced by the five major steel producers amount to a 42 per cent increase over the previous year's investments. In particular, the investment plans are designed to reduce production costs and energy consumption and to expand the output of products with high added value. However manufacturers in the ceramic, paper and pulp, and textile industries are quite reluctant to make investment plans, while their business conditions are deteriorating and inventory adjustment is still continuing.

Looking to 1982 with confidence

Nonetheless among other manufacturers there is confidence, according to surveys conducted by the Nikko Research Centre and the Yamaichi Research Institute, that, by March 1982, profit performance will have turned upwards once more, in response to growing sales of "new" products. Consequently there is a high probability that companies' investment plans will be revised upwards, before the end of fiscal 1981, beyond the various surveys' initial predictions of average increases ranging between 5 per cent and 10.1 per cent. In the long term it is generally expected that the revolution in production technologies will provide wide opportunities for continued equipment investment such as in NC machine tools. A mid 1981 EPA survey of industry concluded that companies are assuming an "offensive" with confidence. Their long range business strategies will give priority to improving technology in 57.6 per cent of the 1,560 companies surveyed, while 39.4 per cent will place major emphasis on strengthening their financial positions. The same survey found that 21.1 per cent of the companies surveyed were planning to expand into new business fields, especially in electronics and in the development of new materials.

A survey of companies' business strategies by the Keizai Doyukai (Japan Committee for Economic Development) similarly found that in the 1980s technological advance will be utilised in order to pursue an offensive strategy aimed at expansion. This kind of strategy follows upon the defensive management policies adopted in response to the oil crises, of cutting back and streamlining operations. Evidently Japanese management now feels able to build upon the reorganisation of the late 1970s, which resulted often in a greater centralisation of power as well as more efficient operations. Thus, as is shown in Table 26, whereas in the 1970s reorganisation was conducted with the aim of improving efficiency, companies in the early 1980s are tending to bring more emphasis on to organisation appropriate for aggressive and adaptive business strategies.

Table 26

Trends in Motives for Companies' Reorganisation[a]
(per cent of responses)

	A: 1973-80	B: 1981-85	B/A
Improving morale	6.9	5.5	0.80
Clarifying objectives & responsibilities	37.3	26.2	0.70
Eliminating sectionalism	8.8	6.0	0.68
Strengthening management control	13.2	11.3	0.86
Encouraging inter-departmental information exchange	7.6	8.6	1.13
Distributing human & financial resources more efficiently	7.3	15.9	2.18

(continued)

113

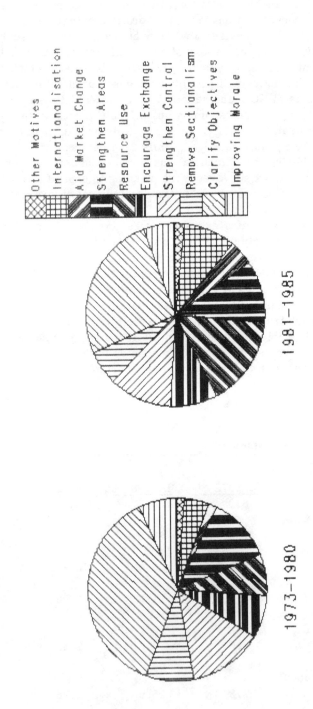

Trends in Motives
for Companies' Reorganization
(per cent of responses)

Other Motives
Internationalisation
Aid Market Change
Strengthen Areas
Resource Use
Encourage Exchange
Strengthen Control
Remove Sectionalism
Clarify Objectives
Improving Morale

1981–1985

1973–1980

Figure 10

114

<u>Table 26</u> (continued)

<u>Trends in Motives for Companies' Reorganisation</u>[a]
(per cent of responses)

	A: 1973-80	B: 1981-85	B/A
Strengthening specific areas of business	11.6	10.9	0.94
Aiding business expansion & withdrawal in certain markets	1.4	4.5	3.21
Seeking internationalisation	4.6	9.3	2.04
Other motives	1.3	1.8	1.38
Total	100.0	100.0	

a Respondents to the survey of 1,400 companies could select as many motives as appropriate.

Source: 1980 <u>Nendai no Kigyō Keiei</u> (Corporate Management in the 1980s), Keizai Dōyūkai, 1980.

THE ROLE OF GOVERNMENT AND OF THE WIDER ECONOMY

Naturally the corporate performance of Japanese industries depends upon the growth of the economy and government policies. On account of trade friction, companies will have to judge their prospects partly according to the strength of domestic demand. The government's role has at times been significant in encouraging strategic sectors, but its influence has diminished.

The influential Keizai Dōyūkai proposed in the spring of 1981 that the government should only handle matters that are beyond corporate control, particularly in respect of the increasing internationalisation of the Japanese economy. Thus industry is seeking government promotion of risk insurance for overseas business ventures and provision of financial assistance for creative technological development, but it rejects the notion of any need now for government protection. Miti's Industrial Structure Council also included among its recommended policies for the 1980s[1] a call for the government to take an active role in high risk technological development areas. The council makes an additional recommendation that the government should consolidate the stock markets and other capital markets so as to enhance corporate capital procurement. Indeed there is some anxiety that the funds shortage in the corporate sector will rise to between 3 and 4 per cent of nominal aggregate demand for outside financing by 1985.

The extent of a funds shortage is naturally dependent upon the government's monetary policy and the state of the economy. It is not the intention in this report to attempt to survey properly the prospects in this area, but a few words on the subject may be useful.

---

1 <u>1980-nendai no Tsūshō Sangyō Seisaku</u> (Industrial policy for the 1980s), Industrial Structure Council, 1980.

There are expectations that the Bank of Japan will continue to ease its control on commercial bank lending to business corporations during 1981/82, as demand for funds heightens. Another policy, intended to discourage the flight of capital from Japan as disparities between Japanese and overseas interest rates widen, has been instituted. This is comparable to the Lombard system whereby the central bank, under a new formula, can lend to banks at an interest rate determined separately from the official discount rate. Thus short term market interest rates are likely to rise whenever the formula is enforced. Such measures are perhaps an inevitable adjunct to the new Foreign Exchange and Foreign Trade Control Law. In the bond market, the city banks are engaged in a struggle with the Ministry of Finance to improve the yields on government bond issues, which may ultimately lead to a more smoothly and efficiently operating securities market. This in turn could loosen some of the informal controls which lead banks have been able to exercise over group member companies.

Moderate optimism in macroeconomic forecasts

In the area of the wider economy, forecasts for real growth in 1981/82 and 1982/83 are generally optimistic. (Those of them using 1975 prices rather than 1970 prices may not appear so, since the change has the effect of reducing percentage growth rates.) Under 1970 prices the government's 1981/82 forecast is for 5.3 per cent real growth, of which domestic demand should account for four percentage points and the external surplus for 1.3. In other words the forecast relies mainly on increased domestic demand, in contrast to the export-led performance during 1980/81. This hope may be justified in so far as the EPA's diffusion index of economic indicators has shown an upward trend since February 1981 and inventory adjustments were completed in the April-June quarter of 1981 - apart from in some sectors including aluminium smelting and PVC production.

However private economic institutes have generally - except for the Japan Economic Research Centre and the Research Institute of National Economy - tended to predict lower growth rates than the government. The average forecast of the 14 leading private organisations turns out to be 4.4 per cent at 1970 prices. It may be that private institutes are more aware than the government of the continued weakness of most smaller enterprises in terms of low profitability and small investment expenditures.

The Mitsubishi Research Institute has also drawn attention to a likely further diminution in the rate of growth in 1982/83. In the domestic market, although demand will be aided by the easing of inflationary pressures, the limited growth in personal incomes and high levels of market saturation for many consumer goods could constrain the recovery of personal consumption expenditure. Meanwhile, the expected revival of the yen in 1982 will restrain export growth.

Also, in the long term, the prospects for domestic demand are likely to be depressed by the expected reduction in the public works budget on account of the insistent pressures for constraining public expenditure. Indeed it is highly probable that the seven year socio-economic plan (1979/80-1985/86) will have to be reviewed again to reflect the decline in public works expenditure. Thus Japanese industry's attitude to the reform of government finances has taken on an ambivalent stance after an early enthusiasm for tax cuts. The OECD, in its 1981 annual review of the Japanese economy, has also noted that a reduction in the volume of public works could jeopardise the anticipated contribution of domestic demand as the spearhead of growth.

116

A new form of dualism in the economy

Nonetheless Japanese companies generally seem to be viewing the future with more confidence than the macroeconomic forecasters. As an indicator of company expectations, the scale of recruitment plans for 1982 graduates has returned to the kind of level existing before the 1973 oil crisis. The Japan Recruit Centre's projection, for the spring of 1982, is that companies will hire at least 12.4 per cent more new employees than they did in 1981. It may be that, while certain industrial sectors, such as those in electronics, can enjoy nearly unlimited good prospects, others are likely to face increasing difficulties as industrial adjustment remorselessly proceeds. The result could be a return to a dual economy, though with different distinctions, as one of the main characteristics of Japanese industry.

OVERSEAS TRADE AND INVESTMENT

If, as the preceding section has discussed, domestic demand is not up to the task expected of it in leading Japan's economic growth, overseas markets will continue to be as significant as in 1980/81 in permitting Japanese industry to expand and advance. Unless overseas companies are able to meet the challenge presented in competing with Japanese industry, the Mitsubishi Research Institute's forecast of a wide disparity in export and import growth rates is likely to be an underestimate. Mitsubishi predicts that imports will grow at rates of only 8.7 per cent and 10.1 per cent respectively in 1981/82 and 1982/83. Its predictions for export growth rates are 15.8 per cent and 13.1 per cent.

The consequent growing surplus on the current account would be aggravated even further, if the yen were to continue to fall against the US dollar as has been occurring in mid 1981. However Japanese commentators expect the US-Japan interest rate differential to narrow, so that the yen should appreciate to reach a level of 190 to 200 yen to the dollar by mid 1982. It is generally acknowledged that at lower rates the yen is undervalued, and so prevents a decline in Japan's export competitiveness. Apart from high US interest rates, a major cause of the under valuation is the large demand for dollars to pay for oil imports.

THE FUTURE OF TRADE FRICTION

As energy conservation measures have reduced the volume of crude oil imports, so has Japan's trade surplus during the first half of 1981 reached a level of $782 mn on a customs clearance basis. Moreover the 13 major general trading companies reported in July 1981 that import contracts have kept declining, apart from those for textiles and machinery. Meanwhile for Japanese exports, the "voluntary" restraints on automobile exports to the USA have been offset by higher exports of colour television sets, VTRs and watches. The Japanese auto manufacturers themselves have not generally suffered adverse effects on account of the restraints, as exports to South America, Africa and Oceania increased substantially during the first half of 1981. For example, auto exports to South America more than doubled over the corresponding period of 1980.

Consequently the Japanese government is becoming increasingly concerned that
the growing trade surplus will exacerbate trade friction and reinforce the charge,
by now largely a myth, that the Japanese market is closed. In July, 1981, measures
to encourage imports of manufactured goods, such as despatching buying missions
to Japan's key trading partners, were announced. Also Keidanren intends to send
a trade mission to Western Europe in the autumn of 1981. Yet it is doubtful whether
such measures will have any real impact on the disparities in manufactured imports
shares. Comparative figures show that the share of manufactured goods in Japan's
total imports was a meagre 22.8 per cent in 1980, whereas the relevant shares
were 56.2 per cent for the USA and 47.3 per cent for the EEC.

Japan urged to champion free trade

These figures seem particularly anomalous, because import tariffs in Japan tend
to be concentrated on agricultural goods. In other areas Japanese officials can
demonstrate that the average level of tariffs shows Japan to be a free trader,
while they also acknowledge that Japan has probably benefited most from the free
trade system. Thus the Gatt director general, Mr Arthur Dunkel, can feel justified in his mid 1981 call to Japan to take the lead and make an active commitment
to reinforce the multilateral trading system. Possibly for Japan to take an offensive in this way would distract attention from complaints and associated trade
friction.

Misconceptions about scrutiny of car imports

Such complaints have tended recently to focus on non-tariff barriers, particularly
in respect of intensive checking, such as that of car imports. News reports,
amounting almost to propaganda, in July, 1981, suggested a breakthrough in that
Golf cars imported from Volkswagen would no longer be subject to individual
scrutiny, but could be admitted under a single thorough check. However this
option has always been open to both importers and domestic manufacturers. The
choice depends on the scale of imports or output, for the individual scrutiny of each
car works out to be less costly below a certain number of cars. The main reason
is that the option of a single examination requires that thereafter the manufacturer
or importer has the inspection facilities required for conducting their own checks.
The popularity of Volkswagen's Golf car in Japan has now made it worthwhile for
Yanase, the major car importer, to set up the special inspection facilities in
Yokohama.

Thus the issue of surmounting non-tariff barriers cannot be simply solved. When
foreign goods have reached an adequate level of competitiveness with domestically
produced goods, some of the barriers will fade away of their own accord.

Will basic materials industries be allowed to decline?

The Japanese also are placing some faith in the decline of certain basic materials
industries. It has been argued by defenders of Japanese trade that industrial
adjustment is being pursued under the Temporary Measure Law for Stabilisation
of Specified Recessionary Industries, partly with a view to enabling an international horizontal division of labour in industrial goods to develop. However it is
possible that before that stage is reached Gatt safeguards will be invoked as non-
ferrous metals, food products and chemicals are considered to be strategic industries.
An alternative may be informal trading rules, amounting to organised trade, as in
the steel industry.

On the export side officials trust that trade friction will become less irritating as Japanese industry begins to concentrate its exports on products with high added value and greater non-price related competitiveness. It is also hoped that higher proportions of plant and machinery exports will ease friction, which tends to emphasise consumer products. In fiscal 1980, excluding cars, motor cycles, TVs, radios, tape recorders and ships, they formed a third of Japan's exports, leaving room for further expansion as Japanese industry advanced in developing new processes and production systems.

Geographical diversification would help

There is also optimism, perhaps unfounded, that the markets for manufactured goods will diversify. As noted earlier, South America and Africa are taking increasing shares of Japan's automobile exports. However the Middle East's share of Japan's total export value actually fell from 11.15 per cent to 10.67 per cent between 1977/78 and 1980/81. Spectacularly large orders for plant exports won by Japanese firms in the Middle East, such as for the prefabricated modular plants to be constructed in Saudi Arabia, may ultimately increase exports to the Middle East by more substantial amounts.

PLANT EXPORTS

Such large projects are tending to be conducted by consortia, often with Japanese government support, in order to lessen the risks involved. Nonetheless plant exporters have often been losing out to US and European enterprises in international bids since 1977, because they do not offer credits on such concessionary terms. Therefore the Japanese government is expected to extend more assistance to economic cooperation projects by utilising yen credits as well as furthering "mixed credits", which combine governmental and commercial loans. The government's interest in promoting more plant exports is partly on account of the fact that trade friction is not thereby aggravated, because the plants create employment opportunities in the importing countries.

The 1980s are heralding two further developments in plant exports. One is the area of project financing, whereby financial organisations participate throughout the corporate plan from the feasibility study stage. The other is the formation of international consortia to make bids for plant construction and financing. An example of both these developments is the consortium formed by Sumitomo Bank with American and European banks to conduct feasibility studies for the Sarawak Shell large scale natural gas drilling project in Malaysia. Such developments are expected to reverse the decline in plant exports experienced in 1980.

DIRECT INVESTMENT OVERSEAS

One expedient being adopted to deflect trade friction is to set up manufacturing plants overseas. Yuasa's projected battery factory in Wales is to some extent the result of a fear of import controls being imposed. Such factors are going to become increasingly important (as shown in Table 27) to a Japanese company's overseas strategy. Whereas in the 1970s 27.6 per cent of companies were not at all influenced by overseas requests for direct investment, in the first part of the 1980s, 17.5 per cent would not entertain any such requests. Similarly, during the first period just over 21 per cent gave consideration to import barriers in investment decisions, but in the 1980s the corresponding figure would be over 31 per cent.

Another interesting aspect of the Keizai Doyukai's survey results in Table 27 is the change in emphasis which will be laid on transnationalising for the purpose of improving efficiency in production and marketing. Japanese manufacturing companies have previously tended to engage in foreign direct investment with reluctance. Their motives have usually been defensive or designed to gain specific and sure advantage in terms of raw material and labour supplies. Now that almost 35 per cent of Japanese companies view overseas investment as making a positive all round contribution to their operations, the emergence of truly multinational Japanese companies may be expected before the end of the twentieth centruy.

Such multinational companies may develop as amalgamations of Japanese and Western companies. In this context, the agreement reached in August, 1981, between Hitachi and General Electric, whereby the former will license, for an undisclosed sum, all its industrial robot technology under a seven year contract, may become clearer in time. Under the contract GE will ultimately have the right to market the microelectronically controlled welding and painting robots through-out the world under the GE brand name. At first it seems difficult to explain these apparently generous terms in Hitachi's licensing its technology. However the agreement is probably part of Hitachi's strategy in competing with the numerous Japanese manufacturers of industrial robots, which amount to about 150 altogether including the small makers. Hitachi's robot technology, however, is rather unique and,so as to compete effectively in the 1990s, the company needs strong partners. Thus the full value of this licensing agreement cannot be properly judged until ten years have expired.

Problems and prospects

In considering the future of Japanese industry, it has not been possible to give adequate attention to likely changes in social factors. It is easy enough to consider the impact of the ageing of the population, which will tend to make industrial adjustment more costly in terms of shunting around and retraining the labour force. Also one can correctly judge that the heightened significance of leisure activities will ultimately result in reduced working hours, even though the full scale transition to a five day working week keeps meeting obstacles. What may be both most significant and most difficult to assess is the future of "Japanese style management" which has produced such enviable industrial relations and work motivation. Yet one does not have to view attitudes to work as emanating from national personality traits. In the Japanese context, the legal support and general respect given to labour unions, coupled with comparatively narrow income differentials between white and blue collar workers, are in themselves sufficient to provide an explanation.

On the other hand, the differentials implicit in a dual industrial economy may be the source of discontent. The slight tendency for a widening in the productivity gap with smaller enterprises, as large companies proceed to install more highly automated processes. could be alarming. However there are indications that parent companies are assisting subcontractors to install industrial robots, in order perhaps to ensure the continuance of the kanban hoshiki system ("just in time" delivery of components).

Table 27

International Business Strategies in Japanese Companies (per cent[a])

Reason for overseas investment[b]	1973–1980					1981–1985				
	1	2	3	4	5	1	2	3	4	5
To widen market	24.5	43.4	4.0	14.8	13.3	34.4	42.5	6.4	8.8	7.8
When requested overseas	4.9	28.8	15.6	23.1	27.6	6.7	38.2	20.0	17.6	17.5
Because of import barriers	3.7	17.9	10.9	22.7	44.8	6.3	24.9	15.4	20.2	33.2
To avoid foreign exchange risks	2.3	10.8	14.0	30.3	42.6	3.0	21.4	20.3	24.0	31.4
To secure cheap labour	2.8	9.6	7.0	23.2	57.4	0.9	12.6	11.0	27.4	48.1
To seek stable natural resource sources	7.4	13.0	9.3	24.5	45.7	11.6	18.3	12.9	22.3	34.9
Transnationalising for more efficient operations	4.9	16.0	13.3	27.2	38.6	10.0	24.5	16.9	22.4	26.2

a Rows add up to 100 per cent over 1 to 5. Respondents to the survey of 1,400 companies had to choose from between 1 to 5 for each row and in each period. b 1. highly important; 2. given some consideration; 3. neither significant nor insignificant; 4. scarcely even considered; 5. of no importance at all.

Source: Sanwa Bank, Economic Letter, December 1980.

122

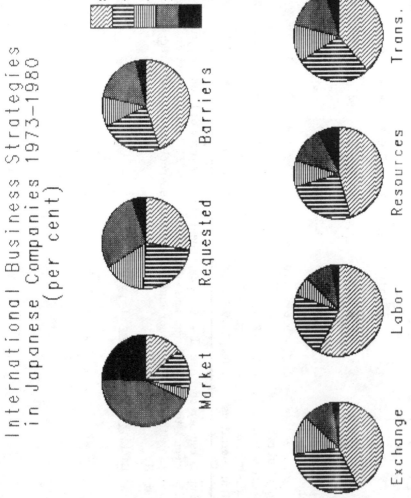

Figure 11a

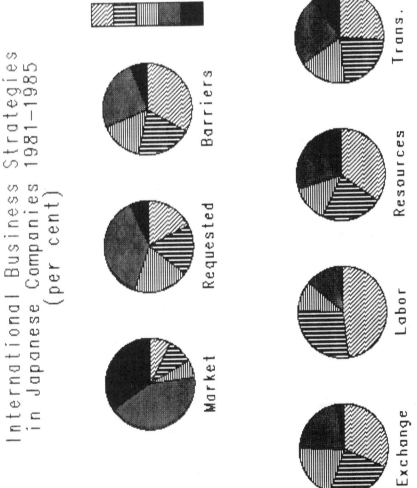

International Business Strategies in Japanese Companies 1981–1985 (per cent)

Market

Requested

Barriers

Exchange

Labor

Resources

Trans.

Figure 11b

123

The emergence of a dualism among large companies, in which some sectors of the basic materials industries are going into a decline, may severely affect industrial relations, as at the Sasebo yard, unless a more fluid labour force, with mid career retraining and recruitment, is established.

The problems in the basic materials industries may be resolved through international alignments, such as are beginning to emerge in the steel industry. In general, the prospects for international cooperation between Japanese and Western firms, both of which can then compete more effectively within their domestic markets as well, are expanding. It would be a pity, however, if the learning of the necessary language skills and the adaptability were to come predominantly from the Japanese side.

Part Two:
Japan s Role in the 1980's

INTRODUCTION

The purpose of this report

This report studies Japan's international position and prospects in the 1980s from a
business viewpoint. It involves an assessment of social and political as well as
economic, conditions and trends. It is no longer possible to make a purely economic
analysis: the economic, social and political scenes must be taken together. And
a broad survey is more useful than model making, which must limit itself to the
economically quantifiable and be based on a few assumptions and variables.

This report outlines the internal situation in Japan, and the motivations and probable
modes of action of the Japanese in the decade which is just beginning, especially
from the viewpoint of their relations with the rest of the world. It sets out to
answer questions such as: "What is Japan really like? What are the aims of the
Japanese? Where does Japan stand today? What are its trends and intentions for
the future? What further impact will Japan have on the world in the 1980s and
what influence will other countries have on Japan?"

Japan as a world economic power

In manufacturing, technology, trade, managerial and organisational capacity,
Japan already ranks as a great power. It is a full member of the group of developed
industrial countries, the OECD. In that respect Japan holds a dominant position
in the Far East and South East Asia, and is one of the front runners in the whole
world. Futurologists like Herman Kahn (inThe Emerging Japanese Superstate,
1971) are optimistic that Japan will be the foremost nation, in econometric terms
such as income or affluence, by the end of this century. That may depend on the
favourite caveat of economists, "other things remaining equal". The rest of the
world will not be static; there are grave difficulties in the Japanese system, and
also unevennesses in its overall excellent achievements.

The areas listed where Japan has established major power status rank in importance
broadly in the order given. Japan has been most successful in manufacturing,
where the Japanese devotion to hard work and tremendous loyalty have proved most
effective. But the Japanese attitude to work is beginning to change as people become
more interested in leisure time activities and this trend will continue during the
1980s. None the less the assiduousness of the people will continue to give them the
competitive edge on other developed and other undeveloped countries. However,
countries between these two extremes which are on the brink of advanced industrialisation and economic development (mainly in Asia) now rival Japan in terms of
a diligent workforce and productive determination. The same applies, though less
strongly, to the element of cohesiveness, in which the Japanese continue to excel.

Second in the list of Japanese successes is technology. The Japanese are still burdened with a reputation for being imitators, but in the world industrial revolution all countries (except the UK in the first phase) began by imitating and adapting; adaptation passed into improvement and innovation, and innovation shades into origination. In some industries, such as photographic equipment, cars, electronics, other optics, and the building of supertankers, Japan has passed through all or almost all the process, while remaining in other areas in the earlier stages.

In both manufacturing and trade, Japan has been hit worse than other countries by the world crisis in oil, on which it is more highly dependent than any other nation. Oil supplies more than three quarters of Japan's power generation, against some 45 per cent in UK, 50 per cent in the USA, 52 per cent in West Germany and 67 per cent in Italy. Trade, however, has been one of the most significant aspects of Japan's "economic miracle". In 1945, when the second world war ended, all Japan's world links had been cut; the restart in the 1950s was mainly from and to the USA, but by the first half of the 1970s Japanese traders had become first class competitors worldwide and over a large product range.

Missing from the list are two important factors. One is finance. Japan is emerging as a capital exporter and money market, and is also extending foreign aid, although on a scale far from commensurate with its trade turnover and industrial output. Internally, the financial system in Japan is in some respects peculiar and traditionally limited: for example, the use of cheques is relatively little developed, with salaries as well as wages often paid in cash. Japan will have little choice but to take a more forward role in international finance in the 1980s, although still not to the degree or in the form that befits the nation's stature; although there is a willingness to do this in some Japanese quarters, others are more conservative.

Another and more flagrant lag between what Japan could do and is actually doing is in the military sphere. Japan's armaments are small in quantity and limited in kind for an island country extremely dependent on material imports and on exporting to pay for them; a country vulnerable to attack by bombing and blockade by the USSR, and one which is sheltered only by its "distant friend", the USA, and by world opinion, which would react more violently to an attack on Japan than to the one on Afghanistan. A comparatively tiny expenditure on national defence was, of course, a main factor in the original "economic miracle" in the post war period when Japan was covered by the US guarantee and to a lesser extent by the other powers in Seato which undertook to protect the sea lanes which are Japan's vital artery to its south west and south. It appears inevitable that Japan's role in this respect must change in the 1980s with some rapidity and efficiency, despite the reluctance to do so.

Any commentary on modern Japan is bedevilled, as it has been for a hundred years past, by the phenomenon called dichotomy. There are always two parts, two levels, two sectors, two way pulls, in the mind and the actions of Japan, which stands between and combines the East and the West, the modern and the traditional: its special position and interest in Asia and the concerns of a world power. This is due to real and identifiable factors, both historically and in the current situation, which must be analysed. Since 1945, Japan has given the impression that it was conscious that it should do something in Asia (besides reconstructing Japan itself from wartime devastation) and take up an international duty but uncertain exactly what to do or how to do it. By 1970, when it had risen to high prosperity, Japan was materially ready to abandon its low posture of the early post war years and
128

act more positively, and the 1980s must now see Japan at last coming fully forward in international affairs.

All these aspects will be examined more closely below, in the light also of the remaining factor in our initial list which applies to all the other activities and may largely be a determinant of Japan's successes. This last is the managerial and organisational ability of the Japanese. It, too, is not equally distributed across all areas of activity, but it is an important factor, especially in the context of Asia to which it must primarily apply, but also in the international setting.

CHAPTER 1.

THE ENERGY SCENE

THE OIL PROBLEM

<u>Oil is the most pressing problem -</u>

The most immediate practical difficulty for Japan is the procurement of petroleum, its scarcity and price. On this everything depends, for Japan even more than for other industrial countries: first survival, next progress and prosperity. The general setting of the problem is the same for Japan as for other countries. However, in this, as in many other things, the ingenuity and painstaking methods of the Japanese, acting with foresight and nationally coordinated directives, pursuing precise targets with unanimity and zest, is the first feature that must be noted. Even before the oil crisis of 1973-74, under which Japan staggered and is only now recovering a certain balance of readjustment, the Japanese were carefully searching the world for new sources of oil, and any means of stabilising or improving the supply to them of that elixir of modern industrial life. This was done, on the whole, both more promptly and in a more coordinated way between private interests with government policy makers than in other countries. In subsequent years, the Japanese have operated with skilful opportunism on the odd lots and free markets in oil around the world. The Iranian crisis was as much a setback to Japan as to other countries - considerable investments were made there by Japan - but in fact, by the time the US hostages were taken in Teheran in November 1979, Japan had already reduced its dependence on Iran from 30 per cent of its total oil intake in 1973 to 20 per cent. This will continue to be the Japanese style of behaviour in the 1980s, even though Japanese realism acknowledges that piecemeal solutions may not ultimately be the best way of dealing with the problem.

<u>- and energy saving plans are being put into operation</u>

Currently Japan has the most specific plan for energy saving of any of the leading countries. This is not merely a paper plan; it has been well received and is being diligently attempted, like all perspective plans of the paternal government of Japan.* These are indicative, not prescriptive or obligatory plans, but all of them have in the recent past been fulfilled ahead of time. The sectors of the energy plan are poetically named: the Sunshine project for developing "new, clean sources of energy", and the Moonlight project for economising the use of power. None of this is, however, moonshine, but rather a careful techno-economic and administrative scheduling.

Early in 1979 the Japanese government scheduled measures to reduce the use of oil by 3 per cent. That was slightly ahead of the agreement by the International Energy Authority (Japan and 19 other members) to save 5 per cent of consumption. Japan moved at once (March 1979) to put the 5 per cent aim into practice. Now, a year later, oil use is being reduced in Japan by over 15 mn kl a year (5 per cent of Japan's total consumption in 1979), by methods which are interesting to list in detail (figures are in terms of crude, throughout). Moderate adjustment of
130

temperatures in offices and workplaces saves almost half the required amount.
Public premises stop central heating a fortnight earlier than previously. Informal
dress is recommended: last summer the (all male) cabinet set an example by wear-
ing safari suits. The saving under this heading is 7.4 mn kl per annum. Switches
by industry to fuels other than oil (coal, liquefied gas, electricity from atomic
power) saves 4 mn kl, mainly in the power stations. Private car users cut 2 mnkl,
achieved by improving public transport, encouraging the use of private, company
and government car pool arrangements, and voluntary agreements for rotas for
commuting together. 800,000 kl are being saved in indoor lighting, by improving
office and plant layouts and maximising the use of window and skylight areas.
Reductions in speed limits (already lower in Japan, as in the USA, than in Europe)
saves about 150,000 kl. Pooling and sharing the use of government and company
cars reduces their consumption by 20 per cent (500,000 kl). A 20 per cent reduction
in the use of lifts and moving stairways saves 100,000 kl; switching off unused
machinery (principally in offices) another 50,000 kl. Minor measures which are
recommended rather than controlled are: less use of neon signs, closing garages
on Sundays, TV broadcasting to cease earlier, and places of entertainment to keep
shorter hours. Subsequently, with the deepening of the oil crisis, more radical
measures are being studied, ahead of need; these include the general imposition of
the five day week (applied so far by few Japanese enterprises), the extension of
daylight or summertime, and the coordination of annual holidays so that everyone
takes them at about the same time. The 1980 programme raises the target to a
7 per cent reduction (by 20 mn kl more) in consumption, but adds no new methods.
The budget for 1980 raises the allocation for energy by 31 per cent. All this is of
interest to show how the Japanese respond speedily in such a crisis.

Per caput consumption of oil is just over 3 tons a year in Japan, compared with 9
tons in Canada, slightly less in the USA, 4.4 tons in West Germany, and just under
4 tons in the UK and in France. The consumption per head is still rising in those
Western countries. It will rise in Japan too (as long as the oil price does not soar
as gold has done), but much more moderately, at least in general use. It must be
emphasised that the current Moonlight project plans, summarised above, relate
mostly to the use of oil by the general public. The use of oil by industry is a problem needing a different emphasis.

ALTERNATIVE ENERGY SOURCES

Other sources of energy must be found -

60 per cent of Japan's total energy consumption is by industry, compared with 35-48
per cent in the other OECD countries. In the industrial sector Japan, in the coming
decade, as consumption rises to European and even North American levels, will
face a formidable energy problem. In heavy industry, the use of energy is already
quite economical; for example, Japanese steelmakers use 20-30 per cent less
energy per ton of output than the British. Technical improvements in heavy industry are said by experts in Japan to promise a reduction of energy inputs per ton
of output of the order of 30 per cent in the 1980s. Light industry and the general
range of factory activities are less economical at present in fuel consumption;
they could reduce their ratio in the order of 50 per cent on average.

Managers and accountants oppose such optimism by saying that the scale of industrial activity will rise by about the same ratio, while the cost of oil will, at the
most optimistic expectation, more than double. The Japanese can depend to a great
extent on their business ingenuity to find and arrange supplies, on the cooperation
of industry and public to economise and rationalise the use of fuel, and on technological advances to find or adapt new types of fuel. The Sunshine project

appropriately stresses first that solar energy will be developed. Secondly, there could be reversion to hydroelectric power; its percentage contribution to the total generation of energy had been reduced in the brief period of oil plenty. The power of the tides can be harnessed. These options are open to other countries, too, and may be used by them to the same extent as in Japan. Technological breakthroughs could make these more valuable oil savers in the future and technical advance is being worked for especially in this field by the Japanese. One other energy source more available to Japan than to most countries is geothermal power, the islands being entirely volcanic.

An important breakthrough would be the full development of safe atomic power. The Japanese authorities and most industrialists and others are determined to ensure the safety of the public, as there is the same popular objection and nervousness about the matter in Japan as in other countries, even more in view of wartime events. But it is likely that Japan will press forward, albeit cautiously, in the 1980s towards the peaceful use of atomic power to a greater extent than other countries. Its first experimental fast breeder atomic plant started to operate in 1977.

Such a change cannot, however, be completed on a comprehensive scale within a decade. Based on existing technology, conventional and neo-conventional sources of power (minerals, the sun, the tides and volcanoes) can at the most maintain the present deployment of the economy. The energy problem is as great and as complicated for Japan as for other countries; and a solution to the problem is a precondition for progress in the 1980s.

It is only possible to proceed by assuming that Japan will solve this problem about as well as other industrial countries are likely to do. It may possibly do so a little better, because – although it starts in a disadvantageous position in that it is more dependent than the rest on oil imported from a long distance – it has shown farsightedness and dexterity in this matter and, as in everything else, it tackles the problem in a nationally concerted way. The same is true of the adaptation of technology – for example, in the late 1970s when oil was first obtained from China by Japan it was found to be of poor quality, but the Japanese lost no time in devising processing methods to deal with it.

– coal, nuclear power and solar energy are possibilities

Long term plans in 1972 set targets for nuclear power generation of 60 mn kw in 1985 and 100 mn kw in 1990, subsequently revised to 33 mn and 60 mn, respectively, and again to "up to 30" and "up to 53". There are, however, now 21 nuclear reactors operating at 14 power plants with a total capacity of 15 mn kw, seven new ones under construction and seven more awaiting official clearance which are likely to operate in the mid 1980s. These 14 would contribute 28 mn kw in 1985. They are in remote areas, under close safety provisions and compensation is offered to local people, but there is intense opposition, especially to the 20 or more additional plants required for the full target.

The manufacture of solar power equipment for buildings began in Japan in 1975. There are now 15 manufacturers, over 2,000 sets have been installed, another 2,000 should be installed by 1984, and 50,000 more by the end of the decade. The overall view (see Table 1) shows, however, that oil must be the main energy source, followed by coal, although coal is regarded as a middle term resource. Japan's home coal reserves are large (22 bn tons, 3 bn accessible), but mining is
132

already deep and geologically difficult, and the price of domestic coal is double that of imported coal. Home production peaked to 61 mn tons in 1961, but was down to 19 mn tons in 1978, and is not given a good future. It could be increased by modern techniques such as liquefaction but at a high cost. The electric power industry would have to be restructured. It relies only 4 per cent on coal at present, mostly in small plants (of 30,000-70,000 kw). Nine major power companies plan to build 1 mn kw plants (i e on the scale of the present oil and nuclear installations). The distribution problem would be massive: 20 new harbours able to take large coal ships would be needed, costing $300-$400 mn each. 53 mn tons of coking coal were imported in 1958, and imports are expected to reach 100 mn tons by 1985 and 150 mn tons in the 1990s. The imports of steam coal are projected to be about 16 mn tons (15 times the present level) in 1985, and 40 mn tons by 1990. Japan has a National Resources and Energy Authority combining responsibility for fuels with raw materials in general.

Table 1

Japan's Long Term Energy Calculations, 1985, 1990, 1995
(mn kl oil equivalent)

	Actual	Projected		
	1977	1985	1990	1995
Total demand for energy	412	660	820	970
Requirements (net of conservation)	412	582	700	807
Supply of energy	412	582	716	825
Composition of the supply				
Exported crude	307	366	366	366
(%)	(75)	(63)	(50)	(43)
Nuclear power (mn kw)	8	30	53	78
(%)	(2)	(7)	(11)	(14)
Imported coal (mn tons)	58	101	143	178
(%)	(12)	(14)	(16)	(17)
Domestic coal (mn tons)	19	20	20	20
(%)	(3)	(3)	(2)	(2)
Domestic natural gas & crude	-	-	-	-
(%)	(1)	(1)	(1)	(2)
Liquefied natural gas	-	-	-	-
(%)	(3)	(7)	(9)	(9)
Hydroelectric power (mn kw)	26	41	53	63
(%)	(5)	(5)	(5)	(5)
Geothermal energy	-	-	-	-
(%)	-	-	(1)	(2)
Solar & tidal	-	-	-	-
(%)	-	(1)	(6)	(8)

THE PETROCHEMICAL INDUSTRY

The petrochemical industry is to be restructured -

Mention must be made here of the large petrochemical industry in Japan. It experienced tremendous growth, from a low base, in the late 1950s (20,000 tons of ethylene capacity), staggered from the oil blow in 1973, but has since, like other industries, to some degree recovered. In fact, immediately after the Opec crisis, it chanced to have a special advantage when there were some general shortages of certain petrochemical products in 1974, and Japanese producers were able to retain in that first crisis year their peak outputs of the pre-crisis period.

At that peak, Japan had nine large petrochemical complexes with a capacity of 5 mn tons and was the world's second largest producer after the USA. Three years of depression followed, with product prices declining, but the cost of the input, naphtha, increasing. Normalcy returned, in the main, in 1978, but meanwhile the Japanese had reconsidered their position. Facilities in Japan being about 20 years old, the need was to bring forward a project that had already been envisaged but now became much more urgent, namely not only the rationalisation but the restructuring of the whole industry. The domestic industry is to be maintained, in quantitative terms, not expanded, but it will be improved in quality. In this field, as well as in others, Japan has begun to look increasingly abroad, primarily to South East Asia at this time. By the mid 1980s, the domestic petrochemical industry will only maintain self sufficiency in the home market, whereas before the oil crisis some 20 per cent of Japan's output was exported. The Japanese are busily promoting downstream activities in South East Asia. The results of these policies will be marked in the 1980s.

This introduces two features that figure strongly in Japan's plans and expectations for the 1980s: the restructuring of industry, the economy and life in general in Japan; and a restructuring of the international economy, in which Japan will play a distinct and increasing part, bringing forward South East Asia especially as a main base. An example is given in the following paragraph.

JOINT VENTURES IN SOUTH EAST ASIA

- with joint ventures in South East Asian countries -

The policy termed "horizontal specialisation" is exemplified by the oil industry in South East Asia. Japan is intending not merely to countenance but to assist self sufficiency by at least two countries in the area. That is the official policy, although the industry in Japan may have some reservations. South Korea changed in the oil crisis from full dependence on Japan for plastics and other inputs to establishing its own ethylene capacity, now over 500,000 tons but aimed to be three times that amount in future. The Mitsui company was a pioneer in this connection and has established two plants in South Korea. The second of these, in which Mitsui has a half interest, is the largest downstream complex in that country. A reminder that Japanese enterprises do not always act in one body is that the Mitsubishi concern withdrew from the same venture as a result of the oil crisis.

Taiwan, which developed its capacity in petrochemicals without so much Japanese help, plans an output of 900,000 tons by 1982. It is interesting that Japan began by developing a retaliatory policy of buying from the West instead of from Taiwan, but now favours multinational coordination; in 1979 foreign interests conferred in Japan and are continuing consultations in Taiwan and elsewhere in 1980.

The Japanese have also developed a third and much greater pivot in Singapore where, alongside other or connected ventures, including natural gas in the general area of Malaysia, they are taking a half share in a 300,000 ton petrochemical complex, due to come on stream in 1983 to serve the whole Asean region. This orbit includes Indonesia, which is so far the largest oil producer in east Asia, with 2 mn b/d. China looms as another possibility in east Asia, in this connection as in others.

- which sets a trend for the future

The Japanese outlook is, however, global; other joint ventures might be embarked on anywhere that appears suitable. Mostly these would be in distant places, on a comparatively small scale. There are two preferences in the Japanese mind, namely South East Asia (because of geographical access and previous investment), and sites combining relative political and social stability with availability of the basic input. In South East Asia, Singapore is deemed to be best from all points of view; it appears highly accessible, politically and socially orderly, and has its own refinery capacity providing the naphtha. This subject cannot, however, be considered without emphasising the importance to Japan of west Asia, the main and crucial source of oil. Among many activities in the region is the Japanese project for a venture (of the same kind and on the same scale as the one in Singapore) in Saudi Arabia, which should begin producing around the mid 1980s. In Saudi Arabia the gas is available and has hitherto been largely burnt off into the air.

Two final points are important. All this expansion is in the face of the prospect of a natural long term growth in demand for oil and its derivatives so great that much more will be required to meet it. The effects of the current and planned investment on the development of Asia in particular and the world economy in general are already distinct, and will grow much larger.

CHAPTER 2.

THE JAPANESE BASE FOR DEVELOPMENT

INDUSTRY AND TRADE

Industry will be devolved -

Japan's view of the future of Japanese industry is that various industries can, should, and will, be abandoned in Japan and developed in less advanced countries. This is no defeatist attitude; on the contrary, it is envisaged that obsolescent activities will be phased out in Japan, and the country progress to newer and higher technologies. The transition would be eased - or induced - at every step by a carefully considered sharing of functions. This is based on both a theoretical view of world progress and on practical proposals already in effect or being planned.

The philosophy reflects that of Arnold Toynbee, popularised in the 1930s in his Survey of History, that European civilisation would "share" the 21st century with the Pacific civilisation, but thenceforward the Pacific would become "paramount". A similar view was put forward by Oswald Spengler in the 1920s in Decline of the West. Contemporary commentators can also be cited, for instance the exposition by Mr Norman Macrae of The Economist that the first industrial revolution took place in the UK with the steam engine and Bessemer steel (1775-1875), the second in the USA with the automobile, aircraft and the computer (1875-1975), but that leadership in the third, which has now begun, will be in the Pacific community, with electronics.

In the last decade the Japanese entered this third industrial revolution, and now purpose larger, more widely considered moves in that direction. A present best seller in Japan is a book by Professor Ezra Vogel entitled Japan Number One. The spirit and modus operandi of the third industrial revolution are those of the modern multinational firm. For Japan, the primary target area is South East Asia, followed by other developing regions. South East Asia means the whole area from Korea to Singapore and from Thailand to Papua New Guinea, plus ultimately - the Japanese and others strongly hope - China. In all these countries Japan must avoid nationalistic suspicions, accusations of reviving its wartime model of a "Greater East Asia Co-prosperity Sphere" or, in the current Chinese term, for striving for hegemony.

- to the newly industrialising countries -

Japan's strategy, to be coordinated with the West, envisages particularly a first round devolution to four east Asian countries which have recently shown swift economic development, advanced rapidly into industrialisation and are about - in association with both Japan and the West - to launch into self sustained economic development. These countries now have standards of living distinctly above their poorer Asian neighbours, reaching the same level as in east and south Europe.
136

They are South Korea, Taiwan, Hong Kong and Singapore. These are termed newly industrialising countries (NICs). There are two other NICs in Latin America, namely Mexico and Brazil.

Behind these first four Asian NICs, a second generation is deemed to be growing up: Malaysia, Thailand, the Philippines and Indonesia. Clearly South East Asia, always vital to Japan's interests, will be a main pivot of action and concern in the 1980s. The Japanese trade organisation Jetro calls the NICs "semi developed countries" and names a third league of "less semi developed countries": Malaysia, the Philippines and Thailand (Indonesia not yet getting into this category), together with Turkey, Argentina and Colombia outside east Asia.

According to UN figures, the semi developed countries are quite near to catching up the developed ones in indicators relating to education, but less so in the rest of the infrastructure, though advancing equally rapidly in the latter. Fig 1 represents the situation diagrammatically. The centre point is the level of the lowest developing countries today. In the educational indicators (to the left of the diagram) the NICs approach the developed level; in physical infrastructure (on the right) they are half way to the developed levels. To indicate the scale in this figure, in developed countries about 80 per cent of people are literate, in the least developed group 42 per cent. The other proportions are, for the same two groups, elementary schooling 88 per cent and 52 per cent, newsprint per head 13 kg and 1.3 kg, electricity output per head 4,250 kw and 350 kw, 30 telephones per 100 of population and 3, 8.5 hospital beds per 1,000 people and 2.3.

Japan will put tremendous effort into the developing countries, providing they fulfil the following qualifications. Political stability is a prerequisite, closely followed by a will to develop on or near the Japanese model. There must be plentiful labour, cheap in relation to its productivity, and able to raise productivity in response to wage incentives. The infrastructure must have matured sufficiently and suitably. Favourable exchange rates would be an additional advantage, and also preferential treatment from developed countries.

These conditions are generally fulfilled by the NICs, which are accordingly to be increasingly interwoven with Japan and the other developed nations, taking large amounts of capital and intermediate goods from them and sending manufactures to them, while developing their own specialisations. A commodity illustration is useful. In electronic components, for example, Japan exports the following to South Korea: resistors (nearly all in parts), transformers, audio parts and switchgear, electron tubes, integrated circuits and other items. But South Korea makes and sends to Japan everything in capacitors or transistors, and much in microphone and loudspeaker parts, complete loudspeakers, mechanical parts, tapes, thermionic receiver tubes, integrated circuits and other items. Although the balance of trade is in Japan's favour in all except electrical capacitors and integrated circuits, some key processes have devolved to South Korea and the two countries are fully interlocked in this industry.

– in a process of horizontal specialisation

This two way business with South Korea represented $0.5 bn at the end of 1970s, and is projected to rise to $1 bn in the 1980s. This process can be described as an industry cycle, like a product cycle, where the advanced products of today are devolving into the hands of the less advanced producers, while the more advanced countries are evolving higher level products. The current jargon in

Figure 1.

INDICATORS OF ECONOMIC DEVELOPMENT

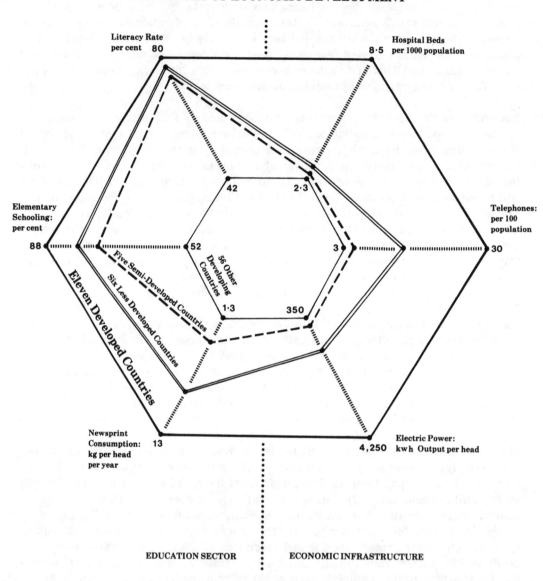

Source : MITI, FUJI BANK

138

Japan is, however, "horizontal specialisation"; evoking the accepted terminology of horizontal combination (the linking of processes at the same stage of production, or cartelisation), in contrast to vertical integration or control of all processes in an industry from the original raw materials to the end products (now associated with colonialism), together with the terminology of division of labour and specialisation (each doing what he is best fitted to do).

Critics consider this is camouflage for the imperialist expansionist purpose of Japan, but it must be taken to be a course Japan is determined on, apparently sincerely. The Japanese see this approach as the way the world will work in the future and think the merits of it outweigh the reservations, and suit particularly South East Asia and other emerging economies at the present time. Thus they consider it a suitable and realistic way of proceeding. A multinational method of operation is inevitable in the 1980s. It could mean international partnership in a "new deal", from the viewpoint of Asian and other developing countries, where there is some support for the concept. Such countries do have reservations but feel strong enough now to check any abuse, given the strength of popular democratic and nationalist sentiments, as far at least as the east Asian states are concerned.

The importance of Asean and other blocs

The South East Asian countries have, moreover, formed a defensive group: the Association of South East Asian Nations (Asean), consisting of Thailand, Malaysia, Singapore, Indonesia and the Philippines. In the inter-war years currency and trade blocs were formed: the dollar, sterling and yen blocs. The present basis is economic - and thereby to some extent political - integration. The USA was the original of this species; much more recently the European Economic Community has appeared, besides common market and free trade area arrangements in Central America and Africa. The trends in the West are regarded as being protectionist; but large blocs can deal with each other, whether across the board or on key issues, much better than a welter of small states. International relations, like national and sectional business dealings, are today largely and essentially a matter of trade-offs and package deals. Thus Asean could deal with Japan, the USA and the EEC, and each with the others much better than the same countries dealing with each other individually.

This development, obviously fitting in strongly with the multinational and horizontal specialisation approach, will be a main feature for Asia and the world in the 1980s. To the list above must of course be added Comecon, the Communist bloc (which includes the USSR and Eastern Europe, but in Asia so far only Mongolia and Vietnam; North Korea, Cambodia and Laos, besides the hostile China, have not been made members). Asean was constituted fundamentally as an association for the exchange of information and the coordination of policy in general terms. Recently it has moved towards more positive integration, a principal example of which is the location of oil processing and downstream activities in Singapore and Malaysia, to serve Asean and the region as a whole.

Japan scans a wider horizon, with projections of a Pacific community embracing all the countries bordering that ocean. Other proposals are for a Pacific free trade area (Pafta), a western Pacific free trade area (Wafta), and there are more. These have their advocates on the North American side, too. While the "super region" proposals interest the developing countries, they are pressing also for a solution on a more global basis. They demand a comprehensive new economic order for the whole world, in such terms as schemes for the stabilisation of the prices of primary products, meaning not fixing prices but gearing them in a just and systematic way with the prices of manufactured goods. Japan is involved with all the other countries in this discussion, in which, and in any practical moves, it could play a major role. The same applies to the monetary and financial problems of the world economy.

In the immediate devolution from Japan to South East Asia, the first industries for Japan to export are those for which sites for large complexes (as in steel, ship-building and petrochemicals) are difficult to find in Japan's small and mountainous islands, those that cause environmental degradation (chemicals), those where factor costs (land, labour and capital) are more favourable overseas, and those with a high input of fuel. This has already occurred to an extent that the Japanese are accused of exporting pollution, in addition to the older charges of plundering resources and exploiting labour. Agitation about degradation has spread to the second generation of NICs, although the developing countries are not as sensitive as Westerners on that score, valuing progress even more than they dislike dirtiness. This is another aspect in which the Japanese are concerned to improve their image, but also another reason for finding second generation NICs willing to be hosts to the basic industries.

Tariff barriers are being lowered

This whole movement will mean opportunities for cooperation against a background of intense competition. The modern Japanese entrepreneur is used to this, of course; he considers protectionism in the West an "undynamic" and outdated way of coping with the competition coming from developing Asia. He can see theoretical justification for an infant industry argument, but almost all the east Asian countries are no longer infants; he can see no virtue in protection for senile, out-moded or uncompetitive industries anywhere. Most Japanese industries are now strong enough to dispense even with the protection (direct or indirect) extended to them by their own government, though naturally willing to let it continue. Japan's tariff barriers are in fact being substantially lowered. Following the Tokyo Round of tariff negotiations, Japan is cutting duties by an average of 50 per cent (from high levels), compared with average cuts of 30 per cent by the USA and 25 per cent by the EEC. After this, Japan's tariff rate overall will be about 3 per cent, compared with 4 per cent for the USA and 5 per cent for the EEC. During the 1980s the rates of all three will coincide, creating something like an OECD customs union; other countries will join to generalise free trade throughout the world. The negotiations are to involve the less developed countries integrally with the industrial ones. Duties on 220 agricultural, fishery and forestry products are being cut by 30-50 per cent. General agreement on tariffs is not of course a complete solution; there will remain wrangling about quotas, details of scheduling, etc. This is only the surface of the question as well; there are problems of non-tariff barriers (administrative difficulties, preference to nationals in public con-tracts, etc), but the machinery of multinational negotiation to which Japan is committed can supposedly cover everything.

The complex process of liberalisation of trade and investment in the 1980s will require extensive regular and expert study in the West, where Japan watching is one activity which needs to grow and improve. The initiative is much the other way at present. For example, the Japanese can provide statistics on everything; 97 translations are made into Japanese from foreign languages for every three in the other direction. There are nine Japanese firms trading from overseas for

140

every foreign firm trading from Japan, and most of the latter employ comparatively small staffs. Direct foreign investment in Japan is no more than 2 per cent of Japanese direct investment overseas. Twice as many Japanese travel abroad for business purposes as do foreigners visit Japan. Foreign, in these cases, means not only Western but others, largely Asian.

The Japanese are eager and ready for changes in the world scene. The Japanese president of the Asian Development Bank has provided an apt simile, speaking of the Japanese kabuki theatre; this uses a revolving platform, which the players step off at times, stepping on again later in a different context or a different role. It seems certain that Japan's foreign policy will be actively and constructively guided on international lines by its present foreign minister, Dr Saburo Okita. He has served his country in many functions as an economist, notably in the Economic Planning Board, in heading the Japan Economic Research Centre, and in other positions. He was associated particularly with the income doubling plan in the 1960s, which proposed that Japan's GNP should be doubled in ten years; it was over fulfilled in a much shorter time. He has been eminent also internationally, in various regional and general bodies and in the UN arena, where he was one of the authors of the Pearson report (1969) advocating the extension and rationalisation of development policy. Before becoming foreign minister late in 1979 he pointed out, among other things, the inevitability of the progress of industrialisation in Asia. The NICs would surely expand their exports in the 1980s, though they could be persuaded to do so in an orderly manner. They have as much right to do this, and to move into new lines of production, as Japan itself. The effect on Japan, he argued, would be essentially healthy, since Japan remains "dynamic".

Dr Okita and others also contribute useful indications as to what orderly progress might mean. At the higher technological level there is scope for specialisation within a widened spectrum of activities. A noted instance is integrated circuits, traded both ways between the USA and Japan; the same applies to a range of other equipment and software. The Japanese are much concerned about continued allegations of Western producers that the Japanese market is largely closed to them; they reiterate, so constantly that they can now hardly revoke on this, that Japan's barriers are being and will be greatly reduced. The national, personal and business sense of honour is involved. At the lowest estimation, an open door policy has to be maintained in east Asia for the West, owing not only to the strength of Western ideas and methods in the ex-colonial countries but also to the unwillingness of the new nations to be dominated by Japan or any other country.

THE DOMESTIC SCENE

Japan's growth rate is higher than in other industrialised countries -

The OECD's projection that Japan will be the leading nation economically at the end of the century is worked out as follows. In the year 2000 Japan's per caput GNP will be $10,577, topping Canada's $10,086, the USA's $9,943 and the EEC's $6,900. In 1970 Japan contributed 6 per cent of the world's total GNP; this is expected to rise to 10 per cent in the year 2000, while the USA's share (in a greatly increased total) will fall from 31 per cent to 19 per cent and the EEC's from 20 per cent to 15 per cent. By then China's share is expected to be 10 per cent. Japan's already comfortable standards of income and living are confidently expected to rise to the utmost affluence. It should be to remembered that in their own estimation the Japanese are better able than other nations to translate high income into fine living.

They feel their aesthetic sense and traditions enable them to pass beyond the merely necessary conditions of more money to a truly elevated life style.

This is the explanation for the agitation in Japan several years ago when a Westerner spoke of the average Japanese being an "economic animal". The trouble was not merely a semantic and contextual misunderstanding of the word "animal" (as equated with sub human); it was an assertion that generally the Japanese consider economic values only part of the question, just a means to higher ends. Even if this is not entirely true, it is a conviction so tightly held as to be a principal determinant of Japanese behaviour. The people are adept at combining practical with aesthetic ability, the east with the west, the traditional with the contemporary, integrity with operational flexibility, and are proud, not ashamed, of this attitude.

Japan's growth rate in the last two decades has been high, enabling a massive build up of internal resources in an atmosphere of general confidence. GNP increased at over 13 per cent a year in 1967-76 (7 per cent in real terms) compared with a usual figure of 10 per cent in that period. The oil crisis caused a 1 per cent decline briefly in 1974: but there was immediate recovery and 5-6 per cent was achieved from 1977 to 1979. It seems predictable that 6 per cent will be the likely growth rate until the late 1980s, rising again to near 10 per cent in the final years of the decade. This 5 or 6 per cent is a much higher rate than in other industrial countries and the headlining of a statement "Japan's growth rate halved" must be regarded in this context. Japan, too, is accustomed to relatively large fluctuations in the growth rate.

– and social care is not far behind Western levels

Japan is now a welfare state, at levels of care comparable with the West (see Table 2). Benefits will grow in line with future levels of prosperity.

Table 2

Social Security Benefits in Selected Countries, 1977

($ per month)	Japan	UK	W Germany	USA	Others	
Pension, married					Sweden	340
couple	391	212	313^a /479^b	365	France	174
% of average wage	41	41	39^a/ 60^b	41	France	34
Welfare payments^c	357	174	263	219		
% of average wage	48	39	42	29		
Medical & health services expenditures as % of GNP	5.1	6.1	7.9	7.7	France	8

a Lowest manual worker. b Highest office worker. c Household with 2 dependants.

Table 2 perhaps distorts the picture in Japan somewhat; there are statistical differences between its figures and those of the other countries and the coverage of benefits is not the same. Nevertheless, it is broadly true that Japan is not excessively behind the West in welfare benefits.

The Japanese see themselves as middle class

Opinion polls and social surveys, to which the Japanese are much addicted, furnish a useful starting point to investigating the outlook of the Japanese people. One point on which the Japanese are near to being unanimous (apart from their patriotism) is that most people consider themselves as belonging to the middle class; the proportion was 72 per cent in 1958, over 80 per cent in 1964, and consistently at 90 per cent from 1970 to 1979. This may reflect a wish to identify with a large and central group (which could also affect the national foreign policy).

The definition of middle class is of course sociologically vague, not least in Japan. Traditional Japanese society, though it was extremely hierarchical, had no concept of class in the European sense, the Japanese language had no word for it and a new one had to be invented, which was fully introduced only about 60 years ago. No fewer than four terms are in use for middle class, all with different implications but all expressing social rather than economic valuations (namely chūsan kaikyū, middle property or middle production class, chūryū kaikyū, midstream, chūkan kaisō or mibun, which resembles the German mittelstand).

In Japan as in other modern societies, the real and effective criterion is the level of income. The Japanese seek to play down the economic motivation, perhaps unconvincingly, since Japan's chief success has been in the economic field. However, when the same question about class was posed in terms of standard of living, stressing the factor of income as well as social criteria, the result was almost the same.

Table 3

Self Assessment Standard of Living by the Japanese
(per cent)

	A little above average	Average	A little below average	Total
1965	7	50	29	86
1970	8	57	25	90
1975	7	60	23	90
1978	7	58	24	89

This middle class consciousness is expressed by people at a European level of industrial living, urbanised and affluent enough to work hard to maintain and improve that condition of embourgeoisement. Their consumption patterns and standards are close to those of other industrial countries and will evolve in the same way. Consumerism is well entrenched and will continue to be high; in this field Japan is expected to follow the same path as Western countries in the 1980s.

The political scene at home –

The political stability of Japan appears certain, short of a world economic crisis similar to or worse than in 1939 (the short term reaction to which, in Japan, could well be one of national patriotic unity), or an attack or blockade by the USSR. Social democratic pressures will, however, as in the West, be great. At centre or left of centre are the liberalist and environmentalist standpoints already mentioned, to which should be added conservationist thinking, which is understandable in Japan's situation of extreme dependence on world resources that are being rapidly depleted. Doomsday prognoses are accordingly in evidence in Japan, as in other countries. The line of the Club of Rome has its adherents, with Foreign Minister Okita one of its notable supporters.

It should be remembered that there is an underlying insecurity in Japan, which is a country liable to natural disasters - earthquakes, volcanic eruptions, typhoons, tidal waves and fires. It is symptomatic that a recent best seller in Japan has been a novel imagining the whole ·country being submerged under the ocean, as a result of unprecedented seismic and volcanic movements in the earth's crust (Japan Sinks! by Sakuo Komatsu; English translation, The Death of the Dragon, Harper 1976 and paperback 1978). Short of such a cataclysm, Japanese reactions show partly traditional stoicism but also nowadays a determination to live more fully through modern technology. The bad effects of hyperindustrialism are obvious in Japan. Public opinion is bound to become even more concerned about them, and the authorities to continue to deal cogently with these problems.

Moving politically to the left, revolutionary elements are not likely to come anywhere near to power, but will continue to make a spectacular showing which sometimes impresses. The Japanese left has a sense of theatre: visually, May Day and other demonstrations, which are sometimes violent (for example the prolonged battles against the opening of the new Narita international airport and of some large industrial ventures), can give the impression of a revolutionary situation. If the processions incorporate a million people, however, this still represents only 1 per cent of the population, and includes participants of all shades of opinion from reformist to extremist, with overt revolutionists a small minority. The occasional pitched battles are mounted by drilled and practised squads in semi-feudal armour with crude hand weapons (though not firearms or blades). Including fellow travellers, militant students, farmers objecting to the purchase of land (or wanting a higher price for it), conservationists and others, this falls short of representing the mass of the people.

The phenomenon of Eurocommunism is now much to the fore. In east Asia there are   varieties of Asian communism. Chinese communism (formerly Maoism), with its Sinic cultural base and its stress on communalism, has appealed to the Japanese, much more than Russian Bolshevism. There is such a thing as Japanocommunism, which is worth studying more than it has been so far. There are also movements of the protean New Left on the fringes of an extremely divided movement. Japan deals strictly, where possible, with assassins. Late in 1979 death sentences were passed on two bomb terrorists and others were given prison sentences.

- the policy abroad

In foreign policy Japan is at a turning point. Diplomatically, politically and militarily the low posture is now as out of date and unsuitable as it is economically. This stance cannot be maintained by one part of the whole and not by the other parts. Japan is already actively involved in all but the military power aspect, and must become much more involved, in all respects, within the next few years. In its own and the world's interests, Japan must realise its full potential as an intermediary between east and west and between advanced countries, in trade and in every other sphere of international relations. Japan has no real option, in the present and near future world situation, but to rearm, although it will do so within the limits of a defensive attitude, as unostentatiously as it can. It is not possible to be a world power economically and in the applied arts and not to undertake the entire role of a world power.

144

In foreign policy there is, therefore, a commitment that Japan must make, sooner rather than later, in the 1980s. Japan has already explored the consequences of such a move and has actually committed itself on a number of smaller issues. It has veered from links with the USSR in respect of Siberian development particularly (not abandoning, but somewhat slowing and reducing its expectations in that direction) towards much more integral and sweeping links with China. Japan has intensified its interest in South Korea and South East Asia. The Middle East and oil, the ocean routes - especially the narrow passes such as the Straits of Malacca, the Persian Gulf, Suez and Panama, where the flows could be cut - are of life or death significance to Japan. Japan has backed Asean and begun to talk of a Pacific Community.

Future historians may possibly locate an actual turning point, for Japan, in Vietnam in 1979, at the time when China announced that it would withdraw its invading forces from Vietnam. It is believed that Japan (with a newly established ambassador in Hanoi and negotiating aid worth 14 bn yen to Vietnam) strongly advised Hanoi against any pursuit of the Chinese across the frontier. Such a pointed demarche would have been unthinkable a few years ago; but this is only a first precedent for the 1980s.

Japan's foreign aid is to increase

In the sphere of foreign aid, Japan announced at the Manila Unctad in 1979 that it· emphasised human resources, education and training. Japan will strive to increase its aid to developing countries in the 1980s, this being a domain in which its image is considered inadequate. In official development assistance (ODA) to developing countries, Japan allocated $2.2 bn in 1978, an increase of no less than 56 per cent, following pledges at the Bonn summit to double foreign aid in three years. This is still far short of the UN prescription of 1 per cent of national income: in fact it brings Japan's foreign aid only from 0.21 per cent of GNP in 1977 to 0.23 per cent in 1978. The grant element had increased, however (from 70 per cent of the aid to 75 per cent in the two years), raising the proportion of grants in the aid commitments outstanding from 38 per cent to 58 per cent. This is mostly bilateral, between Japan and other individual countries, rather than multilateral. The proportion of tied aid is higher than that of other countries and Japan is pledged to reduce it. Japanese aid is widely seen to have been geared until now to its own investment and trade interests and this is another area where Japan is sensitive about having a bad image; in the 1980s Japan's development aid will not only be increased but be in more altruistic forms.

Service industries are on the rise -

Acknowledging the debits as well as the credits of prosperity and high growth, Japan in the early 1970s already realised the need for a restructuring of its economy, and of certain aspects of social policy, and planned accordingly. That was before the oil crisis. The policy for recovering from that crisis embodied not merely restoration of the previous levels, but an extensive and radical rearrangement.

Tertiary or service industries have been the main earners in Japan since 1965, have developed prodigiously and will continue to do so in the 1980s, to the point where they will account, as in the USA, for over two thirds of employment and an even higher proportion of earnings.

Table 4

Net National Product by Industrial Origin
(percentage of total NNP)

	Primary industry[a]	Secondary industry[b]	Tertiary industry[c]
1955	24	30	46
1960	15	37	48
1965	11	37	52
1970	8	37	54
1975	6	36	58
1976[d]	6	35	59

a Farming, fishery, forestry.   b Manufacturing.
c Services.   d 1977 estimates show similar figures.

Table 5, which lists the types of services concerned, shows that Japan in the later 1970s was already similar to Western Europe; and like Europe it is broadly catching up with the USA in the predominance of service functions.

Table 5

Tertiary Industry in Japan and Selected Western Countries, 1975
(percentage of employees in all industries)

	W Germany[a]	France	Japan	UK	USA
Electricity, gas, water	0.9	0.9	0.6	1.6	1.4
Wholesale trade	4.6	...	6.6	3.4	4.0
Retail trade	8.9	...	11.1	9.5	12.5
Restaurants	} 3.0	...	} 3.5	1.9	3.3
Hotels			} 0.9	1.0	0.9
Total of above	16.5	16.3	22.1	15.8	20.7
Transport & communications	5.8	5.6	6.3	6.7	6.1
Finance, insurance real estate	3.1	...	3.4	3.2	3.7
Other business services	1.9	...	1.9	2.7	1.4
Total of above	5.0	5.7	5.3	5.9	5.3
Personal services	1.9	...	2.4	2.3	4.4
Recreation	0.4	...	0.9	1.2	1.0
Medicine, health	3.3	...	2.6	4.3	7.0
Education	3.1	...	3.1	6.1	9.7
Civil service	8.9	...	3.7	5.1	5.3
Other local, social & personal services	2.8	...	4.5	4.5	5.3
Total of above	20.4	23.1	17.2	23.5	32.7
Total tertiary industry	48.6	51.6	51.7	53.5	66.2

a In West Germany the armed forces are included under civil service; in other countries they are excluded altogether. There are other differences of classification, but not such as to affect the comparisons significantly. Later analyses (Table 6) classify services differently, in comparing Japan with the USA; this understates the numbers in Japan in the private sector, but not in the government sector, by excluding enterprises with fewer than 31 employees.

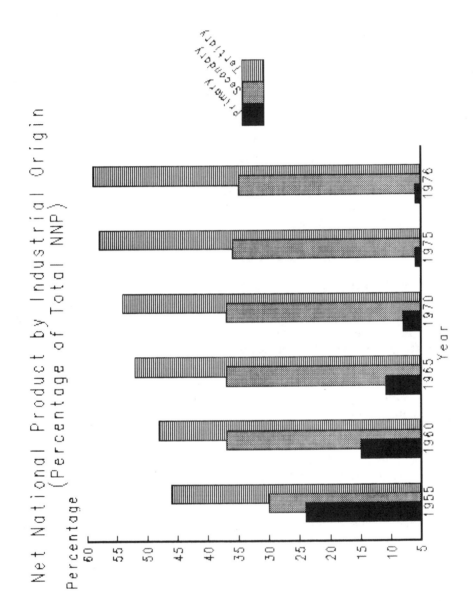

Figure 1a

147

Table 6

Employees in Service Industries as
Percentage of All Employees in Japan, USA, 1978
(per cent)

	Japan	USA
Total in service industries	18.5	27.0
of which:		
hotel	1.5	1.5
private	0.5	1.5
services to companies & establishments	4.0	8.0
education	6.0	8.0
social services	1.0	2.0
entertainment	2.0	2.0
others	3.5	4.0

Table 6 shows that the figures for Japan are similar to those for the USA in the case
of hotels and entertainment, but Japan lags behind in private, office and social
services, although it is catching up rapidly in these sectors.

- and social amenities are being extended

With its domestic background of an advanced and advancing level of living and a
middle class outlook, Japan is heavily committed to great improvements in the
quality of life in the 1980s. This was already determined upon at the beginning of
the 1970s. In the age of its "economic miracle" (1954-74) Japan gave priority to
heavy industry, to the relative neglect of the infrastructure. The infrastructure
meant at first roads and transport and communications facilities but, these having
been rapidly brought forward, the stress has shifted increasingly on to social
amenities, which will be a main sector of advance in the 1980s. Japan, in its
pattern of living at home and its acting and trading internationally, will resemble
West Germany.

The social and the practical facilities are, of course, interconnected. For example,
the extension of the Shinkansen (the famous fast railway between Tokyo and Kyushu)
is being rapidly pursued to bring the railway up to Hokkaido in the north. (The
work is behind schedule, but proceeding at a good rate.) In the farseeing projections which the Japanese authorities issue at frequent intervals - often not
inappropriately styled "visions" - this sort of development is interwoven with
solutions to the problem of urbanisation, including the establishment of hundreds
of new garden city communities.

The government has been sensitive to environmental issues. It studied the problem
in the 1960s, adducing such statistics as the existence in Japan of only 3.5 sq m
of parkland per head of population compared with 30.4 sq m in London. Prime
Minister Tanaka aired the question influentially in his book entitled Reshaping
the Japanese Archipelago, before the oil crisis. In 1973, too, the Economic
Planning Agency pronounced that (the material side being secured) "the need is
now to enable everyone to lead a stable and full life ... (in) the quality of life, in
education, employment, housing, the natural environment, more care for the
elderly, etc". The emphasis on stability is interesting and characteristic. In
1979 one of the Ministry of International Trade and Industry's themes was harmonious relations with other countries as well as within Japan itself, "as a
prerequisite for (the Japanese at home) achieving a decent and satisfying national
life".

The Economic Planning Agency forecast in 1979 a public expenditure of 240,000 bn yen ($1,080 bn) in 1979-85 for fixed investment in environmental improvement, highways, housing, railways, sanitation and social welfare. This represents 11 per cent of GNP, which is a higher percentage than in Western countries (currently 8 per cent in the UK, 5 per cent in the USA). It should be emphasised that 1980 is not the beginning, from 1955 allocations under these headings have represented 5 per cent of GNP, rising by a decimal in the years 1975-79 but now doubled. The prospect is of Japan in the 1980s largely catching up with, and in some respects (on the artistic side) surpassing, the other industrial countries in the field of amenities.

THE FUTURE

New technology is the keynote for the 1980s –

As Japan is set to devolve a large part of its industrial activities into NICs that become ready to receive them (it is intended to retain some processes, especially in assembly work, and to continue some older and more traditional industries, including heavy industries, and some that were new and innovatory not long ago), Japan must find newer and more forward looking occupations at home. These are intended to be technology intensive and especially knowledge intensive. Research and development intensive items come first and they include electronic components, aircraft, electric cars, industrial robots, atomic related industries, integrated circuits, fine chemicals, new synthetics, new metals, special ceramics and the development of the oceans.

Sophisticated assembly items are next: communications equipment, business equipment, pollution control equipment, air conditioners (ultra-large as well as standard), teaching aids, prefabricated housing, automated warehousing, stock and inventory control, large and better construction machinery. Under fashion industries are specified high quality clothing and decorative fabrics, furniture and furnishings, household fittings, electric sound equipment and electronic musical instruments. Last in manufacturing scale but high in potential and in value added are knowledge intensive industries: information processing and retrieval, software in general, video, systems engineering and consultancy services. (See Kiyoshi Kojima, Japan and a New World Economic Order, English translation, Boulder and London, 1977.)

All this involves a great extension of education, especially of technical education. The equivalent of $1 bn is being earmarked at the beginning of the 1980s for recasting the system of instruction and training to place more emphasis on the required competences. The stir in the higher scholastic world in Japan is some-what reminiscent of that in the UK in the 1960s after the Robbins report urged teaching more technology and inducing graduates to go into industry instead of into the bureaucracy and the professions. There are, however, great differences: we are now 21 years further on, and world technology and management standards have become much more advanced. The move is led by a more specific and determined agency (Science and Technology) of the government and the stress is more on basic advanced science than on its application. The remit includes research and development as well as education, posing problems that cannot be completely resolved in ten years but will be largely met in that time. Most interesting is the stress, a novel one in Japan, on the need to enhance the capacity of individuals to be innovative and inventive personally as well as collectively, and on human relations as well as institutional ones.

- and will be an important item of trade

Technology is, of course, an import and export business for Japan, as for other industrial countries. The multinational orientation is important, but here Japan has distinct difficulties. Most essentially, its ability is still to adapt rather than to invent. A major function in the last two decades has been as an entrepot for technology between the West and Asia, because of Japan's understanding of and connections with both. This position has been eroded for some time past. While Japan was catching up greatly in technology with the West, it did not reach some of the highest and most rapidly advancing levels, and meanwhile the NICs were beginning to need sophisticated rather than intermediate technology, and turned directly to the West to obtain it. (It is a matter of pride for developing countries to insist on the latest models, refusing secondbest even if it is almost as good and possibly more suitable for them.)

It does not by any means follow that Japan is losing this trade. 40 per cent of Japan's technology exports still go to Asia, and this percentage will be retained in a market that will grow enormously. The NICs are not dropping Japanese technology, but mainly seeking to diversify their sources and types of supply (evading Japanese domination) and also now needing the highest grade items. For example, South Korea between 1962 and 1976 made 737 agreements for taking foreign technology on licence. Japan supplied 487 (two thirds), the USA came next with 158 (just over one fifth), then France with 23 (3 per cent), West Germany with seven (1 per cent), and the rest of the world (effectively the rest of Europe) provided 9 per cent.

Some of this has been big business; for example, in 1965 in the early days of this trade, Mitsubishi set up in South Korea with licensed foreign (mostly European) technology what was at that time the largest urea fertiliser plant in the world (Samsung). In the 1980s there will be wider horizontal specialisation, with a larger and more variegated demand and supply. The Japanese excel at dissemination, which depends on organisation and collective effort; they now need to achieve the same level in origination, which depends on a more individualistic ability. This may be the greatest revolution they have ever envisaged, but it is not impossible considering what Japan has done to change itself in the last hundred years. It may be another of the targets for the year 2000; but it is one of the priorities, likely to be more than half fulfilled by 1990. Japan's international network is large and complicated. Table 7 gives the recent position and shows the solidity of the basis.

Table 7

Japan's Exchange of Technology with the World:
Value of New Licensing Arrangements and Renewals of
Existing Contracts for Techniques and Processes, 1976
(bn yen; $=300 yen approx in 1976)

Imports to Japan			Exports from Japan			Balance
West		%			%	
USA	112	(64)	USA	8	(10)	-104
			Canada	5	(6)	5
West Germany	19	(11)	West Germany	1	(1)	-18
Switzerland	13	(7)				-13
UK	11	(6)	UK	1	(1)	-10
France	7	(4)	France	1	(1)	-6
			Italy	5	(7)	5
			Netherlands	2	(2)	2
			Other Europe	12	(14)	12
East Asia						
			China (Mainland)	8	(9)	8
			South Korea	7	(9)	7
			Taiwan	5	(6)	5
			Indonesia	4	(5)	4
			Other east Asia	8	(10)	8
Rest of world						
			Brazil	5	(7)	5
			Others	11	(14)	
Total	12	(7)		16	(21)	4
Grand total	177	(100)		83	(100)	-94[a]

a Total as published; includes USSR, Eastern Europe and small
countries.

Industry is becoming more flexible

Among the Japanese virtues, some have become almost legendary: a capacity for
hard work, productivity, thrift, self discipline and collective disciplines.   These
will be considered further below, together with the probability of their continuing
in the 1980s.   It is difficult not to exaggerate the impression of the Japanese working in one monolithic body, like an efficient army.   There is much to support such
a depiction, but also a lot of contradictory evidence.   An important point to make
is that increasingly, as life and business become more complicated,   involving a
larger number of different countries and types of activity, the more varied Japanese
industry becomes.   Flexibility is of paramount importance.   Firms, policies and
plans diverge; products are not uniform.   For example, in the context of South East
Asia and of electrical products, Matsushita transferred its production of refrigera-
tor compressors to Singapore while Sanyo was increasing its output of the same
component in Japan.

Another significant point is that traffic is reversible.   Black and white television
sets, which went overseas in the 1970s, recently began to return to Japan - for
use in a new Japanese line, videos combining small screens with recording
machines - but emigrated again when the NICs learnt this technique also.   These
and other examples emphasise that technology is really the key; and technology,
largely but far from exclusively, is held by Japan.

Politics may intrude. Japan had largely favoured Taiwan in the 1960s, but turned away from it in the 1970s to try to please mainland China, where major prospects were seen. Japan Airlines ceased to serve Taiwan, but it was not long before another Japanese service was created to replace that link. There is now some aversion to South Korea because of its government's restrictions on joint ventures and other investments, the high rate of inflation and other features (industrial competition at some points). Hong Kong is an open economy, but comparatively costly, because of high site costs (except for compact operations such as Hitachi transistor watches). Land costs are also high in Singapore, but there are govern-ment encouragements as well as an open economy (including allowance of complete foreign ownership of manufacturing enterprises). So Singapore is among the lead-ing NICs in this sector. Matsushita, Hitachi and Toshiba all have substantial operations there at present, but so do US companies. All these factors are relativi-ties; the Japanese can take advantage of the shifting balances between them, but so can others. If wage costs or other factors become expensive or troublesome, other localities will be chosen for the overflow of Japanese industry's enterprises. In east Asia Japan cannot have, does not need and does not seek any totalitarian sort of monopoly. Elsewhere it just seeks a reasonable entry. Worldwide capi-talism is largely in the era of monopolistic competition, product differentiation, output and market sharing multinationalism. Cut-throat competition is outmoded: the race is to the swift innovator and the able negotiator. Such is the philosophy in the Japan of the 1980s, and one that will be widely supported and applied.

CHAPTER 3.

ATTITUDES TO WORK AND LEISURE

How Japan's standard of living compares

Income comparisons between countries depend on the rate of exchange of currencies and the internal purchasing power of each currency. Disregarding any quality of life comparison, in late 1978 Japan's GNP per head was, at the then current exchange rate of 176 yen to the dollar, actually above the USA's. Subsequently the yen depreciated and a calculation early in 1980 would show the money GNP per head in Japan about 10 per cent below the USA and about 10 per cent above the West European average. A realistic assessment, however, requires some discounting for the so called quality of life - amenities, the satisfaction of people's aspirations - and takes into account the differences between nations' ways of living. On this basis, the Japanese standard of living has overtaken that of the poorer European countries, rivals the highest of countries in the EEC and approaches North American standards. It will continue to do so, and may reach US levels in the 1980s.

It is necessary, therefore, to have an idea of the Japanese pattern of living, and particularly of how much the comparisons should be weighted to allow for the supposed qualitative difference. The Japanese themselves reckon on the quantitative rise in their standard of living continuing significantly in the 1980s, at rates distinctly above those in the West, in money terms, but not at anything like the 10 per cent per year and more that Japan achieved before the oil crisis, indeed at only between 4 per cent and 6 per cent. This is evidently no cause for despair, bearing in mind that the UK in 1980-82 faces zero growth or worse, and the USA a low percentage growth. This is inherent in mature economies at the top of the curve of development when greatly diminished rates of growth are experienced onward from the achieved affluence. The Japanese count on excelling in the 1980s not only in money terms but also in the quality of living, so removing the discount that is made against them on that score.

Hard work is still esteemed -

The Japanese are renowned for their diligence, their high and constantly increasing productivity, and even for enjoying working hard and well for its own sake. The phrase "dignity of labour" is meaningful in Japanese society, for a worker is ashamed of unsatisfactory work for which he loses face personally and for his group. Collectivity is strong - not on the paternalistic basis of the past, where the structure of the firm approached a family relationship, nor on the former patrimonial basis of inheritance by the eldest son (or, if he failed, by a better man who became the adopted son).

Collectivity persists in an up to date form of teamwork appropriate to modern industry. There is little of the Western divisiveness between management and workers. Workers are elated at their firms' successes (and receive substantial bonuses in proportion to them). They participate in management committees. Businessmen and employees alike are inclined to serious reading on economic and social matters. In this, and in the joint management and trade union arrangements, the nearest Western parallel is in West Germany. The former distinction in Japan (almost a caste distinction) between manual and office workers is rapidly fading, as is the hierarchical preference for graduates of traditionally superior schools, at both the managerial and technician levels. What is expected to be the attitude in the 1980s?

The accusation of addiction to work now gives rise to indignation in Japan. The gaffe of the EEC in 1979, referring to the Japanese as workaholics dwelling in rabbit hutches, was sharply resented. The phrase was quickly modified to "diligence and frugality". The former term was more acceptable in Japan, though still considered to underestimate Japanese positivism and imply slavishness. Frugality seems slightly absurd taking into account the luxuriant displays in Japanese department stores; it reflects again the general ignorance about Japan in most of Europe. In the last few years it has been the people in the South East Asian NICs that have appeared to the Japanese to be work addicted since they work longer hours and exhibit patriotic zeal.

- but the pattern of living has become more Westernised -

The growth of tertiary or service industries (see Table 5), which now approach the US level, shows the trend in Japan's pattern of living. The following aspects are especially significant. The catering industry, always a large one in Japan ,has developed phenomenally. Its sales grew 9 per cent in 1977 and 13 per cent in 1978, when, at 13,000 bn yen, its earnings outstripped those of the Japanese motor industry (10,000 bn yen). The great gainers were the chains of "fast food" establishments, of US style or US origin (including Macdonald's and Kentucky Chicken, now prominent in Japan). Family housekeeping, however, remains broadly on Japanese lines. Husbands do not take their wives out much and there is little entertaining of guests to meals at home. Diet is increasingly becoming Westernised, but far from totally.

In shopping and in family life the market psychologists stress that Japanese life has become child centred to an American degree. The Japanese have, in fact, always indulged their children, and the modern marketplace gives ever more scope. Disposable incomes are set on a rising trend, days off are more numerous, and menus more extensive. The market not merely follows but leads the evolution of the pattern of mass consumption. Supermarkets have recently doubled their share in retail trade to 12 per cent. Department stores have only 8 per cent of the total turnover, but have formative influence; they handle half the imported consumer goods, against only 1 per cent by supermarkets. Distribution patterns are expected to experienced major change in Japan in the 1980s - there is great scope for improvement in this sphere. The gap between wholesale and retail prices is often greater than in other countries and the trends of the two more disparate. 80 per cent of retail trade is in small shops. Foreign goods still try to rank as luxuries, and have a high mark up in Japan, but luxuries become conventional necessities with affluence. The whole Japanese home market is thoroughly sophisticated, particularly at the top end. New products, in advanced lines, are geared

154

simultaneously to the home and export markets. For example, early in 1980 new home computer units came on the market in Japan; it may indicate export readiness, rather than culture lag, that the instruction manuals were available at first only in English.

Opinion polls (if critically regarded) are a useful indicator of Japanese life, frequently and exhaustively probing the public mind. They reveal, not surprisingly, that everyone wants a higher standard of living. In 1978, as in 1973, 30 per cent of the people equated this with housing, clearly the top priority by far. Loans for house purchase are widely available, but at rates of interest which would put the cost well above the 20 per cent of income that is the theoretical maximum for the cost of housing. Yet there is no slackening in the demand to acquire and improve dewellings. The rapid change of the family, from the extended to the nuclear, will continue to intensify this feature. From 1960 to 1975 the proportion of households consisting of a married couple with children remained steady at 42 per cent, but the number of children per family fell. The next most numerous category was that of the household containing other relatives or non-relatives, but its percentage fell from 37 to 21 per cent in the same period. Meanwhile, households containing only a married couple increased steadily from 8 per cent to 12 per cent of all households; and the number of persons living alone increased still more sharply, from 4 per cent to no less than 19 per cent. These trends became even stronger after 1975.

To keep up with rising standards and rising prices, more wives are now in paid employment. Published figures state that before the war nearly 89 per cent of the real income of households came from the husband's earnings, falling after the war to 83.5 per cent in 1977. The wife's earnings represented only 1.5 per cent of the family income before the war but 6.7 per cent in 1977, while other income (from children or property) remained the same at just under 10 per cent. This seems to understate the wives' contribution, which may be accounted for by some Japanese husbands not liking to report their wives' earnings.

The motivations for earning more are primarily to have more to spend on educating children, to obtain more and better durable consumer goods,and to improve homes. A significant indicator is the decline and disappearance of public bathhouses, which once served as local centres of social life; they have been largely replaced by launderettes (as social centres) and most houses now have their own bathrooms. "Do it yourself" facilities are spreading, as a necessity rather than a cult. Japanese homes and the Japanese streets will become much more like American and European ones in the 1980s - though on a much smaller physical scale.

- and leisure pursuits are increasingly popular

An equally important angle revealed by the polls is the increasing appreciation of leisure and its use. The Japanese still work hard for the firm during the day, but finish much more punctually in the evening, and are now more interested in leisure and recreation pursuits, Industries concerned with the latter have not only survived bad recession, but have grown enormously. In 1978 restaurants and catering became the biggest single industry in Japan. The travel business flourishes. All means of transport - buses, trains, planes, passenger and car ferries - and accommodation at resorts are prebooked and packed out at holiday times. Foreign travel has increased at a great rate; in 1978/79 just over 3 mn Japanese went abroad, 84 per cent of them on organised tours. The phenomenon of highly regimented groups of Japanese tourists following a leader with a flag, in the West especially, has dwindled. Although tourists still like to travel in groups, they are now more at ease in Western surroundings and less in need of shepherding there. Flag led groups are, however, still to be seen in Japan, especially in popular centres such as Kyoto.

Outdoor and active or participant sports are now widespread. Tennis, skiing, running, and other sports have grown and in some cases displaced the formerly dominant spectator sports such as baseball and Japanese wrestling. Golf is important, though mainly for the elite. The ubiquitous saloons for pachinko (pinball machines) - a game of oriental fatalism in a mechanical form, with more chance in it than skill - have declined somewhat. A portent of the technological age is that the pinball machines have been replaced to a great extent by new electronic ones, of the "Star Wars" and other war games types (war games being acceptable as long as they are hypothetical, in the stratosphere far away from Japan). The electronic machines require mental alertness and personal decision, which the old sprung ball on the whole did not. In this and other domains, individualism is strongly entering into the Japanese way of living, especially perhaps in the Japanese way of playing. Quick changes in fashion are characteristic of modern Japan. In the present example, a space invader video game was in vogue in 1979 and nearly a quarter of a million machines installed; later in that year the number was reduced to 100,000, the rest being replaced by new spectacular devices.

Business and social entertaining has always been largely outside the home. This continues to enlarge in scale, and rise in the national expenditure. Marriages, commemorations and other ceremonies are increasingly held in restaurants, etc. It can cost up to £500 to hire one of the widely advertised traditional bridal outfits for one day. The cabaret and hostess system is well known to foreign visitors, not least for its high cost. It is famously supported by expense accounts, Japanese firms allowing lavishly for entertainment. Estimates indicate that companies in Japan spent 2.6 bn yen (about $10 mn) on business entertainment in 1978, which represents about 2 mn yen (or $8,000) per firm per day on average; large firms averaged more than 25 times that figure and the very largest no less than 400 times it. There are obviously opponents of the expense account system, but nevertheless, it is good business; every 5 yen (2 cents) disbursed from an expense account generates 1,000 yen (about $4) of sales.

In 1960, 4,100 bn yen were spent on all leisure activities in Japan, in 1970 9,600 bn, and in 1975 18 bn yen (one eighth of the total GNP). The trend will continue strongly, although not at this rate of doubling in every five years.

Economic and social attitudes are changing

At the beginning of the 1980s productivity in Japan is rising at "only" about 4 per cent a year against between 10 per cent and 20 per cent a year in 1968-73; value added is increasing by a similar proportion in 1980 but that is distinctly more than in the pre-crisis boom, when it rose very little. Both are expected to rise more significantly during the next decade (Fig 7) even though (alternatively some observers say because) working hours are expected to be reduced. A five day working week has been advocated by the public, by organisations and in opinion polls for many years past; the majority clearly in favour of it is now 70 per cent and its enactment is a probability for the 1980s. According to some sources it is applied as yet by only 6 per cent of firms in Japan, although other figures put the proportion as high as nearly a quarter. The explanation is that nearly half of all firms have some kind of compromise system giving occasional days off. Annual holidays are much shorter than in the West (five to ten days) but again there are practical adjustments and vacation time will surely be extended in the next few years. 20 per cent of the population took a winter holiday last year.

Social dissolution is seen by some in the increase of divorces revealed by a recent social survey, the first on the subject for ten years. The number of divorces reached a record in 1979 at 132,000 decrees granted. 56 per cent of the divorced women said they did not wish to remarry, a reversal of previous attitudes. Yet alimony is rare in Japan and most divorced women have to work. The conclusions of the survey add a useful epitome of the demography of an advanced society with a large and ageing population; there is a divorce every three minutes, a birth every 19 seconds, a marriage every 40 seconds and a death every 46 seconds.

Japan in the 1980s will become similar to other advanced countries, although it is aware of some of the unfavourable features in the Western models and hopes to avoid them. This does not mean it will lose its special characteristics any more than it did in the modification undergone in the past 100 years. In the process of still further Westernisation, there will be some strong reactionary currents which will also be seized upon by the critics. Neither political nor intellectual trends show any great tendency to reactionary thought, but it is interesting to sample once more the opinion polls of recent dates. Regarding attitudes to foreigners, the Japanese have recently shown their national confidence. Asked in a poll in 1953 "are the Japanese superior or inferior to the Occidentals?", the "inferiors" and "superiors" were equally balanced; 25 years later the "superiors" had come into only a slight majority, but the discussion was much more sophisticated, with counter questioning on "superior in what?" Early in 1980, the younger generation attached much more importance than was shown in earlier surveys to the traditional values such as a child's duty to its parents. A reaction against materialism and towards fatalism, and a feeling that aggressive attitudes on life should become less uncompromising, is interpreted from one series of responses to the remarkable question "should man, in order to be happier, obey, capitalise on, or conquer Nature?". Before 1960, 27 per cent falling to 20 per cent, said "obey", 50 per cent falling to 45 per cent, said "capitalise" and the number answering "conquer" rose from 23 per cent to 34 per cent. In 1978, contrastingly, 31 per cent of respondents thought "obey", 52 per cent "capitalise" and only 17 per cent considered that the path to happiness was to "conquer" Nature.

There is much more uncertainty about materialist values shown also in answers to the question "should children be told that money is the most important thing in life?" In 1953 65 per cent responded "yes" and 35 per cent "no"; in 1978 only 24 per cent replied "yes", 40 per cent answered "no" and 36 per cent were uncertain. The proposition that "the fruits of science and technology are making human beings less human" has been supported by a small but increasing majority. It is probable, however, that many responses reflect higher prosperity; people can now afford more culture and leisure; the marginal utility of money has diminished and fewer people need to overcome immediate adversities. Respect for temporal authority was strikingly reaffirmed recently when 90 per cent of the people were willing to accept cuts in fuel consumption. Inwardly the Japanese are not so Americanised as they are outwardly; nevertheless, the outward and extrovert side is going to make a formidable showing in the 1980s.

Some of the most hardened myths about Japan are subject to change. A leading one, in Western commentaries, is that of loyalty to the firm being a centuries old or almost generic feature of Japanese life. It is certainly strong, as one of the group loyalties that strongly affect the Japanese. Employees like to join a successful and prestigious firm in which they can spend their whole working lives in secure employment on a defined ladder of promotion. This attitude, except for a few at the top and some highly dependent workers at the bottom, dates only from the period around the first world war. It became general in the 1920s under the pressure as much of the trade unions, which were demanding job security, as of the employers. Thereafter it suited the military and fascistical outlook of those who cam to power in the 1930s. Even this element may be eroded in the changing Japan of the 1980s, although the currents will be conflicting, as the opinion polls show; personal security or reassurance is being sought in new rather than traditional forms. At present the older generation of Japanese managers, approaching retirement and looking for successors, frequently aver that they cannot find successors who are not only qualified to replace them but also motivated to do so. With every allowance for the outlook of the middle aged man in that position, it is clear that the rising generation is in favour of a more balanced life.

Hours of work -

The index of total industrial production (Table 8) rose in the second half of the 1970s in Japan about 16 per cent more than in the UK, France and Italy, 9 per cent more than in West Germany and 4 per cent more than in the USA. Japan is expected to maintain that lead in the growth of output.

Table 8

Index of Industrial Production

(1975=100)	1973	1978	Jul 1979
Japan	117	123	134
USA	110	124	130
West Germany	109	113	123
UK	110	110	116
Italy	105	116	116[a]
France	104	111	115[a]

a   June 1979.

The fall in industrial production after the oil crisis has thus been much more than recovered in Japan, and output is expected to rise by a quarter or more in every five years. The intensity of working of plant capacity (Table 9) fell, as a result of the oil crisis, much more than did output, but this too has shown a marked recovery; even in the most depressed sector, iron and steel, it is now almost back to 1975 levels, although still more than a quarter below the 1973 peak.

Table 9

Operating Rates in Japanese Industry

(1975=100)

	1973	1978	Aug 1979
Total	128	111	113
Above average			
Non-ferrous metals & products	153	132	134
Chemicals	131	109	124
Pulp, paper & products	130	114	120
Petroleum & coal products	129	114	120
Machinery	130	118	115
Below average			
Ceramics	132	113	112
Textiles	115	104	108
Fabricated metal products	146	103	107
Iron & steel	128	91	99

Industrial capacity is accordingly well utilised, but with great variations between industries. The use of workers and plant is swiftly and smoothly being switched from the less active and less promising activities to the busier and expanding ones. The big firms naturally take the lead in this; Mitsubishi, for example, has switched workers and equipment from its shipbuilding yards to automobile, engine and other works. But is is not limited to the giant plants; it extends to medium and even small industry as well in the highly interlocked Japanese structure.

The number of hours worked in Japan (Table 10) show a broadly similar picture. After a fall of some 20 per cent in 1975 compared with 1973, over all industries, the figures are nearly back to their 1973 peak. The rising labour intensity is especially marked in the manufacturing sector, where the hours worked are fully back to the 1973 record. Overtime constitutes 7 per cent rising to 8 per cent of the hours worked in industry generally, and in manufacturing 8 per cent rising to 9 per cent. It is notable that overall the number of overtime hours worked is still 14 per cent below the 1973 maximum, but in manufacturing it has risen again to the 1973 level.

Table 10

Monthly Hours Worked in Japan

All industries	1973	1975	1979[a]
No. of hours	182.0	175.2	176.0
of which: overtime	15.4	12.3	13.3
%	8.8	7.0	8.0
Manufacturing			
No. of hours	182.0	175.6	182.5
of which: overtime	16.8	13.7	16.4
%	9.0	8.0	9.0
Indices (1973=100)			
All industries			
Hours	100	96	97
of which: overtime	100	80	86
Manufacturing			
Hours	100	96	100
of which: overtime	100	82	98

a Estimated rate for the year 1979 based on returns up to July.

– pay for leisure activities

The tables above show the working pattern. What is the exact pattern for the leisure hours? Table 11 analyses the expenditure of the average household in Japan, in recent years, on leisure activities. The amounts are at current prices, including inflation, but all outlays have increased in real terms, and there are some interesting shifts in the relative emphasis on travel and other categories of expenditure. All these trends are continuing strongly. The future portends a work hard, play hard mode of life for the Japanese, but with play gaining distinctly on work. The Japanese will continue to enjoy work, but grow more serious about their play.

Table 11

Expenditure of Average Japanese Household on Leisure Pursuits

	1973		1975			1979[a]	
	'000 yen	%	'000 yen	%	Index (1973=100)	'000 yen	Index (1973=100)
Publications	22	17	42	19	189	46	211
Listening & admissions[b]	7	5	10	5	149	14	201
Recreational goods	27	21	49	22	180	54	199
Travel	21	16	40	18	153	54	263
Day trips	14	11	21	10	193	...	...
Use of leisure facilities[c]	6	5	12	5	198	...	...
Sports & hobbies	11	9	15	7	134	...	...
Meals taken with family outside home	18	15	30	14	161	...	...
Total	126	100	218	100	173	...	...

a Rate for the year 1979, estimated from returns for the first seven months.
b Radio, theatre and cinema tickets, etc.   c Entry charges to gymnasia, etc, and hire of gear.

CHAPTER 4.

TRENDS IN TRADE

Japan's exports are widely distributed

Fig 2 illustrates the relative dependence of Japan and other countries on each other in terms of exports. It takes the degree to which countries or groups of countries depend on exports for their national incomes together with the proportions of Japan's exports that go to each country or area, and the proportion of the latter's exports that go to Japan. Japan's exports represent some 12 per cent of its GNP, while those of the others vary greatly. Japan's maximum dependence (on the USA) is relatively low and all its other dependences very low. Japan's exports are widely distributed. The Middle East's export dependence on Japan is high because it is dependent on exports (oil) for half its GNP and it exports much to Japan. China's export base is very narrow (as yet) but much of its exporting is to Japan. The growth rates of east Asian countries, and of Australasia, are closely correlated with the growth rate of Japan, since a rise in Japan's GNP enables it to buy more, particularly from them. Japan is dependent on exports for up to 14 per cent of its GNP, compared with the UK's 31 per cent, West Germany's 28 per cent, Canada's 24 per cent, France's 20 per cent and the USA's low 8 per cent.

The geographical and commodity pattern of Japan's trade is summarised in Table 12 and 13 (see pages 36, 37). Table 12 shows Japan's exports shifting rapidly away from simple metal goods and light industry products into machinery; it now sends more to North America and South East Asia, and less to Latin America, Africa and Oceania. Table 13 shows Japan's imports also rising greatly in total but the proportion from the USA and that from Africa is falling and the percentages from South East Asia and Europe rising a little. Fig 3 shows the trend and the balances of trade. Japan had surpluses with all its trade partners, except for a relatively small deficit with Oceania and a large deficit with west Asia. The deficit with west Asia has been reduced by some 14 per cent, however, as a result of a near trebling of Japanese exports to the oil states. The deficit should continue to be reduced, but by no more than a half in the 1980s for, even assuming no more runaway rises in the price of oil, west Asia will not be able in that space of time to absorb so many of Japan's products.

Future trade patterns depend on world economic development

International trade imbalances, already an acute problem, will intensify in the 1980s if the present trend continues. A number of extrapolations from the trend in the 1970s are given below, in illustration of the extremely one sided situations that could arise from various countries if they continue to incur such large and increasing deficits in their trade with Japan. But extensive economic development in east Asia and other less developed regions could change the whole picture by multiplying the turnovers of all concerned. The matter is suitably depicted by the well known S-curve of economic development (see Fig 4).

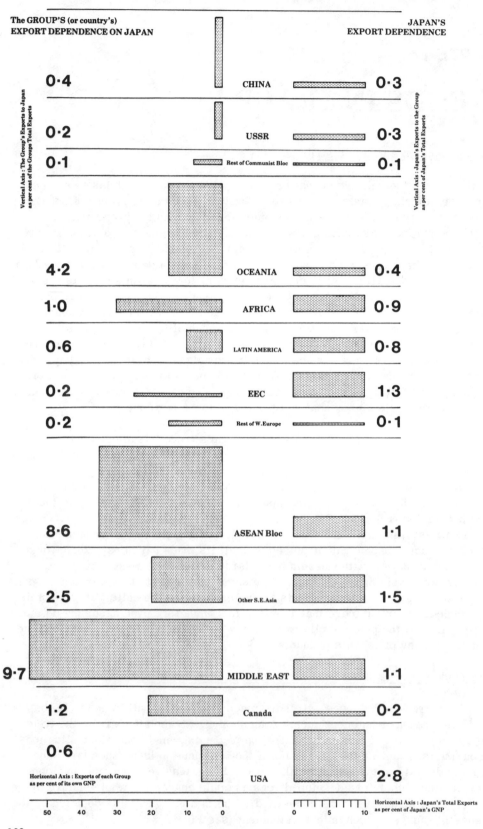

Figure 2. **INTERDEPENDENCE ON EXPORTS : $ Values, 1977** AREA OF RECTANGLE GIVES THE INDEX :
Shown by the large arabic numeral

The GROUP'S (or country's)
EXPORT DEPENDENCE ON JAPAN

JAPAN'S
EXPORT DEPENDENCE

Vertical Axis : The Group's Exports to Japan
as per cent of the Group's Total Exports

Vertical Axis : Japan's Exports to the Group
as per cent of Japan's Total Exports

Group's dependence		Japan's dependence
0·4	CHINA	0·3
0·2	USSR	0·3
0·1	Rest of Communist Bloc	0·1
4·2	OCEANIA	0·4
1·0	AFRICA	0·9
0·6	LATIN AMERICA	0·8
0·2	EEC	1·3
0·2	Rest of W.Europe	0·1
8·6	ASEAN Bloc	1·1
2·5	Other S.E.Asia	1·5
9·7	MIDDLE EAST	1·1
1·2	Canada	0·2
0·6	USA	2·8

Horizontal Axis : Exports of each Group
as per cent of its own GNP

50   40   30   20   10   0

0   5   10   Horizontal Axis : Japan's Total Exports
as per cent of Japan's GNP

162

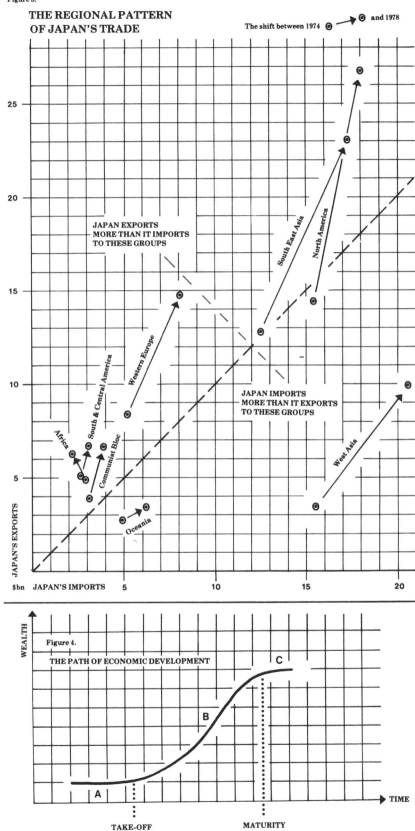

Figure 3.

THE REGIONAL PATTERN OF JAPAN'S TRADE

The shift between 1974 ⊚ ⟶ ⊚ and 1978

JAPAN EXPORTS
MORE THAN IT IMPORTS
TO THESE GROUPS

JAPAN IMPORTS
MORE THAN IT EXPORTS
TO THESE GROUPS

South East Asia

North America

Western Europe

South & Central America

Africa

Communist Bloc

West Asia

Oceania

JAPAN'S EXPORTS

$bn   JAPAN'S IMPORTS   5   10   15   20

25

20

15

10

5

WEALTH

Figure 4.

THE PATH OF ECONOMIC DEVELOPMENT

A

B

C

TAKE-OFF

MATURITY

TIME

163

Table 12

Japan's Main Exports by Type and Region, 1974 and 1978
($ bn)

	% of all Japanese exports		North America		South East Asia		Western Europe		West Asia		Communist countries		Central & South America		Africa		Oceania	
	1974	1978	1974	1978	1974	1978	1974	1978	1974	1978	1974	1978	1974	1978	1974	1978	1974	1978
Foodstuffs	1.0	1.0	0.2	0.3	0.2	0.3	–	–	–	0.1	–	–	0.1	0.1	0.1	0.1	–	–
Raw materials & fuels	1.0	1.0	–	–	0.3	1.8	–	–	–	1.0	–	–	–	–	–	–	–	–
Textiles	7.0	5.0	0.2	0.8	1.4	1.8	0.3	0.3	0.4	0.7	0.5	0.4	0.1	0.2	0.4	0.4	0.2	0.2
Ceramics	1.0	1.0	0.2	0.4	–	–	–	–	–	0.3	–	–	0.2	0.2	–	–	–	–
Other light industry products	8.0	7.0	0.7	1.4	0.7	1.5	0.6	1.2	0.3	0.5	–	–	–	–	0.1	0.2	–	–
Chemical goods	7.0	5.0	0.6	0.6	1.6	2.5	0.6	0.6	1.0	2.0	0.5	0.7	0.3	0.2	0.1	0.1	0.2	0.2
Metal goods	25.0	16.0	3.7	3.8	3.0	4.2	1.3	0.8	1.4	2.2	1.3	2.8	1.6	1.1	0.6	0.8	0.5	0.4
General machinery	50.0	64.0	1.0	2.9	2.0	4.5	0.8	1.5	0.3	1.7	0.2	0.3	0.6	1.0	0.3	0.8	0.2	0.4
Electrical machinery			2.4	5.0	1.4	3.6	1.3	3.2	0.3	1.7			0.4	1.0	0.3	0.7	0.3	0.5
Transport machinery			3.9	9.6	1.5	3.3	2.2	5.0	0.4	2.1			1.5	1.4	2.9	3.3	0.6	1.1
Precision machinery			0.5	1.6	0.3	0.8	0.5	1.4	–	0.4			0.1	0.2	–	–	–	0.1
Re-exports & unclassified			0.2	0.3	–	–	–	0.1	–	–	–	–	–	–	–	–	–	–
Total	100.0	100.0	13.6	26.8	12.4	24.3	7.6	14.1	4.1	12.7	2.5	4.2	4.9	5.4	4.8	6.4	2.0	2.9
% of all Japan's exports			27	30	24	25	10	9	6	11	7	7	10	7	9	7	5	4

164

Table 13

Japan's Main Imports, by Type and Region, 1974 and 1978
($ bn)

	% of all Japan's imports		North America		South East Asia		Western Europe		West Asia		Communist countries		Central & South America		Africa		Oceania	
	1974	1978	1974	1978	1974	1978	1974	1978	1974	1978	1974	1978	1974	1978	1974	1978	1974	1978
Foodstuffs	13.0	14.0	3.2	4.4	1.5	2.6	0.5	0.9	–	–	0.3	0.9	0.9	0.8	0.5	0.6	1.0	1.4
Textile raw materials	3.0	3.0	0.4	0.4	0.1	0.2	–	–	–	–	0.3	0.4	0.3	0.4	0.3	0.1	0.5	0.6
Metallic raw materials	8.0	6.0	1.3	1.0	1.0	1.0	–	–	–	–	–	–	0.8	0.9	0.3	0.3	1.7[c]	1.6[c]
Other raw materials	12.0	11.0	3.2	4.1	2.3	2.6	–	–	–	–	0.7	0.8	0.1	0.1	0.3	0.2	0.3	0.4
Fuels[a]	40.0	40.0	2.1	1.5	–	–	–	–	–	–	0.7	1.1	–	–	–	–	0.9[d]	1.7[d]
Chemical goods	4.0	5.0	1.0	1.5	–	–	1.0	1.5	–	–	–	–	–	–	–	0.1	–	–
Machinery & equipment	8.0	8.0	2.6	3.1	–	–	1.7	2.6	–	–	–	–	–	–	–	–	–	–
Other manufacturing goods	–	–	1.4	1.8	–	–	1.5	2.0	–	–	0.8	0.9	0.5	0.6	0.1	0.4	–	–
Petroleum products	–	–	–	–	1.0	1.0	–	–	0.8	1.0	–	–	–	–	–	–	–	–
Crude & semi refined oil	–	–	–	–	3.7	4.4	–	–	15.4	20.6	–	–	–	–	0.9	–	–	–
Other mineral fuels	–	–	–	–	0.2	1.1	–	–	–	–	–	–	–	–	–	–	–	–
Manufactured goods	–	–	–	–	2.4	4.2	–	–	–	–	–	–	–	–	–	–	–	–
Others	12.0	12.0	–	–	–	0.1	–	–	–	–	0.2	0.2	–	–	0.4[e]	0.2[e]	–	–
Total	100.0	100.0	15.4	18.0	12.5	17.3	4.7	7.0	16.2	21.6	3.1	4.3	2.7	3.0	2.9	1.9	4.9	6.2
% of all Japan's imports			25.0	23.0	20.0	22.0	8.0	9.0	25.0	27.0	5.0	5.0	4.0	4.0	5.0	2.0	8.0	8.0

a See also entries below; classifications vary. b Includes sugar $0.6 bn in 1974; coffee $0.2 bn in 1978; animal feeds $0.1 bn in 1974; and others $0.2 bn in 1974; $0.6 bn in 1978. c Of which: Iron ore $1 bn in 1974 and $1.1 bn in 1978. d Of which: coal $0.7 bn in 1974 and $1.5 bn in 1978. e Copper and copper alloys.

165

China and other less developed countries are at the start of the curve, where swiftly increasing returns are not yet in sight. Japan, like the West, is on the higher plateau where increasing returns are again difficult. The swift risers are on the middle of the curve; these are countries like the NICs. If all the less developed countries reach this segment of the curve, the picture would be transformed, and it is on this calculation that Japanese optimism for the future is based. Japan is more closely involved than other countries in the possibilities and problems of worldwide development; in its own estimation, and that of its admirers, it approaches this whole question more purposefully, with more local knowledge and more efficiently than others do.

The Pacific Basin could play a larger role in Japan's trade

Japan's horizon as a nation helping the less developed countries industrialise - obscured only by the more immediately crucial preoccupation with the oil problem - is a wide one. One of the most interesting of the concepts of the pattern of development, already mentioned above as being to the fore in Japan, is the pan Pacific concept. Its origins may stem from the time when the USA, after the Vietnam war, fell back militarily to the easternmost perimeter of Asia - a line including Japan, the Philippines and Australasia - and in reaction to European efforts at integration. Such shifts were, however, clearly far from total, east Asia continuing in business and all other respects to be fully connected and involved with both parts of the West and with the whole of the rest of the world. At the same time the USA established more optimistic relations with China.

Discussion in terms of the Pacific Basin does not imply that that hemisphere will turn away from the rest of the world. The eight countries and regions in the Pacific, with the exception of Japan, have increased the proportion of their trade that is with non-Pacific Basin countries. All of them remain dependent to a high degree on links beyond the Pacific, as Table 14 (see below) shows. It gives the ratio of the trade of each country within the Pacific Basin to the trade of each with non-Pacific Basin nations (the latter as 1.0). All conduct more trade within the Pacific Basin than outside it; some are increasingly doing so, some decreasingly. The figures for China are exceptional, that country being at an earlier stage of entering into international trade; it is expected to be more Pacific minded in future, but the percentage figures for China in this table are, of course, relative. There is a weighting in the figures towards the "rest of the world", swaying the ratios for Japan, especially, in that direction, in the need to get oil from west Asia and to export as much as possible to pay for it.

Table 14

Trade Within and Outside the Pacific Basin, by Value
(Trade within the Pacific Basin as a multiple of trade outside it)

	Exports			Imports		
	1967	1977	% change	1967	1977	% change
Japan	1.8	1.5	-17	1.6	1.2	-25
China	1.0	1.5	50	0.75	2.0	167
Other Far East	2.0	2.0	-	3.5	2.8	-20
Asean	2.3	2.6	13	1.8	1.8	-
USA	1.0	1.0	-	1.5	1.2	-20
Canada	3.0	3.8	27	4.3	4.3	-
Latin America	1.0	1.2	20	1.7	1.5	-12
Oceania	1.1	1.6	45	0.9	1.5	67
Total	1.5	1.7	13	1.6	1.8	13

This Pacific Basin thesis is, however, only one of the lines of thought in Japan. Its usefulness is limited. The dependences in Table 14 are more directly indicative, against the background that Japan is dependent on oil from the Middle East, raw materials from Asean, Oceania and elsewhere, and technology from the USA and Europe, while the Asian NICs are moving closely into a Japan-like condition. Table 15 (see page 41) which gives a simplified overall view by reducing all the entries for a recent decade (the most up to date complete returns available) to round figures to the nearest billion, shows that the total world trade of the eight countries and areas increased about five times in that period (at current prices), but that of the Asian Pacific countries increased seven to nine times, that of the North and South Americas increased four times, while that of Australia and New Zealand only doubled. The shares of the USA, Canada and Latin America in the world total have accordingly fallen but Japan's has nearly doubled, the NICs have increased their percentage shares and China is moving up the table.

Growth expectations for the 1980s –

The trends shown above are still operative in 1980, but what are the prospects for the rest of the decade? In ten years there can be many changes, but not such as to upset the existing pattern radically, especially as far as international trade is concerned, not such as to change fundamentally the trends of the preceding decade. New trends could set in, but are unlikely to become very powerful or widespread within a ten year period. The assumption is adhered to - in Japan at any rate - that things will continue (in terms of the general health of the world economy and the conditions of industries and markets) broadly the same as at the end of the 1970s in the economic sphere. The course of Japan's trade from 1974 to to 1978 is summarised in Tables 12 and 13. This assumption derives from careful consideration of the favourable and unfavourable factors, which are expected broadly to be in balance, or even to incline towards a determined and energetic nation like Japan which is clear minded about both its handicaps and its opportunities. On that basis the conclusions on the expected pattern of trade for the Pacific Basin countries are given in Table 16, as a simple extrapolation for 1987 from 1977 of the continuance of the trends from 1967 to 1977. The figures are in 1977 values.

The expectation is that the USA will retain the largest share in the trade of the whole zone, although a diminishing one, with Japan closely approaching it and quite likely to catch it up by 1990; the NICs and Asean countries are expected to follow much the same course as Japan. Latin America is expected to achieve a similar trade expansion, particularly its NICs Mexico and Brazil, but that trade will be largely within the Americas and elsewhere rather than across the Pacific. China will move forward, but is not expected to become a major component in international trade until some time later. Its reliance on exports for income is low (Fig 2), and industrialisation there is no easy task.

Table 15

Exports of the Pacific Basin, 1968 and 1978
($ bn at current prices)

To:	Japan		China		Other Far East[a]		Asean		USA		Canada		Latin America		Oceania		Total Pacific		Rest of world		Grand total		Increase
From:	1968	1978	1968	1978	1968	1978	1968	1978	1968	1978	1968	1978	1968	1978	1968	1978	1968	1978	1968	1978	1968	1978	1978/68
Japan	-	-	0.3	3.1	1.5	12.8	1.2	8.7	4.1	25.4	0.3	1.9	0.6	5.9	0.5	3.5	8.5	61.2	4.5	37.2	13.0	98.4	x7.5
China	0.2	1.9	-	-	0.4	2.1	-	0.8	-	0.3	-	0.1	-	0.1	-	0.2	0.6	5.4	0.6	3.1	1.2	8.4	x7
Other Far East[a]	0.3	5.1	-	0.1	0.1[b]	2.0[b]	0.3	2.8	1.1	12.5	0.1	0.9	-	0.8	0.1	1.0	2.0	25.1	1.0	11.5	3.0	36.7	x12
Asean	1.0	8.9	-	0.3	0.2	2.5	0.2[b]	5.0[b]	0.9	7.6	-	0.2	-	0.3	0.1	1.1	2.4	25.9	1.3	9.8	3.7	35.7	x9.5
USA	3.0	12.9	-	0.8	1.2	7.1	0.9	4.6	-	-	8.0	28.4	4.7	20.2	1.0	3.5	18.8	77.5	15.8	66.2	34.6	143.7	x4
Canada	0.6	2.7	0.2	0.4	-	0.4	0.1	0.3	8.5	32.5	-	-	0.3	1.6	0.2	0.4	9.9	38.3	2.7	9.6	12.6	47.9	x4
Latin America	0.6	2.3	-	0.3	-	0.4	-	0.7	4.0	15.6	0.4	1.7	1.4[b]	7.7[b]	-	0.1[b]	6.4	28.8	5.2	21.6	11.6	50.4	x4
Oceania	0.9	5.1	0.1	0.6	0.1	1.1	0.2	1.4	0.6	2.3	0.1	0.4	-	0.2	0.4[b]	1.9[b]	2.4	13.0	2.2	6.3	4.6	19.3	x4

a Hong Kong, South Korea and Taiwan.   b Trade within the group.

Table 16

Total Trade[a] of Countries of the Pacific Basin
($ bn in round figures)

| | 1967 | | 1977 | | 1987 (projected) | | |
	$ bn	% of total	$ bn	% of total	$ bn	% of total	Increase 1987/77
Japan	22	15	152	20	1,100	27	x7
China	2	1	13	2	200	4	x15
Other Far East	6	4	59	8	450	12	x8
Asean	10	7	62	8	350	9	x3
USA	59	39	277	36	1,300	32	x5
Canada	21	14	84	11	350	9	x4
Latin America	21	14	93	12	450	5	x5
Oceania	9	6	26	3	100	2	x4
Total	150	100	766	100	4,200	100	x5

a Exports plus imports.

- could be marred by conflict -

From Japan's viewpoint it is clear that there are many potential points of conflict
along this path of further trade expansion.   The prevailing atmosphere is of wide
and vigorous competition, but against a background of multinationalism and
negotiability as stressed above.   An additional aspect is terms of trade: the
prices of exports in relation to the cost of imports.   The aspect that most concerns
the developing countries in modern times is the same one that has historically given
most concern; the ratio between the prices of raw materials and the prices of manufactured goods.   Today all countries are concerned with the terms of trade for oil.
Another area of anxiety is the price ratio between the simpler manufactures and the
more sophisticated ones.   The terms of trade question is very much on the agenda
for the 1980s; the developing countries linking it to the wider perspective of planning
a new international economic order.   Japan, particularly, will be widely involved
in this. As an industrial country it holds the same position as the West in such
matters.   The NICs, as the appellation implies, are also moving into that position.
The Asian NICs do not have large home markets or indigenous raw material resources.
The non-Asian ones, Brazil particularly and Mexico to some extent, are comparatively well off in those respects.   The Asian NICs have a high propensity to export:
notably, Hong Kong has a higher figure for exports per head of population than any
other country in the world, and Singapore ranks high in this regard.

- over trade imbalances with Japan

Another area of particular importance to Japan - and to the east Asian countries
in general - is protectionist responses in the rest of the world.   At the present
level of trade turnover and business the recriminations and machinations in this field
are already of major concern; the prospect shown in the above tables of seven to
ninefold increases in the exports of Japan and east Asian countries greatly magnified
that concern.   Issues will focus especially on the imbalances in trade; the excess
of imports over exports that it is apparent from Table 19 (which makes projections
to 1989) would become very large in several key cases if the 1974-78 trend
continued.   Only Oceania has a trade surplus with Japan (Fig 2).   Owing to differential rates of trade growth, the adverse balances with other Western areas are likely

to double by the late 1980s. That might strain the tolerance of public opinion and vested interests in the debtor countries to the extent that protectionist or retaliatory measures were taken.

The only possible answer, as the Japanese in particular see it, is international discussion aimed at multilateral agreements, understandings and programmatic actions. One sphere where this is thought almost inevitable is in regard to oil. The Opec countries share the quandary of the monopolist - the balance between maximising profit and maximising sales. They do not want world economic decline which affects the poor countries as much as or more than the rich. They are also aware of the possibility of oil running out within one or two generations, during which time they need in any case to secure other bases for their own economies.

A regional pact?

The situation in east Asia seems likely to lead to a general move to a collaborative solution. The area contains a majority of the world's population, mostly poor, but extremely diverse - in levels and kinds of development, culture, political trends and aspirations, social and other situations. It is vitally concerned with many of the world's problems. China's emergence into global trade and politics, while modernising its own internal structure, affects the area on more than one level. China has a special influence in South East Asia, because of the large and enter-prising population of overseas Chinese. The matter of China could, moreover, be perilous to east Asia because of the deep antagonism and rivalry between China and the USSR, carrying risks of war that seem the more real after recent events in Indochina and Afghanistan. Islam, and the current perturbations within it, affect the whole region from the Middle East, Pakistan and Afghanistan through Bangladesh, Thailand and Malaysia to Indonesia and the Philippines. Most of the South East Asian countries in this further crescent have Moslem minorities (as do China and the USSR), with restive or even secessionist elements among them. Indonesia is mainly Moslem, but has other restive elements. In addition there are the worries caused by the situations in divided Korea and in Taiwan.

All the east Asian countries are undergoing swift economic development, at rates much above those of the Western countries, and are at a phase of development that is stressful economically, politically and socially. A regional pact or scheme for South East Asia's peace and progress is therefore advisable; it is not a fanciful idea, given all the pressures, that moves in the direction of a general regional and inter-regional understanding may mature in the 1980s. (For a more detailed exposi-tion, see the article by Stuart Kirby in Brassey's Defence Yearbook, RUSI, London 1980.) Such moves would have to be cogently prepared and coordinated. The present UN organisation cannot initiate them, although it might be able to help in servicing them. Besides the nations interested and concerned in the region (the USA, the EEC, Japan, China, Asean and all the countries in South East Asia or vitally linked with it) this could involve a relevant array of other essential partici-pants (Opec, the OECD, and business institutions and organisations). There is certainly some thinking in this direction in Japan, where the future is seen as fiercely competitive, but in the modern, systematic and technologised way, as befits a multinational era.

Table 17

Japan's Trade, by Region, 1974-78

| | Exports to: | | | | | Imports from: | | | | |
| | 1974 | | 1978 | | Increase | 1974 | | 1978 | | Increase |
	$ bn	(% of total exports)	$ bn	(% of total exports)	1978/74	$ bn	(% of total imports)	$ bn	(% of total imports)	1978/74
South East Asia	13	23	23	24	x1.8	13	20	17	22	x1.3
West Asia	3	6	10	10	x3.3	15	25	21	26	x1.4
North America	14	26	27	28	x1.9	15	25	18	23	x1.2
Central & South America	5	9	7	7	x1.4	3	4	3	4	x1.0
Africa	5	9	6	7	x1.2	3	5	2	3	x0.7
Oceania	3	5	3	4	x1.1	5	8	6	8	x1.2
Western Europe	8	15	15	15	x1.9	5	8	8	10	x1.6
Communist countries	4	7	7	7	x1.7	3	5	4	5	x1.3
Total	55	100	98	100	x1.7	62	100	80	100	x1.3

Projections for the next decade -

The Japanese are, therefore, surprisingly and persistently optimistic, as a result
of their confidence in their own ability and their conviction that international agreement can resolve difficulties and enhance economic development. If crude projections
are made on recent trade figures (as in Tables 17 and 18) huge increases and
imbalances are in sight internationally. The Japanese are (with few dissenters)
broadly confident that although trade imbalances are likely to occur in the 1980s
they will be digestible, or even agreeable, to the other nations. Japanese optimism
draws on careful study of the issue, as well as expressing the strength of Japanese
entrepreneur spirit.

At the end of the 1970s, Japan's exports and imports were distributed regionally
(by value) as shown in Table 17. South East Asia accounted for 25 per cent of Japan's
exports and   20 per cent of Japan's imports, North America for 25 per cent of
both the exports and imports of Japan, and Western Europe for 15 per cent of Japan's
exports and 10 per cent of its imports; the shares of the other regions were smaller.
West Asia's oil weighed heavily on the debit side from Japan's point of view,
accounting for a quarter of all Japan's imports in value; the whole of Japan's exports
to North America were just about sufficient to pay for this.

- leave Japan with a large trade deficit with west Asia -

Table 18 presents a simple extrapolation of what the figures for 1983 and 1989
would be if the trends in 1974-78 continued unchanged into the following five year
period, and again into the one after that. (The figures are, throughout, in terms
of price levels at the end of the 1970s.) This means that Japan's exports will rise
70 per cent in each quinquennium, while Japan's imports rise at the much lower rate
of 30 per cent per five years. The consequences for the balance of trade can be
seen in Table 18. The extrapolation is at once unacceptable as far as west Asia
is concerned. The high figures for Japan's exports to west Asia reflect the enormous
effort in the late 1970s by Japan to make an export drive into the oil countries,
when Japanese exports there more than tripled. Despite the absolute wealth of the
Near East and its great need for economic development on a wider basis, it is most
improbable that it can absorb a tripling of its shopping from Japan in each of the
next two five year periods. A result of the extrapolation is that west Asia will
take 50 per cent more goods from Japan than the whole of South East Asia in 1989,
and have a trade deficit with Japan by 1983, which would become a large one by
1989; this is hardly admissible as a realistic projection. Moreover, Opec has
already impaired the basic assumptions in the calculations that the situation would
continue as in the base period of 1974-78 when it imposed a further round of oil
price increases for 1979/80. The cost of Japan's oil imports from west Asia
in the next few years may well be higher than the assumed rise of about 10 per cent
a year, even if price rises become more moderate than at present.

As already noted, the Japanese hope for a multilateral or international settlement
of the world oil supply problem some time in the 1980s, and in the meantime hope
to arrange some bilateral solutions, or at least helpful arrangements for Japan
itself (for example: proceeding with the large Mitsui petrochemical complex in
Iran in exchange for assured deliveries of oil, and the exemption already obtained
by Japan from the Iranian ban on oil deliveries to the USA). A fair assumption may
perhaps be that the value of oil imports by Japan from west Asia will rise in cost
terms by 70 per cent rather than 40 per cent during the 1980s. So in Table 18 the

172

Table 18

Japan's Trade by Region, Extrapolation of 1974–78 Trend
($ bn)

	Exports to: 1978	1983	1989	Imports from: 1978	1983	1989	Balance 1978	1983	1989	Exports/imports 1978	1983	1989
South East Asia	23	41	74	17	22	29	6	19	45	x1.4	x1.9	x2.6
West Asia	10	33	110	21	29	41	-11	4	69	x0.5	x1.1	x2.7
North America	27	51	97	18	22	26	9	29	71	x1.5	x2.3	x3.7
Central & South America	7	10	14	3	3	3	4	7	11	x2.3	x3.3	x4.7
Africa	6	7	9	3	2	1	3	5	8	x2.0	x3.5	x9.0
Oceania	3	3	4	6	7	9	-3	-4	-5	x0.5	x0.4	x0.4
Western Europe	15	28	54	8	13	21	7	15	33	x1.9	x2.2	x2.6
Communist countries	7	12	20	4	5	7	3	7	13	x1.7	x2.4	x2.9
Total	98	185	382	80	103	137	18	82	245	x1.2	x1.8	x2.8
Revisions												
West Asia	10	20	30	21	36	61	-11	-16	-31	x0.5	x0.5	x0.5
Total	98	172	302	80	110	157	18	62	145	x1.2	x1.6	x1.9

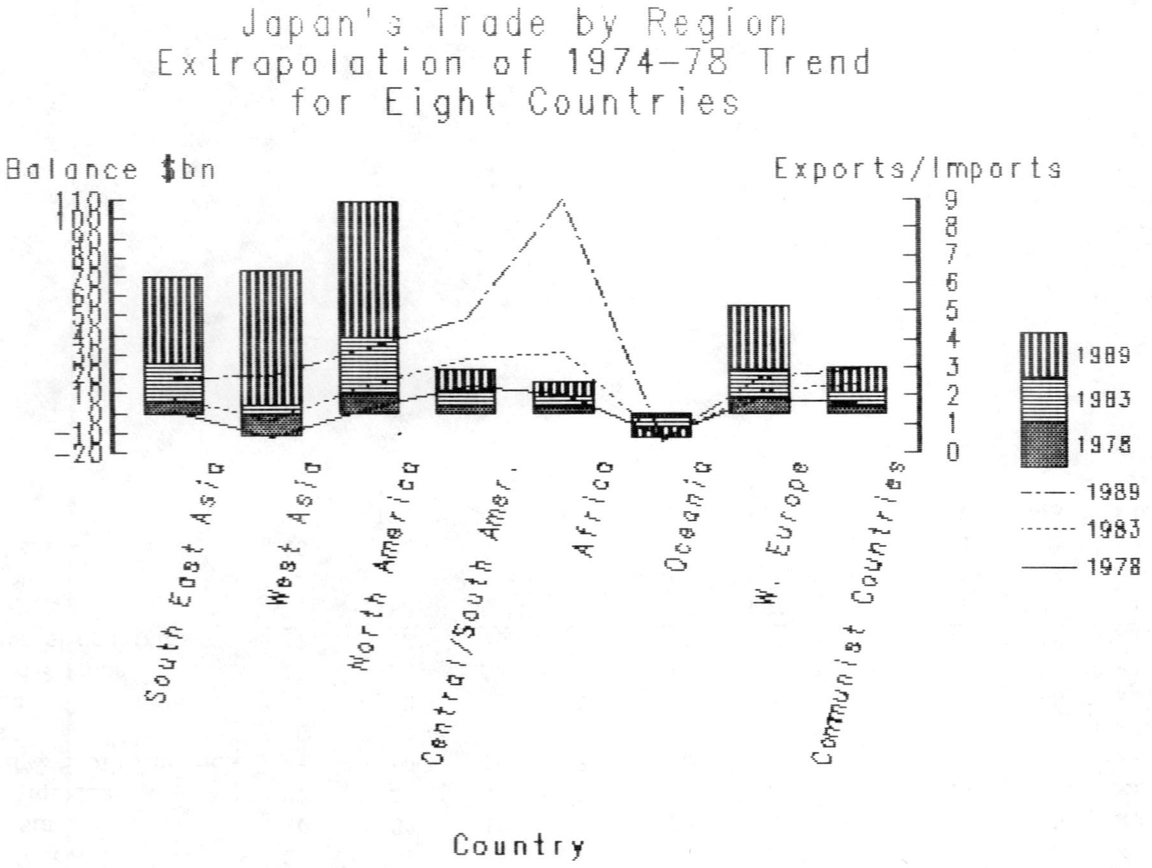

Japan's Trade by Region
Extrapolation of 1974–78 Trend
for Eight Countries

Figure 4a

174

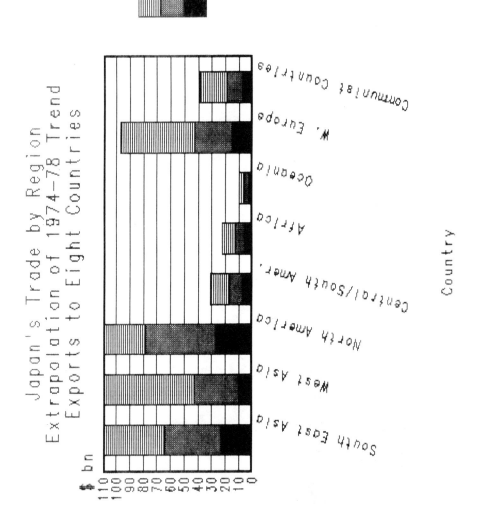

Japan's Trade by Region
Extrapolation of 1974-78 Trend
Exports to Eight Countries

Country

Figure 4b

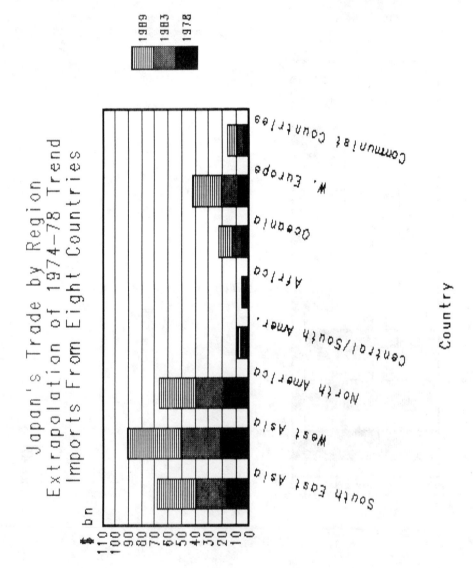

Japan's Trade by Region
Extrapolation of 1974-78 Trend
Imports From Eight Countries

1989
1983
1978

$ bn

110
100
90
80
70
60
50
40
30
20
10
0

South East Asia
West Asia
North America
Central/South Amer.
Africa
Oceania
W. Europe
Communist Countries

Country

Figure 4c

176

figures for west Asia and the totals must accordingly be readjusted to bring them nearer to the likely reality - as in the revisions noted at the foot of the table. This results in the more reasonable perspective of Japan continuing to cover half of its oil intake from west Asia by its exports to that region.

- but large surpluses elsewhere

The result,nevertheless, leaves Japan with a continuing heavy trade deficit with west Asia, which it must cover by increased efforts elsewhere; and Japan would still have huge surpluses with other regions which they may find intolerable. Another (minor) adjustment in the figures should also be noted. Those for Africa are abnormally low, because 1978 saw a particularly large drop in the main component of Japan's exports there, namely sales of ships, while, with possible progress towards more peaceful economic development in Africa, Japan may import substantially more from this continent in future. Africa is, however, a relatively small entry in the account, and there is not much need for another revision of Table 18 on this score. It must be stressed, however, that even the revised figures at the foot of Table 18 are widely considered to be too high. They are crude extrapolations, needing further discounting in the light of developments in the 1980s, but they are useful in highlighting the problems.

The major difficulties of imbalance are with west Asia, the USA and Western Europe. The prospects indicated up to the mid 1980s can perhaps be comparatively tolerable to the Western countries; a mere doubling of Japan's exports to North America while Japan's imports from it increase by only 25 per cent, leading to North America's adverse balance tripling; and,similarly, an approximate doubling of Japan's exports to Western Europe while its imports from there increase by about 50 per cent. But these perspectives will surely cause anxiety and friction. If, however, the same trends continued in the second half of the 1980s, the outlook would become much more disconcerting: Japan's exports would double again both to North America and to Western Europe; Japan's imports from North America would increase by only 25 per cent, although Western Europe's sales to Japan might rise 50 per cent. This would lead to colossal deficits for both the Western regions, and possibly to a disalignment in their attitudes to Japan.

Development in South East Asia and China will influence trade prospects

The prospects for world trade in general and Japan's in particular thus hinge primarily on solutions or accommodations to the oil crisis, secondly on an adjustment of trade relations with the two great Western groups, the USA and Europe. Of equal importance as the West to Japan is South East Asia. A "great (but soundly based) leap forward" in economic development in that region could transform the situation. This is a major focus of Japanese efforts and aspirations. The figures for South East Asia, in the tables here, show a rapidly increasing export surplus for Japan in that region. It must be stressed, however, that these exports consist largely of development goods (equipment and facilities for economic development) whereas Japan's exports to the West consist mostly of durable consumer goods. South Korea, Taiwan, Hong Kong and Singapore have already entered the stage of industrialisation, too, and another generation of NICs will enter it in the 1980s. A full industrial and commercial revolution can hardly be effected in South East Asia within the decade, but considerable progress is in prospect there, sufficient to ease the situation substantially for all concerned, but primarily for Japan, which has put the most into that region, in energy, capital and foresight.

The other emergent nation in east Asia is obviously China. The planned economies are not the easiest for the rest of the world to make predictions about. The considered judgment in this report is that China, too, will achieve considerable but slow development on its massive base, but not within the period attain a high position in international trade. The figures for the communist countries in Tables 17 and 18 constitute almost entirely the USSR, which has not dealt altogether smoothly with Japan and expresses bitter hostility to Japanese concepts and practices. But above all the USSR is hostile to China, and is suspicious of any move that might help China, and vice versa. The East European countries also have large and expanding relations with Japan. Japan is ably pursuing economic development relations with Vietnam, and is interested in collaborating with North Korea (which is industrially important), Laos and other minor elements in the Asian complex, contributing to an economically minor but politically important easing of tension in what is called by one Japanese writer the infra red part of the spectrum.

Japanese policy may be summed up here, from the trade point of view, as follows: to maintain the Japanese hardworking attitude and efficiency; to pursue concordats, which would have to be multinational if not worldwide, for the solution of the oil problem and of the problems of trade balances; to stress the development of South East East Asia; to evolve a new and positive relationship with China; and at the same time to restructure the economy and society of Japan itself, particularly to liberalise the home market with freer international trade, to change the production structure more deeply and more widely, to meet the new needs of the late 20th and the 21st century.

Invisible earnings may rise

Such restructuring raises another essential issue: the quality or composition of trade. Tables 17 and 18 assume the existing mix (in kind and value) of commodities, and cover only visible exports and imports. Japan expects greatly to develop its knowledge intensive and automated lines, which have high value added, while devolving the simpler and more traditional lines to South East Asia and other developing areas. A rise is probable in Japan's net invisible earnings through business services of all kinds and overseas investment. This can be of key importance, as illustrated in the UK, which broadly makes up its international deficit in visible trade by its invisible earnings. The city of Tokyo can hardly be expected to rival the City of London in this respect, but it can move somewhat in that direction (as also Hong Kong and Singapore can and are doing). In finance especially, this is obviously another sphere of international coordination and collaboration.

The figures used are, of course, for exports fob and for imports cif, and they are grossly rounded in the tables. Much of the cif (more accurately, much of the insurance and freight) goes to other countries. Only about 2-4 per cent of Japan's exports are at present priced in yen. In patent dealings, consultancy and other business service matters, Japan is a customer rather than a seller. Japanese enterprise is moving into these areas, both directly and in overseas associations. The field of finance involves some conflicts of interest within Japan, including the exchange rate question; some like a strong and supported yen, others dislike it. The Japanese government has so far remained cautious about opening the Japanese economy too widely, to international monetary instability. The question of inflation is a wide one which cannot be covered in the scope of this report; essentially, the Japanese standpoint and policy on it are close to those of West Germany.

178

The likely outcome

Expectations for trade are in general optimistic, as outlined above. Current projections are on the lines of Table 19. The USA's share will decline, as its trade with Japan increases less than total trade. South East Asia, which is about to play a much more important role in international trade than a crude projection from past trends shows, will top the USA in Japan's exports as well as Japan's imports. China will become of greater significance, not with startling rapidity but taking, say, twice as much as a straight projection from the end of the 1970s predicts. The USSR is also a large unit, but comparatively sluggish as far as international trade is concerned. Eastern Europe is more active, but at a lower quantitative level.

Japan's quest for basic resources may increase its dealings with Australasia, Latin America and Africa more than a crude extrapolation indicates, but these countries, too, cannot contribute so greatly to the volume of trade as the Western countries do. There remains the all important west Asia; Japan's exports to that region exceed $10 bn a year at present, and need to be multiplied by a factor of about eight to balance imports from it in ten years' time. Such a trend was actually taking place at the beginning of 1980, but it is widely doubted whether west Asia's intake from Japan can continue to be absorbed at such a high rate; perhaps a three-fold or fourfold increase is more feasible within the decade as a whole.

Table 19, therefore, represents a broad consensus of expectations in Japan at the beginning of the 1980s. It seems to give a reasonable prediction for the first half of the 1980s, but to imply such huge surpluses in the later 1980s, against the USA particularly, that the hoped for negotiability of such imbalances will be beyond the political and economic tolerance of the trading partner. The envisaged exports to non-Western destinations would be less unacceptable, because they are of development goods. Some of the Western markets, especially the USA, however, would be provoked to resistance more than they were encouraged by the consequent increase in global trade and development. However, for the first half of the 1980s at least, the figures in Table 19 do not seem unrealisable. In the meantime the world as a whole needs to work out a better and more thorough approach to Asia and world economic problems than it has so far contemplated. Japan will be a major agent in such rethinking.

Table 19

Japan's Trade by Region: Projections for the 1980s
($ bn at 1978 prices)

	Exports to:		Imports from:		Balance		Exports/Imp	
	1983	1989	1983	1989	1983	1989	1983	1989
North America	45	60	25	21	20	39	x1.8	x2.9
South East Asia	45	82	30	35	15	47	x1.5	x2.3
Western Europe	12	20	12	16	–	4	x1.0	x1.3
West Asia	27	55	28	37	–1	18	x0.9	x1.5
China	3	15	2	5	1	10	x1.5	x3.0
Comecon	10	12	4	5	6	7	x2.5	x2.4
Central & South America	8	10	3	6	5	4	x2.7	x1.7
Africa	8	10	3	5	5	5	x2.7	x2.0
Oceania	4	5	1	4	3	1	x4.0	x1.25
Total	164	269	108	134	56	135	x1.5	x2.0

CHAPTER 5.

BEYOND 1980

Prospects for inflation

One of the most immediate preoccupations in Japan is inflation. The Japanese do not worry about inflation as much as the West Germans, but they are,nevertheless, deeply conscious of the problem. In most countries it is common to blame rising prices on foreign countries and many Japanese believe high prices for their imports to be the main difficulty. This is certainly true as far as oil is concerned, but the view is less justified in the case of other imports. However, it is important that foreign suppliers should show themselves open to negotiation on the prices and the facilities they offer. Fig 5 shows how the rate of increase in dollar prices led the price increases in Japan during the oil crisis (1973-75), but after that (1976-78) their effect was greatly diminished, since dollar prices dropped much more than the indices of Japan's internal prices. In 1980 the graph of import prices is again rising above the zero line, but it is believed that in the next few years the rates of wholesale and consumer price rises will not accelerate again, whether from internal factors or from the external factor of the cost of imports, to anything like the crisis figures of 1973-75. The expectation is that they will run at around the 10-15 per cent level in the next four or five years.

The official view, which is broadly accepted, is based on confidence in the ability of the mixed economy to keep matters under control. The causes of price inflation are taken in Japan to be the following, in order: supply and demand relations (pull), costs (push), foreign influences (primarily prices of imports) and monetary factors. This ranking shows Japan remains a free economy, putting supply and demand first in the causal categories, but still a Keynesian mixed economy confident of adjusting itself through appropriate policies. Monetarism is not dominant, the currency supply being the last factor in this list. Fig 5 does not include the money supply.

Fig 6 presents the recent trend, showing the components of the inflation in wholesale prices in the 1970s. In 1972-75 foreign factors were the chief influence; demand fell rapidly in 1974/75 but labour costs pulled the graph of price increases upwards. Comparative stabilisation followed in 1975-79. By the first quarter of 1976 the increase in wholesale prices was about 3 per cent a year, adverse factors being the exchange rate, accounting for about one percentage point in the 3 per cent, and rising labour costs and rising demand which added about two percentage points each, while other, favourable, factors brought the figure down by two percentage points. By early 1979 wholesale prices were declining slightly (about 1 per cent per annum) when the inflationary effects of import prices (representing nearly 7 per cent upward pressure) and rising demand (another 2 per cent upward pressure) were offset by a much more favourable exchange rate (about 7 per cent, thus counter-balancing the effect of import prices) and other factors which improved matters by about five percentage points. The graph for the future course of wholesale prices in the 1980s is expected to repeat the pattern for the period from mid 1975 to mid 1979, with similar rises and falls in the rate of inflation; but these swings

INTERNAL AND EXTERNAL PRICES

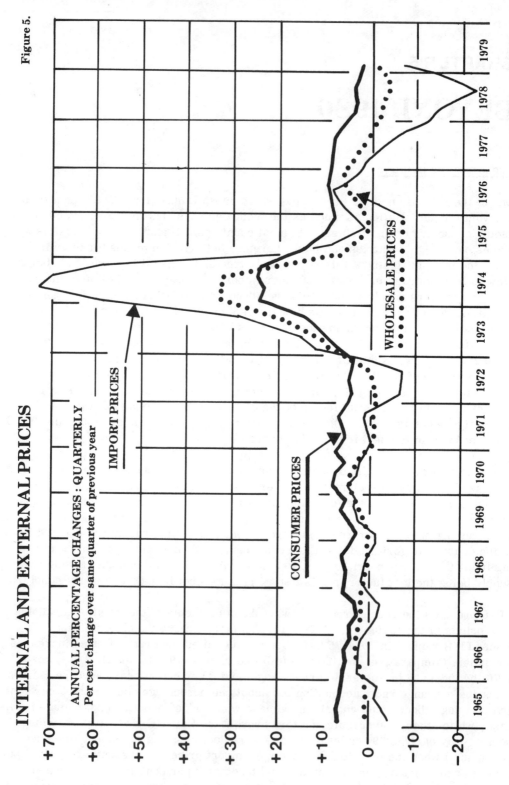

Figure 5.

ANNUAL PERCENTAGE CHANGES : QUARTERLY
Per cent change over same quarter of previous year

IMPORT PRICES

CONSUMER PRICES

WHOLESALE PRICES

Source : MITI and FUJI BANK

182

are expected to be of greater amplitude, as shown by the projection in Fig 6. The curve's shape depends on the components; labour costs, import costs, demand pull, the exchange rate, monetary policy and other responses.

Increased productivity is to be the counterbalance

Labour costs per unit of output represent the internal factor through which it is hoped principally to reduce the adverse effects; the aim is to improve productivity still further while giving labour a rising share in national income. That larger share, with total income rising, will give the workers substantial raises which will satisfy them while at the same time ensure that productivity rises even more. Fig 7 gives a further illustration. It shows the rate of increase, year by year, in the average worker's wages; the rise in productivity, which offsets the wage rises; the rate of increase in prices, which offsets the workers' wage gain, but is again offset by the increase in the workers' share in total national income; while the rate of increase in value added is the other factor in the total result. The effect of the oil crisis (end of 1973 through to the first quarter of 1979) is again obvious. Subsequently all the graphs in this set evened out again, generally to their pre-crisis levels.

It is believed that in the 1980s the trends will continue moderately favourable, on the following reasoning. Wage rises, at present moderate, may resume their pre-oil crisis level and course. Productivity should, however, rise even higher and accelerate. The wage gains will be negated by price increases. Labour is expected to accept a moderate though distinct increase in its share of the growing national income. Wage increases in the "spring offensive" in 1979 (the annual season when general wage settlements are rather comprehensively negotiated in a more orderly way than in Western economies) were about 6 per cent overall. The spring settlements in 1980, not yet in train as this report was being written, may show greater increases, but rates like those in the UK, where up to 20 per cent is now normally demanded, are not in sight in Japan. Last, but it is hoped not least, value added is required to rise much above its present static trend of merely maintaining its (not altogether low) level.

The projection lines in Fig 7 therefore demonstrate a calculated optimism, and Japan has achieved such rising trends before. The analysis is much more well thought out and more widely discussed in the media than in other countries.

Economic summary

Japan thus entered the 1980s in an optimistic spirit. The government's target for the growth rate was 6 per cent or less but, particularly as overtime working was again increasing, the actual rate appeared to be some 7 or 8 per cent. Effective or hard core unemployment is believed in business circles to be distinctly less than the official figure of about 5 per cent if deductions are made at one end of the scale for the increasing numbers retiring and at the other end for the increasing number of young persons continuing into further education (about 45 per cent of school leavers now go on to some form of college education, some of whose studies will emphasise knowledge intensive industrial lines).

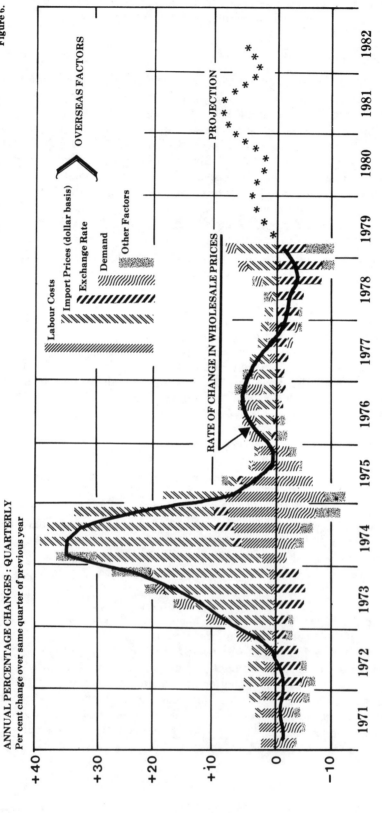

PRICES IN JAPAN : COMPONENT FACTORS

ANNUAL PERCENTAGE CHANGES : QUARTERLY
Per cent change over same quarter of previous year

Figure 6.

184

WAGES, PRODUCTIVITY AND INFLATION

Figure 7.

ANNUAL PERCENTAGE CHANGES : QUARTERLY
Per cent change over same quarter of previous year

W : Total Expenditure on Labour ✳
<u>L</u> : Total Number of Employees

A. RATE OF INCREASE IN PER CAPITA WAGES

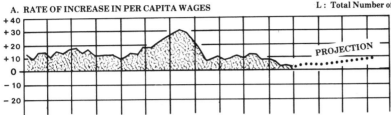

O : Output (volume)
<u>L</u> : Total Number of Employees

B. OFFSET BY INCREASE IN PRODUCTIVITY

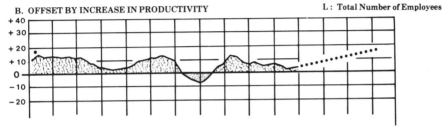

P : Price Index for Manufactured Goods

C. OFFSET BY PRICE INCREASES

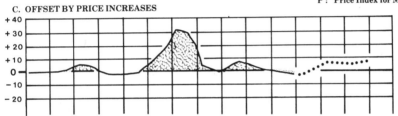

W : Total Expenditure on Labour ✳
<u>V</u> : Value Added ✲

D. OFFSET BY INCREASE IN INCOME DISTRIBUTED TO LABOUR

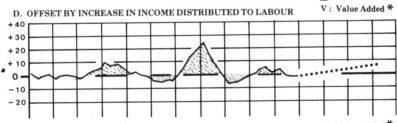

V : Value Added ✲
<u>S</u> : Sales

E. OFFSET BY HIGHER ADDED VALUE

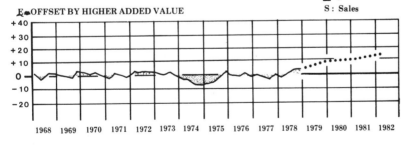

1968 1969 1970 1971 1972 1973 1974 1975 1976 1977 1978 1979 1980 1981 1982

✳ includes amenities and facilites   ✲ Current Profits plus Interest and Discounts Paid
minus W plus Depreciation

Source : FUJI BANK REVIEW

A new wave of inflation early in 1980 had no demoralising effect. In general, over the last few years, the rise in the money supply has been kept at around 10 per cent. Inflation peaked momentarily in the late 1970s at 28 per cent and was followed by large wage increases, reaching nearly 33 per cent at their maximum. In March 1980 inflation rose to about 20 per cent. Nothing like these figures is forecast; and wage settlements are expected to be relatively moderate, and monetary pressure to slacken.

Investment in plant rose 10 per cent in 1979; it was to a marked extent led by the smaller firms. It is expected to amount to 17 per cent of output in 1980/81. The rate of personal saving is high, though consumer spending has again been on the increase since September 1978.

Labour productivity is encouraging. It rose between 1967 and 1973 at an annual rate of 19 per cent on average, and it is believed that there could be a gradual reversion to that rate; it was 8 per cent in 1978 and 10 per cent in 1979. In the West in 1978, only France had a rate above 10 per cent; West Germany's rate was similar to Japan's at 7.9 per cent, while the figure for the USA was 5.1 per cent and for the UK 4.2 per cent. In 1977/78 average hours worked per week were 40.8 in Japan, 38.3 in the UK, 37.9 in France, 36.8 in the USA and 36.3 in West Germany.

The value of exports is high. Two years ago the Japanese were able to compete at 190 yen to the dollar; in early 1980 the yen was considered to be much undervalued at about 250 to the dollar. The volume of exports has been maintained, so dollar earnings remain satisfactory. Profits were roughly 40 per cent in 1979, reportedly 25 per cent in March 1980 and expected to be 30 per cent in 1981. The exchange rate question is thus a constant concern, but with the emphasis on the ability to compete (like West Germany and Switzerland) even if rates of exchange are high. The correct rate of exchange for the yen was considered in March 1980 to be about 210 to the dollar. Some observers see it reaching about 109 to the dollar in the 1980s.

With the prime rate in the USA and elsewhere running high (17.25 per cent to about 20 per cent in the USA in March 1980), an outflow of fu ¹s from Japan to take advantage of the higher interest rates abroad is a natural reaction. In 1978/79, some observers estimated such outflow to have been as much as $7 bn; most put the figure at something less than this, but all agreed it was large. Against this, investors expecting the yen to rise are moving into Japan.

Recent history shows the deficit on the visible trade account for the first month of 1980 at $2.25 bn and the deficit on invisibles at nearly $1 bn (the largest total deficit ever). On long term capital account, an actual net inflow into Japan during January 1980 of $900 mn was recorded and reserves rose 3 per cent in that month to $21 bn.

Future trends -

These are short term results, which will show fluctuations of various kinds, including responses to policy actions elsewhere. In March 1980, for instance, (just before the UK budget) there had to be a reaction from Japan to President Carter's new anti-inflation programme. This was in part defensive but, since in this report it is the longer term prospects that are being considered, what was presented
186

in Tokyo by the government was a larger seven point government anti-inflation plan, expected at the time of writing to include raising the bank rate in Japan to about 9 per cent, raising the reserve requirements, and other measures.

It is optimistically believed that the recent oil price increases have carried the oil bill to its payable maximum, or somewhere near the maximum Opec can impose on Japan unless greater prosperity is generated in Japan. Government expenditure is sure to increase greatly in the 1980s from its present relatively low percentage of GNP; fresh commitments imply an increase, as a proportion of national income, during the decade, to the levels of the USA.

In the public sector, too, emphasis is on quality as well as quantity. A minor but significant component, military expenditure, has recently been discussed. Japan's peaceable stance has been reaffirmed; defence expenditure appears to be pegged at 0.9 per cent of GNP.   Armament will, however, be improved, and the arithmetic of the percentage needs to be borne in mind. If GNP rises (by near 8 per cent at present but unofficially expected to be 11-12 per cent in the next few years), the defence outlay rises pro rata, that is it would double in the 1980s. In the much larger civilian public sector quality is equally stressed, notably in housing, with further revelations that the older style provision in large blocks is disliked to such an extent that, despite a housing shortage, some of it remains unsold or unleased. The EEC should note that the contemporary Japanese (who have always been house proud) are by no means content to live in "rabbit hutches".

Company policy has become more modern and enlightened in recent times. The rotation of tasks is emphasised, with every manager and worker taking his turn at all the relevant tasks. Consultation and suggestion meetings are held with all concerned in common session. The aloofness of Western managers, who "do not even say good morning to employees, and may not know their names or their tasks" is a constant source of surprise to Japanese visitors to Western plants; in Japan there would be not only the exchange of bows and niceties but conversation about the work in hand. The average worker's wage in Japan is near $10,000; it is claimed that good firms spend over $8,000 a year on human capital support expenditure of all kinds (amenities, training and general facilities) and the average firm about half its wage bill. The 1980s will see the emergence of a highly competent and motivated Japanese workforce, competent and motivated also to enjoy a high standard of living. This is often held to be synonymous with the lifestyle of the American people who are high producers and high spenders, but in Japan it is more likely to be similar to the lifestyle of West Germans, retaining, of course, the Japanese setting.

- are not expected to be all rosy

On this bright background, there are, however, shadows. At the opening of the 1980s, the weakness of the yen against the dollar was marked. At the peak rate in October 1978, only 175 yen were required to buy $1; the yen weakened in the latter part of 1979 to 240-250 yen to the dollar and the import bill rose accordingly. For the fiscal year just ended (April 1979–March 1980), the Japan Foreign Trade Council, representing industrial and exporting interests, projected imports at $118 bn, up almost 40 per cent on 1978/79, and exports at $107 bn, an increase of only 8 per cent, resulting in a deficit of $11 bn. The $14 bn trade surplus of 1978 would thus be nearly reversed. For 1980/81 the official expectation is of imports rising at a much lower rate, by only just above 10 per cent to $130 bn, while exports rise much more sharply than before, by 15 per cent to reach $123 bn and thus reduce the deficit to $7 bn. The Japanese government has given as actual results for calendar 1979 exports up by less than 6 per cent to $103 bn, and imports up by nearly 40 per cent to $110 bn, leaving a deficit of $7 bn.

Growth in GNP in Japan is officially estimated to be 4.8 per cent in 1980 and 5-6 per cent thereafter, which reflects the government's caution. Oil is, of course, the largest single difficulty. The Foreign Trade Council's 1980/81 forecast makes the somewhat optimistic assumption of the oil price being only $26 a barrel; it was only a dollar or so below that at the end of 1979. Reduction in oil use will not be great, so the oil bill will be up nearly 20 per cent. Exports benefiting from the low yen exchange rate are principally industrial equipment, chemicals, cars and ships. The market for ships remains depressed, despite some revival in Japan early in 1980, but the other exports are doing well. Credit liquidity is high; when the US bank rate reached 12 per cent, Japan's was 5.25 per cent. Subsequently (March 1980) the rates went to 20 per cent in the USA and 9 per cent in Japan. Car sales and profits are high, especially with good domestic sales, good servicing both at home and abroad, and success in the small car market in the USA. The US majors are massively gearing up for the car of the 21st century, but it will not arrive immediately; meanwhile Japanese interests are setting up some plants in the USA. Manufacturers of electrical products avow that 205-210 yen to $1 is a cost plus exchange rate, so are comfortable at more than 10 per cent above that. The steel industry shows no such elation, in view of the rising costs of iron ore and coking coal; nevertheless it estimates exports in 1979/80 at nearly $14 bn, from raw material imports of $9 bn, earning nearly $5 bn. All the big oil refiners and dis- tributors in Japan are registering losses; they consider the correct rate of exchange to be 218 yen to $1. In 1978/79 they budgeted for a 203 yen to $1 rate but had to face much higher prices.

The government and consumers are the most afraid of inflation - of cost push more than demand pull. Retail prices rose only 4.2 per cent in Japan in the 1979 "spring offensive" (the annual period when general settlements mostly clear the wage agreements for the year) when wages were raised by 6 per cent. Wholesale prices are, however, up by nearly 13 per cent, and will work themselves through in 1980. Japan is none the less convinced that the inflation killer is productivity. The average Japanese worker's annual value added for 1978/79 was 5.717 mn yen (about $24,000), 10.4 per cent up on the preceding year. He was rewarded by an earned income of nearly 4 mn yen (about $17,000), 8.1 per cent up on the preceding year.

Official policy for the 1980s -

The Ministry of International Trade and Industry (MITI) produced in November 1979 its "vision" for the 1980s (Report on the 1980s by the Trade and Industry Study G Group), a basic draft for a long term calculation, wider and deeper than similar exercises in the past. In the 1960s MITI clung to the development philosophy of the earlier generation, stressing heavy and chemical industry growth. In the 1970s it backed the next generation of development thinkers, advocating knowledge inten- sive industries, though by implication rather than explicit headlining. It is interest- ing that on the threshold of the 1980s it stresses the world view outlined at the beginning of this report: transition from "US hegemony" to "multi-polarisation of the world structure and the post oil civilisation". It starts by pointing out the hard facts that Japan depends on the rest of the world for 88 per cent of its energy imports and 53 per cent of its food. Japan has reached Western standards in material terms but is still behind in the quality of life.

Three things, MITI continues, must be done by Japan in the 1980s: first, to make an international contribution in proportion to Japan's economic strength, aiming at stabilisation and growth (stabilisation in the Japanese mind tends to mean equilibrium - a moving equilibrium - rather than resting at the present level); second, to reduce Japan's vulnerability in respect of its extreme dependence on imported resources; and third, while maintaining the Japanese impetus, to improve the quality of life in Japan, especially in terms of leisure (this means more housing, a five day week and good holidays, and catering for an ageing population). Japan must shed its small nation complex and the stress on achieving economic security which dominated after the oil crisis; the report emphasises the importance of free trade, international interdependences and global arrangements, new fuels, and new techniques.

The cost will be heavy on the people, but represents a necessary investment to secure the future, the report continues. Japan must face protectionism abroad by emerging as a champion of economic freedom, non-intervention and non-discrimination, opening therefore its markets to the world, and helping to create new ones overseas. Industries will devolve to other countries; a principle is cited, attributed to the OECD, of international adjustment of industry. Foreign aid should be increased to 3 per cent of GNP. There should be a large investment in equipment and large imports. By the methods mentioned earlier in this report, MITI schedules a 15 per cent saving in the input of (fuel) energy, more than double the 1980 plan. Fuel prices should be allowed to find their market level; price rationing is the weapon not government tinkering.

- the emphasis is on a technological revolution -

Another part of the MITI report is concerned with technology. Japan must change from importing and adapting or improving foreign technology to evolve its own independent, creative technology. MITI rejects the postulate of diminishing returns to advances in technology at a high level, considering that startling innovations are possible. The government will back such developments with tax concessions. Research and development allocations will double in the 1980s, from 1.7 to 3 per cent of GNP (this is not, however, overwhelmingly ahead of Western countries, which are moving towards 2.5 per cent). MITI's previous "vision" of ten years ago, for the 1970s, had stressed intensification ("concentration") of industrial knowledge largely in terms of implanting into Japanese industry, on its existing basis, much more high grade knowledge, methods and information. There was success in those directions; advanced processing and assembly activities developed, the availability and handling of information were greatly improved, while the older labour and energy resource intensive activities showed a relative decline.

This is now to be carried much further, to a qualitative, not just a quantitative change. A "dynamic order of precedence" is to give priority to the activities showing the best growth. A second criterion for priority, and presumably for rewards, will be the contribution made to improving the quality of life. A third criterion will be the contribution made to energy saving, and a fourth effectiveness in reducing dependence on imported inputs. This is not an absolute schedule: trade offs are envisaged as far as possible whereby a gain under one heading will secure a concession under another. Besides the fuel processing industries, other beneficiaries are named as sophisticated aircraft, computer, telecommunications and data processing activities. These will be areas of dispute with the other developed nations, which could be resolved by wide discussion, the report says.

Meanwhile the less developed countries will compete sharply and extensively, not only in textiles and everyday goods but in items of machinery; Japan must open its markets to these, but use its influence to achieve a harmonious evolution. The MITI study tries to identify the new features in technology. Basic material industries such as steel and petrochemicals should find new high performance materials and more specialised uses, aiming at quality rather than quantity of output. This trend is already exemplified in the automobile industry in the use of strong steels which reduce the tare and lower fuel consumption. Processing and assembly must become more electronic and use more software. Examples are the use of microcomputers in household electronic goods, and automation of production in smaller but higher quality batches, for fashion goods and so on. The same should apply in social services, public health and education.

Actual outlines are given (to an extent that critics could point to government officiousness) on an array of industries: textiles, household products, paper and pulp, cement, glass, chemicals, non-ferrous metals, iron and steel, general and precision machinery, vehicles, electricals and electronics, data processing, aircraft, aerospace, housing and leisure pursuits. Government planning in Japan is widely said to be to only a minor extent prescriptive, and largely indicative; to this must be added that it is didactic. The technology situation is, according to official circles, critical. The public does not altogether agree with that alarmism, but sees the need for change and the opportunities for improvement and gain. The official prescriptions, taken in detail, seem to some to be too much like orders, and to carry requirements such as reform of education and recasting of research and development, which the bureaucracy may be unable to fulfil satisfactorily. The view holds that it would be better to leave the basic implementations to the free economy and for the government to limit itself to an encouraging and facilitating role.

There is also some suspicion of empire building on the part of MITI, which was particularly powerful in the 1960s and early 1970s with its stress on heavy industry and higher knowledge inputs, but has been less influential in the last few years when liberalisation of business and investment has prevailed and MITI has had to defer to intensified anti trust regulations. However, it is evident that there is an awareness of the technology problem on all sides in Japan and a preparedness to help deal with it.

– but the business world has more faith in improving existing technology –

The business world sees a slightly different horizon from official circles regarding technology. Businessmen take a longer term view of striking developments in new fields of technology – as being more likely to be on the agenda for 1990 than 1980. Meanwhile, they would press for better use of existing technology rather than aiming at a technological breakthrough. This applies differently, of course, in different spheres; bankers are more cautious about revolutionary techniques than the research and development men. Most of the managerial class reflect along the lines that if the 1980s mean pursuing a great array of small, specialised and quality controlled lines of production, that puts managerial ability at a premium (with much more coordination required) and at the same time costs become the touchstone.

Previously competitiveness was achieved by cutting costs through mass production; now it comes by making cost savings on each of a million specialised operations or on tailor made products. One periodical spoke recently of the riddle of increasing productivity under conditions of static output, the answer being quality. Demand is now not merely large, it is diversified and even personalised. The last word, personalised, is most striking; it is normal or even laudatory to the Western mind, but more startling in Japan where it goes distinctly against the traditional outlook.

In sum, a Brave New Technological World is seen for the most part as a middle to longer term aim, though a good and necessary one, for 1994 perhaps rather than 1984. Meanwhile the focus will be on detailed improvements on certain critical processing activities within the current rather than the long term cycles of production and of change.

- and looks for economic stability as a priority

The exchange rate recurs as much more the day to day preoccupation among businessmen. The cheap yen favours exports but, because imported inputs are dearer, not in the longer term. Supporting the exchange rate is costly, as many countries know. During 1979 Japan's foreign exchange reserves fell from about $33 bn to $20 bn. The yen was supported at various times, such as at the end of November 1979 when it fell below 151 to the dollar and again in the early part of 1980. Although the reserves have fallen, they can hardly be called low at around $20 bn. The price of imports is a more acute question than that of exports. The Japanese, like the West Germans and the Swiss, are not especially afraid of their currency being dear; they did well before when the yen was high, and could do so again. There is no demur against the policy of raising productivity and raising value added on the score that it will raise the yen's exchange rate. The government's technological approach is thus well accepted.

It is feared that the emphasis on quality means cost inflation; and cost push is considered the relevant factor, rather than demand pull. Analysts (especially those on the cautious side, such as bankers) point out, however, that under slow growth even a moderate increase in demand may outrun the capacity of supply, which is no longer on the mass production basis, to meet it. There will be bottleneck inflation. Firms will not benefit from inflation, except in the short run. A low price ceiling means that booms will not last long and depressions will be protracted. The world situation, particularly in respect of oil, means that any boom will increase the pressure on oil and raw materials, forcing prices up and soon leading to recession, whereupon, according to the textbook, prices should fall, but in the real world this does not happen.

Japan as a whole is therefore seeking primarily for security in the 1980s, its alert entrepreneurs planning for staying power rather than a venturesome spirit. This does not exclude a keen lookout for opportunities, and a readiness to seize them. Broadly the outlook is the same as in the advanced countries generally, of which the Japan of the 1980s is distinctly one. Although the current stress is on stability and order rather than on competitive edge and expansion efficiency, the introspective Japanese wonder whether the former really suits them as well as the latter. Resting on the high plateau of the advanced economies, could Japan avoid the troubles that afflict the other members of that group?

Social trends disturb some Japanese, especially the growth of individualism (called by traditionalists selfishness or self centredness), but hardly yet to such an extent as to conclude that Japan must succumb to the Western malady. The other cause of the malady is held to be over enlargement of the public sector and the role of the government; on that score the Japanese are generally satisfied with their country's version of the mixed economy. That economy must now rationalise and consolidate the transformation that was effected just before the oil crisis and in the recent recovery from it, when the channels of money supply diversified, personal and company liquidity greatly increased, financing became more internationalised and freer and more flexible interest rates became necessary.

Small firms have a large role

The role of small enterprises, which are still prominent in Japan, is vital. There have been qualitative changes in this sector: smaller firms are highly integrated with the big concerns; the day of unitary cottage workshops is long past and they have for some time been thoroughly linked in a highly modern sub contracting system. Small enterprises constitute an actual majority of undertakings and of workers, in shops, in sales and also in industry. They compete - some successfully, some unsuccessfully - among themselves, with Japanese enterprises of the medium size (though hardly with the largest) and with imports.

In light manufactures and processing the small firms are particularly important. The larger among them have recorded high growth rates, especially those processing heavy and chemical industry products. The successful ones grow into medium sized firms, or develop useful specialisations. If Japan is calling for the devolution of industry to Asia, there is room for the same process at home; this need not lead to increasing polarisation between large and small enterprises, given the high degree of integration between them. The technology policy therefore has the small industry structure very much in mind, with possible arrangements for training its managers and workers, assessing and coordinating the experience they have, their credit and purchasing facilities and other requirements. To raise efficiency in this sector as much as in the giant factories would be of great benefit. Because the small industries are rural (or in modern Japan the correct description may be least urbanised), it is considered that their further modernisation might also raise the quality of life.

Trade in technology is becoming more favourable to Japan

Japan's high ambitions depend particularly on the intention to develop technology. The present level is far from low. It is only in aerospace and nuclear reactors that Japan is not fully equal to other industrial nations, as far as understanding of and ability to use known techniques is concerned. Where Japan lags is in innovation and invention. Thus Japan imports technology, paying out much more in royalties abroad than it receives under this heading. Technology exports have, however, risen considerably in recent years (nearly three and a half times from 1971/72 to 1977/78), while imports have risen just under one and a half times in the same period. Japan's adverse balance of payments on this account has fallen: royalty receipts on licences covered a little over 2 per cent of payments out in 1960 but over 10 per cent in 1965/66, nearly 14 per cent in 1970/71 and nearly 23 per cent in 1977/78.

The foregoing are the Bank of Japan's figures. A recent survey by the prime minister's office, with a different coverage and by other methods, provides another set of figures, which shows the same overall trend. It claims that receipts covered payments, on this account, by over 20 per cent in 1971/72, nearly 36 per cent in 1974/75 and almost 50 per cent in 1977/78. The main explanation is that Japan's exports of technology are largely re-exports; Japan has been an entrepot, principally for east Asia (including the USSR), in this matter. It may be recalled that in the days of British rule in India, British products, designs and methods were often marketed there with the annotation "modified for India". Japan has largely been operating a "modified for Asia" marque, adapting technology for developing countries.

The Japanese distinguish between dealings in new technology (receipts and payments on new agreements) and existing technology (on existing agreements). On that basis, in 1977/78 about half of Japan's industries had a favourable balance in respect of new technology. Star performers among these were the construction industry, reversing an unfavourable balance in new technology of 76 per cent in 1972/75 into sales nearly two and a half times purchases in 1977/78; iron and steel, moving in the same period from a 93 per cent deficit to receipts nearly double the outlays; and textiles, transforming a 76 per cent deficit into a 13 per cent surplus. Nevertheless, over the whole field, large payments continue to other countries, in respect especially of existing and continued contracts (see also Table 7, page 24).

Research and development expenditure is rising -

On the research and development (R & D) front, the directions in which Japan is looking are clear. Total R & D expenditures in Japan on the natural sciences rose between 1967/68 and 1977/78 at an average annual rate of over 18 per cent, from 606 bn yen to 3,234 bn yen. This is still below the proportion of GNP devoted to R & D in Western countries: it is just over 1.5 per cent in Japan compared with about 2 per cent in the West. The period taken here covers a static year during the oil crisis, 1974/75. Just before that, investment in R & D had risen sharply; but for the whole period 1973/74 to 1977/78 it rose at 13 per cent per annum on average.

Of course, not all enterprises in Japan carry out R & D: only 15 per cent of the myriad Japanese undertakings did so in 1977/78. Naturally the big firms and plants are the main practitioners: in chemicals and in machinery from one eighth to two thirds of firms in various lines engage in R & D work; over the whole range of industry nearly all the giant trusts do so, and up to half the medium sized firms, but only one eighth of small units. A major aim for the 1980s is to extend, if not the actual practice of R & D, at any rate full access to it, to the numerous smaller enterprises, while the leaders carry it to the highest international standards. Table 20 shows the extent and distribution of the R & D effort at the end of the 1970s.

- and will be concentrated on improving quality

While, as is apparent from the table, R & D expenditures represent high percentages of sales in various industries, in the chemical and engineering industries they reach particularly high proportions. This investment will bring substantial returns in the 1980s.

Table 20

Research and Development Activities by Manufacturing Industries, 1979

	Percentage of all firms engaged in R & D				R & D expenditures as % of R & D sales			
	Large enterprises[a]	Medium-sized firms[b]	Small enterprises[c]	Average	Large enterprises[a]	Medium-sized enterprises[b]	Small enterprises[c]	Average
All manufacturers	83	56	13	15	180	130	140	170
Chemicals	88	80	56	62	270	240	260	260
General machinery	93	68	21	24	200	160	250	200
Precision machinery	96	70	19	22	350	230	210	290
Electrical machinery	93	62	12	17	400	210	160	360
Transport machinery	85	46	10	15	240	90	140	230
Non-ferrous metals	93	55	5	11	110	70	90	100
Metal goods	73	55	9	11	120	90	160	120
Textiles	72	25	8	9	60	70	40	60
Iron & steel	77	24	9	8	110	70	70	110

a With capital of 1 bn yen or more.   b With capital of 100 mn to 1 bn yen.   c With capital of less than 100 mn yen.

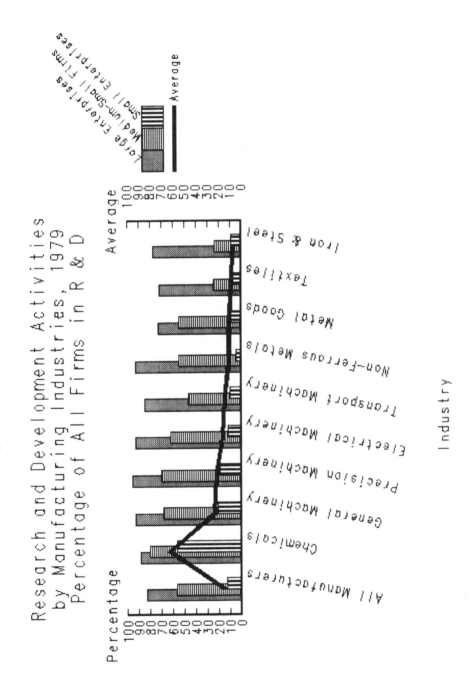

Figure 8a

195

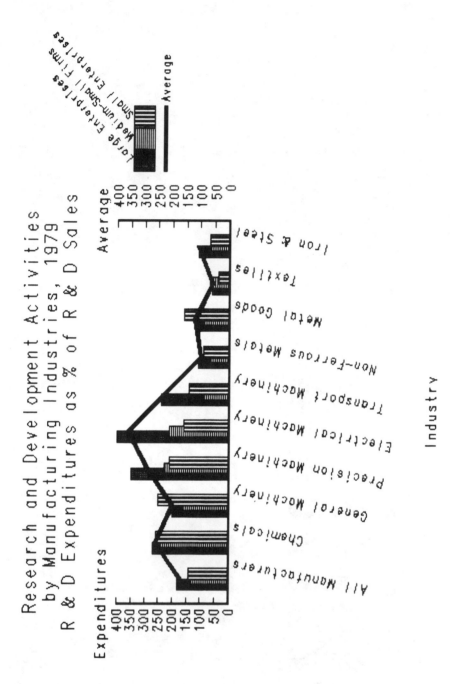

Research and Development Activities
by Manufacturing Industries, 1979
R & D Expenditures as % of R & D Sales

Figure 8b

196

Quality is the main consideration in research and development. In the later 1960s Japanese manufacturing, rapidly growing, concerned itself mainly with basic and applied research for fundamental long term development. In 1967/68 the application of basic research represented nearly 40 per cent of the research outlay but in 1977/78 only 24 per cent. This reflects partly the greater need at present to secure more immediate profits and to concentrate therefore on quick gain lines, but partly also a maturing of the economy, and a wider implementation of knowledge already gained. In the 1980s, it is asserted, official policy will promote more basic research, but to a greater extent interlock the two spheres of activity, abstract investigations with current applications.

Table 21 is the list given by the government (MITI) Agency for Industrial Science and Technology of principal headings for research and development work in the 1980s, with indications where the responsibility for them will lie - with the government, private interests, or a collaboration between them.

The silicon chip has not been specifically mentioned so far, but it certainly needs mentioning in a study of the prospects for the 1980s, which are widely expected to be the "chips with everything" decade. This is too wide a subject for this report, but the chip will obviously feature in many of the programmes listed in Table 21.

New sources of raw materials must be found

In the 1980s Japan will intensify its worldwide search for raw material and fuel resources. Table 22 summarises actual commitments at the beginning of 1980 in this respect. It excludes one major possibility, China, which is expected to figure in the later 1980s. The list covers a great range of commodities: oil, oil shale, aluminium and bauxite, cobalt, copper, lead, iron ore, chromium, natural gas, uranium, special metals, rare earths, etc. To select uranium as an example, Japan imported 3,000 tons in 1978, about 30 per cent from Canada, 16 per cent from South Africa, 11 per cent from West Africa, 4 per cent from the USA, 4 per cent from Australia, about 7 per cent from France and much enriched material from the UK. As Japan plans to increase the number of its operable nuclear power plants from the present 19 to 37 by 1985 (representing 12.6 mn kw now and 33 mn kw in 1985, i e 20 per cent of electric power requirements in 1985), its uranium needs will be more than doubled. Thus the Japanese are competing with the French in Mali for uranium, are interested in a large new find in British Columbia and another vein in New Mexico, are investing in activities in Queensland, and more. The list, moreover, does not include every activity of Japan in searching for minerals. There are additional operations in Zambia, Zaire, the Philippines, Papua New Guinea, Indonesia, Brazil, the USSR, Thailand, among others.

Care will be needed in relations with other countries: with China –

Japan's relations with all parts of the world will evidently take into account a number of different considerations in shifting priorities: politics, defence, trade, investment, cultural and others. Japan, in common with most other countries, is ready to be especially accommodating to China. Mr Ohira, visiting China at the end of 1979, announced that Japan would start preferential tariff arrangements for China in 1980. Political considerations weigh heavily here. In the talks, the necessity of maintaining peace in Korea was stressed. Japan's foreign minister recommended that Japanese loans to China be untied, to allay any foreign fears of Japan's cornering the China market. China's response is not yet fully clear,

Table 21

Japan's Principal Intentions in Technological Research and Development

Category	Improvements to existing technology[a]	New technology
Semiconductors, computers	JR: VLSI[a] JR: new generation computers, developing software and terminals for VLSI circuit computers. G: pattern information processing systems, input-output indicators, use of Japanese-Chinese script, drawings.	G: photosensor measurement and control systems, especially for steel industry and power plants; use of fibre optics (transmission of light signals through glass fibres, with much larger throughput than coaxial cables)
Domestic electrics	FM: facsimile reproduction. FM: telephones in vehicles FM: multiplex TV; FM: small videos; FM: mini-computers	FM: pulse code modulation recording (digital)
Nuclear power	G: new converters (intermediate between light water and fast breeder); G: high temperature gas reactors (1,000 C); G: uranium enrichment	G: fast breeders (to be the future basic type)
Precision machinery	FM: self focusing cameras	JR: robots
General machinery	...	G: laser applications
Medical	JR: artificial kidneys, supersonic diagnosis, laser surgery	JR: cancer treatments
Cars	FM: electronic fuel control. FM: electric driven car[b]	G: a car driven by magnetic induction
Aviation	JR: passenger jet to be produced in Japan	–
Iron & steel	FM: heat and corrosion resistance for ships and nuclear	G: use of waste gas and nuclear power for direct ore reduction
Oil	FM: cracking of heavy oil. G: deep-sea production G: olefines (ethyl) from heavy oil (first fraction residues)	
Cement	FM: new, low fuel kilns	
Food	...	FM: new protein foods
Oceanography	JR: sea water distillation (osmosis, electrolysis)[b] JR: manganese from seabed[c]	
New sources of energy	JR: geothermal; JR: gasification of coal	JR: solar battery (amorphous), solar housing, solar power
Systems engineering	G: automobile and traffic control	–
New materials	G: regeneration; JR: use of waste heat	FM: new ceramics (non-oxide compounds, high purity, resistance, hard cores, for electronic uses)

Note: G: to be handled by the government.   JR: joint efforts between government and private interests.   FM: free market; available for either of the above, or for private initiatives.

a Very large scale integration.   b Large basic research project completed 1977//78.   c Large scale integration.

198

Table 22

Current Japanese Activities in Seeking and Developing New Supplies of Raw Materials

Region	Area	Product	Company	Investment commitment ($ mn)
East Asia	South Korea	Petrochemicals	Mitsui	...
	South Yakutia (Siberia)	Coal	Nichimen	...
	Laos	Zinc refining	Kyowa	0.6
		Others	Marubeni	...
South East Asia	West Malaysia	Forestry	C Itoh	1.3
	Sarawak (East Malaysia)	Forestry	Mitsubishi	1.0
	Philippines	Copper	Mitsubishi	6.2
		Chromium	Nichimen	...
		Agriculture & forestry	Mitsui	...
	Indonesia	Plastics, oil, timber	Mitsui	...
Oceania	Australia	Coal	Nippon Coal	80.0
		Coal	Sumitomo	...
		Coal	Mitsubishi	...
		Bauxite	Kobe Steel & others	...
		Coal	Mitsubishi, Nissho Iwai	...
		Copper	Sumitomo	...
		Aluminium	Mitsubishi, Yoshida	...
		Others	Sumitomo, C Itoh & others	...
	New Zealand	Aluminium	Showa & Sumitomo	10.9
		Titanium, magnetite	Nichimen	...
South Asia	India	Gas	Mitsui	...
West Asia	Iran	Petrochemicals	Mitsui	(large)
	Abu Dhabi	LNG	Mitsui	...
North America	USA–Alaska	Oil	Teikoku (& many others)	3.3
	USA–Seattle	Timber	Shin Asahigawa	0.2
			Sumitomo	1.0
	USA–Utah	Uranium	Taihei	...
	USA–Arizona	Copper	Nichimen	...
	USA–Kentucky & Tennessee	Zinc	Nichimen	...

/continued

Table 22 (continued)

Current Japanese Activities in Seeking and Developing New Supplies of Raw Materials (continued)

Region	Area	Product	Company	Investment commitment ($ mn)
North America (contd)	Canada–Alberta	Oil & gas	Japan Oil Sands, Fuyo, Marubeni	8.6
	Canada–British Columbia	Forestry	C Itoh	12.1
		Minerals	Nichimen	0.5
		Coal	Mitsui	4.6
		Coal	Nippon Coal, Kawasaki, Mitsubishi, Sumitomo	22.6
	Canada–other areas	Coal	Nichimen	...
		Uranium	Mitsui	...
Latin America	Mexico	Copper	Sumitomo	0.2
	Panama	Copper	Mitsui	0.45
	Guatemala	Mining	Toho & C Itoh	0.1
	Colombia	Oil	Teijin, Mitsui	7.7
	Bolivia	Zinc	Nichimen	...
	Brazil	Steel mill	Nichimen	...
		Chrome ore, copper	Mitsui	...
	Peru	Zinc	Toho	(small)
		Copper, lead	Mitsui	1.55
			Nippon	0.04
Africa	Chile	Iron ore	Mitsubishi	(small)
	Guinea	Iron ore	Nichimen	...
	Mali	Uranium	Nichimen	...
	Zaire	Oil	Mitsui, Teikoku	...
	Zambia	Cobalt	Mitsubishi, Mitsui	...

despite many encouraging signs. After the reign of Mao, China made quite a sudden turnround and some feel that it could do so again. There is internal dissension, and the Taiwan question remains. On this Japan continues to maintain an uncommitted position, hoping to combine a large material interest with the role of intermediary. Developing China is no small task, requiring not only time and patience but huge infrastructural investment, adjustments and ingenuity.

Dealings with such a highly centralised and bureaucratic state are complex and uncertain, through an abundance of regulations and intricate channels. Paradoxically, although China proclaims the desire to help the masses of poorer people rather than wealthy capitalist interests, it is only big firms that can deal with the plethora of documentation, procedure, credit and other arrangements. In Japan's structure small and medium sized firms are well integrated with larger companies and national policy, so consortia can be formed, but that means in effect that the bureaucratic nature of communist state trading is building up rather than diminishing the role of what the Russians call monopolies (meaning big capitalist interests).

There is much empathy with China in Japan, mainly for cultural reasons and through "Asianism". It is a somewhat vague attachment, once tinged with war guilt until a new generation,for whom the war was merely history, grew up. The world has been waiting to form commercial and cultural links with China for a long time; it now promises to open its doors, but what is inside is still somewhat a mystery.

Japan's trade balance with China will remain a problem for while China has an impressive shopping list of needs it is unclear what it can or will offer in payment. The prospect is now better than in the days when China could offer only odd items like tung oil, pigs' bristles, some tin,and there was also a currency problem. Primarily, China has oil, but the development of this is not simple, and its own industrialisation programme will claim much of the oil and of other natural resources.

The situation is complicated by the bitter quarrel between the USSR and China, the course of which is crucial to future events in Japan. Some observers regard the Sino-Soviet dispute as a passing phase; but others consider it to be lasting, if not endemic, for a number of reasons. There are elements of a religious war over the leadership of the communist faith in the liberation of mankind, between a "Vatican" in Moscow and "Protestantism" in Peking; of irredentism (large territories taken from China by Russia); of lebensraum (resources appropriate for China's industrialisation existing not far away in Siberia); of cultural and racial clashes (see <u>Russian Studies of China</u>, by Stuart Kirby, London 1975).

- with the USSR -

The USSR has a large presence and armament looming over Japan. It occupies former Japanese territory a few miles away from northern Hokkaido, the retrocession of which it blankly refuses to consider or discuss. No full peace treaty has been signed between the USSR and Japan. Japan's signature to a treaty with China including a clause against the hegemony of any nation has angered the Moscow government. The USSR is harsh in other ways in its attitude towards Japan. It denies the reality of the Japanese economic miracle, is antagonistic to Japan's capitalist outlook, emits a stream of defamatory propaganda denouncing Japan as full of reactionary, feudal and revanchist elements, resuscitated by the USA to form a springboard for the designs of American imperialism to restore fascism and launch a new war - despite the resistance of the impoverished masses of Japan, who are represented as ripe for revolution. In the Japanese opinion polls, the USSR always scores as the most disliked nation (see Russian Studies of Japan, by Stuart Kirby, London 1980).

The extent to which politics can intervene materially is illustrated by the case of BAM, the Baikal-Amur railway. Japan was interested in helping to build this great northern branch of the Trans-Siberian mainline, running from north of Lake Baikal to the Russian coast of the Sea of Japan and opening up large areas of natural resources, but it withdrew from the project. There were the usual working difficulties, and China was concerned about the strategic implications, the consequent strengthening of its heavily armed local adversary and main political opponent. The Russians determined to build it themselves, and will complete it in 1983. Regarding the USSR itself, that gigantic federation is not by any means free of internal stresses which could, in the view of some expert observers, soon become disintegrative.

- with east and west Asia -

Oceanic east Asia, as mentioned earlier, is also a sensitive area politically, although a main zone of economic development. Japan's relations with Asean are good. The South East Asian nations are particularly uneasy about involvement in the Sino-Soviet clash, having among their problems those of active and important overseas Chinese minorities (in Singapore's case a Chinese majority) and indigenous communist or Moslem separatists or secessionists.

The China Seas contain major offshore oil deposits which the Japanese are interested and competent in developing, but those waters are demarcated by claims of national sovereignty, with actual or potential conflicts between all the countries concerned - Vietnam, Taiwan, the Philippines, Malaysia, Indonesia, Thailand, Cambodia and others. Vietnam is Soviet supported, but is of great practical interest to Japan and Asean; it cannot, any more than the other countries of the area, take only a one sided view.

On the business side, certainly, Japan (especially its major capitalists) has been attracted by the possibilities of participation in developing the vast resources of Siberia, now artificially withdrawn from sharing fully in the development of east Asia and the world. Much has been done with Japanese participation in Siberia, but not as much as had been hoped. Difficulties of attitude and of procedure, and so on (with the Russian centres of decision a hemisphere away in Moscow) have impeded the matter. Japanese proposals for Siberian development (often jointly with the USA and other interests) have totalled something in the order of $5 bn; about $1 bn of investment has been realised. The USSR thereby imported a good deal of technical knowledge. A full study on this is given in Japan's Role in Soviet Economic Growth, by R S Mathieson, New York 1979, although it is limited to official data on both sides, and lacks field knowledge of the workings in either Russia or Japan. Relations with the USSR are thus likely to be sustained, but not dramatically extended or improved. China is now the more attractive of the rivals.

Turning to Japan's relations with the rest of the world, these have been more broadly discussed earlier. The west Asia problem (oil) is perhaps not completely soluble within a decade, but Japan has devoted special concern and attention to it, showing economic flexibility but also some readiness to make political concessions, for example regarding the Palestinians.

202

– and with the West

This report has been optimistic that an extreme trade balance problem between Japan and Western Europe is unlikely, following the Japanese view on this question. At least it is unlikely to lead to an immoderate, non-negotiable protectionist reaction by the Western Europeans. This optimism is based on the assumption that in Western Europe, particularly, Japanese market penetration (in terms of percentage market share at least) has already reached something like its maximum for the next few years; there will be some innovation, but principally consolidation, with concentration on servicing the already acquired market (in which the Japanese reputation is generally good).

Relations with the USA are still the most vital by far; they are too complex for full investigation here, and there are many commentaries available already. Other aspects of Japan's international relations have therefore been covered more fully in this report. Other regions are becoming as significant to Japan now, principally South East Asia, or east Asia as a whole. Clearly Japan will take a leading role in that hemisphere. It has good reasons for undertaking this responsibility willingly; if it does not the role may be thrust upon it by the balance of circumstances.

The cultural element of Japan's international relations must not be forgotten. There is immense interest worldwide in all aspects of Japanese culture, in the arts and the applied arts, ranging from aikido (a form of jujitsu) to Zen. This area of international exchanges will continue and could well expand.

This study is necessarily made on the large assumption that no cataclysmic changes such as a major war or a world economic depression severe enough to break or bend the framework of the projections will occur. Within these limits Japan should play a remarkable and significant role in the 1980s in the inauguration of a new era in the world economy and world affairs.